Capable Women, Incapable States

The Other One Percent
Sanjoy Chakravorty, Devesh Kapur, and Nirvikar Singh

Social Justice through Inclusion
Francesca R. Jensenius

Dispossession without Development
Michael Levien

The Man Who Remade India
Vinay Sitapati

Business and Politics in India
Edited by Christophe Jaffrelot, Atul Kohli, and Kanta Murali

Clients and Constituents
Jennifer Bussell

Gambling with Violence
Yelena Biberman

Mobilizing the Marginalized
Amit Ahuja

The Absent Dialogue
Anit Mukherjee

When Nehru Looked East
Francine Frankel

Capable Women, Incapable States
Poulami Roychowdhury

Capable Women, Incapable States

Negotiating Violence and Rights in India

POULAMI ROYCHOWDHURY

OXFORD
UNIVERSITY PRESS

OXFORD
UNIVERSITY PRESS

Oxford University Press is a department of the University of Oxford. It furthers
the University's objective of excellence in research, scholarship, and education
by publishing worldwide. Oxford is a registered trade mark of Oxford University
Press in the UK and certain other countries.

Published in the United States of America by Oxford University Press
198 Madison Avenue, New York, NY 10016, United States of America.

Library of Congress Cataloging-in-Publication Data
Names: Roychowdhury, Poulami, author.
Title: Capable women, incapable states : negotiating violence and rights in
India / Poulami Roychowdhury.
Description: New York, NY : Oxford University Press, [2021] |
Series: Modern South Asia series | Includes bibliographical references and index.
Identifiers: LCCN 2020016073 (print) | LCCN 2020016074 (ebook) |
ISBN 9780190881894 (hardback) | ISBN 9780190881900 (paperback) |
ISBN 9780190881924 (epub)
Subjects: LCSH: Family violence—India. | Women—Violence against—India. |
Women's rights—India. | Women—Legal status, laws, etc.—India. |
Discrimination in criminal justice administration—India.
Classification: LCC HV6626.23.I4 R69 2020 (print) |
LCC HV6626.23.I4 (ebook) | DDC 362.82/920954—dc23
LC record available at https://lccn.loc.gov/2020016073
LC ebook record available at https://lccn.loc.gov/2020016074

1 3 5 7 9 8 6 4 2

Paperback printed by Marquis, Canada
Hardback printed by Bridgeport National Bindery, Inc., United States of America

for Anita & Ashis Roychowdhury
my Ma and Bapi

CONTENTS

SECTION IV   APPENDICES

ACKNOWLEDGMENTS

Books can be long, lonely affairs. I could not have written this book without financial support or without the generosity of others. And I would not have wished to write it without the company of family and friends. First: financial support. The department of Sociology at New York University accepted me, gave me a degree, and paid me to read, learn, and run around the world for five years. When those five years proved to be insufficient, the department provided further support through the Georgette Bennett dissertation writing fellowship. The National Science Foundation and Fulbright saw promise in what in hindsight appear to be relatively unpromising research proposals. I hope this book testifies to the value of funding long-term qualitative research, research that may not be easily quantifiable or have simple policy solutions attached to it but which seeks to expand the reader's emotional and intellectual horizons.

After I returned from India, the Consortium for Faculty Diversity allowed me to spend a blissful year writing in residence at Smith College, where the Department of Sociology provided a cozy office and collegial atmosphere. Once I became an assistant professor at McGill University, the Canadian federal government and Quebec's provincial government understood the value of qualitative work in international settings. I am thankful to the generous funding provided by the Social Sciences & Humanities Research Council of Canada and the Fonds de Recherche du Québec.

Second: generosity. Countless people occupy the pages of this book. They cannot be named, but without their time and attention, I could not have completed this research. They invited me into their homes and places of work, talked to me openly about experiences that are difficult to talk about, and put up with my inquisitive and at times overbearing presence as they went about their daily lives. I am indebted to them and sincerely hope to have translated their lives honestly and sympathetically.

Another set of hidden actors made this book possible. They do not show up on these pages, even under pseudonyms. But they helped craft the intellectual currents that allowed me to write. Without them, this book would make much less sense. First and foremost, my advisor Lynne Haney: my academic role model and someone I enjoy having drinks with. I always feel smarter and more energetic after seeing you. Judith Stacey, Sally Merry, Steven Lukes: you were all active and substantive members of my dissertation committee. I think about gender, social inequality, and law differently because of you. Ann Orloff: you ceaselessly organize reclusive academics, encouraging us to support each other and think about the direction of the field. You do not have to provide all this effort and care, but you do it anyway. Shelley Clark, my mentor at McGill: you set an example of unwavering commitment to research, honesty, and warmth. Raka Ray: you took an NYU student under your wing and provided advice from afar. Patrick Heller: you took the time to meet an unknown graduate student so many years ago and believed in this book. Ashutosh Varshney: thanks for publishing the book. Harsh Mander, Pratiksha Baxi, Radhika Govindrajan, Madhav Khosla: thank you for reading an early manuscript and providing insightful and kind comments. Blair Peruniak: the index would have been a complete mess without you. Martin Chandler: you deserve full credit for the lovely maps.

Third: friends and family. This is a blurry category, which significantly overlaps with those who helped mold my intellect. Dwai Banerjee, Nishaant Choksi, Misha Chowdhury, Sandipto Dasgupta, Durba Mitra, Debashree Mukherjee, Matt Murrill, Jyoti Natarajan, Francesca Refsum Jensenius, Andrew Rumbach, Neelanjan Sircar, Pavithra Suryanarayan, Nishita Trisal, Anand Vaidya: conducting research and writing about it would have been much less enjoyable, not to mention feasible, without you. You sustain me with humor, advice, and *adda*. Issa Kohler-Haussman, Alison McKim, Daniel Aldana Cohen, Ashley Mears, Abigail Weitzman, Madhavi Cherien, Nadda Matta, Max Besbris, Anna Skarpelis, and all the members of my cohort: you made NYU a respite from the occasional indifference of the city. Mike Levien, Smitha Radhakrishnan, Gowri Vijayakumar: you enliven the sociology of South Asia, and I am glad to have you as comrades in the discipline. Abigail Andrews, Savina Balasubramanian, Marie Berry, Jennifer Carlson, Anna Korteweg, Jordana Matlon, Rhacel Parrenas, Celene Reynolds, Leslie Salzinger, Evren Savci, Nazanin Shahrokhni, Laurel Westbrook: your contributions to the sociology of gender and your company at our annual gender meetings sustain me. Michelle Cho, Merve Emre, Shanon Fitzpatrick: our writing club was short-lived but crucial. I miss those of you who moved away and will physically bar those who have not from leaving.

Trying to summarize my thanks to my parents, Ashis and Anita, in a few short sentences seems a slightly pointless exercise. But I will say this: thank you for always putting my education first and for setting an unattainable standard of kindness. It was through your example that I came to wonder and care about the lives of others. I am not necessarily the kind of doctor you wanted me to be, but hopefully you are amused that instead of saving people's lives, I can engage them in detailed intellectual debates. Finally, my best friends and dearest loves. Sohel, I wrote this book despite your efforts to make me into a sleep-deprived zombie. But you are still the best thing that ever happened to me. Brandon, thanks for reading what I write and providing substantive feedback. I am sorry I have no idea what you are doing at that computer of yours, though I have a sense you are helping people access affordable healthcare. I am a lucky lady indeed, getting to end and begin each day with you.

LIST OF ABBREVIATIONS

ADM	additional district magistrate
CPI(M)	Communist Party of India (Marxist)
DIR	Domestic Incident Report
DM	district magistrate
DSP	district superintendent of police
FIR	First Incident Report
GD	General Diary Report
IC	inspector in charge
IPC	Indian Penal Code
mahila samiti	women's association
OC	officer in charge
panchayat	elected village council
PO	protection officer
PWDVA	Protection of Women from Domestic Violence Act, 2005
shalishi	community-based arbitration
SP	superintendent of police
TMC	Trinamul Congress Party
125, CrPC	Section 125 of the Code of Criminal Procedure, 1973
498A, IPC	Section 498A of the Indian Penal Code, 1983

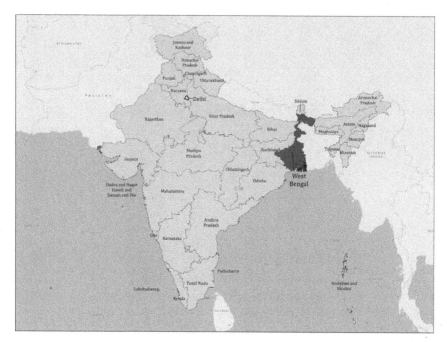

States of India map.

Scale [ca. 1:27,290,000]. Data layers: Vijay Meena: GIS file of India State, District and Tehsil Boundaries; Esri, HERE, Garmin, OpenStreetMap, and the GIS User Community: World Light Gray Canvas Base [computer files]. McGill University, Montreal, QC: Generated by Martin Chandler, April 3, 2020. Using: ArcGIS Pro [GIS]. Version 2.4.2. Redlands, CA: Esri, 2019.

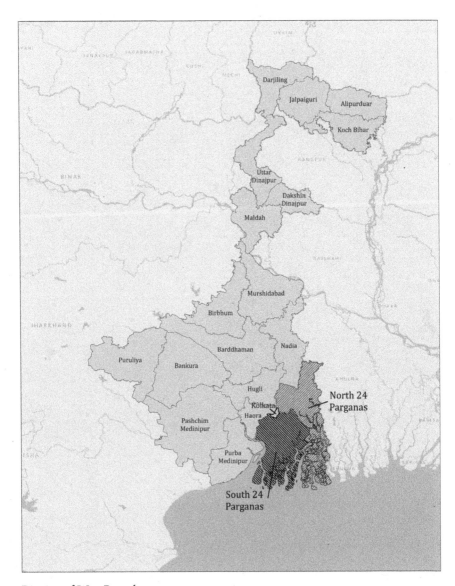

Districts of West Bengal map.

Scale [ca. 1:1,750,000]. Data layers: Vijay Meena: GIS file of India State, District and Tehsil Boundaries; Esri, HERE, Garmin, OpenStreetMap, and the GIS User Community: World Light Gray Canvas Base [computer files]. McGill University, Montreal, QC: Generated by Martin Chandler, April 6, 2020. Using: ArcGIS Pro [GIS]. Version 2.4.2. Redlands, CA: Esri, 2019.

SECTION I

OPENING

Introduction

Endeavor

By eleven o'clock in the morning, the courthouse was already running behind schedule. Located in the neighborhood of Alipore in Kolkata, the South-24 Parganas District Magistrate's Court resembled a postcolonial rendition of Dickens. The plaza in front of the main building buzzed with lawyers, typists, and vendors doing a brisk business in *luchi* (fried bread) and *ghoogni* (split pea curry). The atmosphere inside the courthouse was decidedly less festive. Bundles of yellowed, brittle paper lined each cube-shaped room: tangible reminders of all the legal suits that had been filed and forgotten. Frustrated litigants clogged the hallways. They shuffled up and down struggling to follow their lawyers' legal jargon and coalesced in small groups in doorways and staircases, seeking solidarity against the endless indifference.

Navigating past the constable who manned the front door, I made my way to the courthouse's top floor. Rupa was waiting for me, zealously guarding a seat on a broken bench. Despite its missing legs, the bench was favorably positioned below a ceiling fan that provided respite from the heat. We had entered May, one of the least benign months on the Indian calendar. A hundred years back, the British would flee the city at this time, driving pell-mell for the hills to escape the burning plains. But far from running away, Rupa had traveled to the city from her village. Inhaling exhaust and braving two hours of traffic, she endeavored to make progress on her domestic violence case. And so she waited, perched precariously on a sloping bench.

In her early thirties, Rupa had the appearance of someone older. Fine lines creased her forehead. Her eyes evidenced an exhaustion her energetic movements seemed calculated to defy. She had a penchant for bright colors and dark lipstick. But for her days in court, she aimed to look more conservative. Wearing carefully pressed tunics, her long hair neatly confined in a ponytail, she moved and spoke slowly and tried not to raise her voice. Outside the courthouse, she proudly recounted her rebellious nature. Born into a poor, lower-caste family and educated until the sixth grade, Rupa's rebellion started at the

Capable Women, Incapable States. Poulami Roychowdhury, Oxford University Press 2021. © Oxford University Press
DOI: 10.1093/oso/9780190881894.001.0001

age of fourteen when she defied her parents and ran away with her boyfriend. By her mid-twenties, she found herself on her own with a young son to take care of, her husband having abandoned her after years of sexual abuse.

Knowing little about her rights and lacking the language to articulate her experiences as violence, Rupa unintentionally moved toward a legal claim. One of her neighbors, an older woman with political connections, introduced her to a *panchayat* (village council) representative known to work on women's behalf. The *panchayat* representative pointed her to a *mahila samiti* (women's association). The *mahila samiti* referred her to a women's nongovernmental organization (NGO). The NGO provided rights education and legal counseling for women experiencing various forms of gender-based violence. Soon after Rupa entered the NGO, she found herself registering a case under Section 498A of the Indian Penal Code, the criminal law against domestic violence.

By the time I met her, Rupa's case was in its tenth year. On that particular morning, she was in court because her ex-husband had filed an appeal. The original court decision had been in Rupa's favor. He claimed to have unearthed new evidence to prove his innocence. Rupa worried about the time, money, and emotional costs her case had exacted. Yet, despite such burdens, Rupa continued to believe in the promise of rights and insisted that things were changing for women.

What was changing was sometimes unclear to her. But in her own words, she claimed "I have capabilities in the palm of my hand." She understood she had been abused and deserved compensation. She was friendly with powerful people, could navigate government offices, and knew how to work the system. At the NGO that supervised her case, she had trained to be a caseworker. She now made a living helping other women claim rights against violence. Through her casework, she had become something of a person of consequence in her village. And the very act of doing what she referred to as "running a case" (case *calano*) felt empowering. Her exertions produced a sensation of personal influence over the legal process. And at the end of it all, like the horizon that always receded, there lay the dream of legal redress: the more enchanting for its perpetual unattainability. It was all rather seductive.

Unfulfilled Promises

Rupa arrived at the courtroom that morning by braving hours of exhaust and traffic. But her journey into the rooms of the Indian criminal justice system mapped a longer history of women's struggle. Fifty years back, she would not have been sitting on that bench because India did not recognize domestic violence as a crime. Now, she was technically entitled to protection and compensation for the harms she had suffered. But it was unclear when, and if, she would attain those promises.

States ostensibly guarantee rights in exchange for obligations, such as paying taxes and voting (Bloemraad et al. 2008). Rights, however, have historically faced a discrepancy. You can have them on paper but not in practice. The discrepancy between rights on paper and rights in practice plagues women experiencing gender-based violence today. As I write these words, at least 144 countries have passed laws against domestic violence (UN Women 2019). Yet, law enforcement personnel implement rights unevenly, and women who claim rights face retaliation, ill health, and social isolation (Choo 2013; World Health Organization 2013).[1]

India provides a key example of this more general disjuncture. Legislators have passed both criminal and civil reforms. Section 498A of the Indian Penal Code criminalizes "physical and emotional cruelty" within marriage.[2] The Protection of Women from Domestic Violence Act (PWDVA) provides civil remedies to women in a range of domestic relationships. Sadly, legal reforms are poorly administered.[3] Law enforcement routinely suppress charges, refuse to initiate mandatory procedures, leave investigations pending, and fail to enforce verdicts (Burton et al. 2000; Mahapatra 2014). By 2018, Section 498A had the lowest conviction rate of all crimes prosecuted under the Indian Penal Code, and 10.9 percent of tried cases were illegally "compromised" out of court. Meanwhile, PWDVA cases had a higher chance of leading to a court order than 498A cases. But a mere 616 PWDVA cases were registered countrywide (National Crime Records Bureau 2018).

Noting the deadly consequences of this enforcement void, women's rights organizations have gotten involved in the nitty-gritty of case processing. Activists and caseworkers accompany women to court, pressure law enforcement to register complaints, and form alliances with other civil society groups to advocate on women's behalf. Routine intervention at the level of individual complaints has made domestic violence an increasingly politicized issue not just at the legislative level but at the level of local criminal justice institutions. As was the case for Rupa, diverse organizations with multiple and at times contradictory agendas weigh in on individual complaints.

This book is about women like Rupa, women who approach the Indian criminal justice system for rights against domestic violence. It examines the aftermath of legal reforms, asking how they have altered women's lives and relationships to the state. And through this in-depth analysis of the Indian case, the book poses a larger question about the possibilities and pitfalls of rights in vast areas of the world: places where gendered violence is a political issue, yet criminal justice institutions remain incapable and unwilling to enforce legal mandates. How do women claim rights within these conditions, and what happens to them when they do? How do law enforcement respond to their claims, and why? What kinds of governmental regimes and gendered citizens emerge in these contexts?

Collective Claims, Official Failures, and Extralegal Gains

For two years, I ethnographically tracked seventy women who were experiencing domestic abuse. I also conducted in-depth interviews with law enforcement personnel and a range of civil society actors who provided legal assistance. This research generated three key findings. First, women rarely claimed rights on their own. They distrusted law enforcement and feared they would either be ignored or further violated if they directly appealed to the criminal justice system. Instead of seeking rights as individuals, women systematically approached the state through organized groups: NGOs, *mahila samiti*, political parties, criminal networks.

Second, very few women received formal legal remedies in the process of claiming rights. Of the seventy women I tracked, only ten secured some kind of criminal or civil remedy and did so only after interminable waits. My qualitative findings mirrored country-level trends in case disposition, conviction, and enforcement. Since the 1990s, domestic violence cases have remained pending for longer periods of time, conviction rates have fallen, and fewer court orders are enforced. I found that these official failures structured the daily lives of the women I met.

Third, women who tried to access legal rights made notable extralegal gains. By approaching law enforcement through organized channels, they learned how to be financially independent and became knowledgeable about the public sphere and, at times, physically aggressive. They negotiated financial settlements, forcibly repossessed children and jewelry from abusive husbands, accessed paid employment, expanded their social networks, built women's groups, and became involved in politics. And they made sense of their transformations through a gendered discourse of self-transformation and empowerment.

How did all of this happen? Initially, the women I met wished to avoid a legal case. Lacking concrete definitions of "domestic violence," they nonetheless felt aggrieved. Most of them responded to their aggrievement by hoping their abusers would reform so that they could "run a family": continue to share a household with their abusers and jointly take care of children and aging parents. They looked to various local authorities for mediation and conflict resolution: neighbors, family, friends, political party members who lived in their area. They hoped these people would scold their husbands and fix their relationships.

They also believed that their gender entitled them to financial care and physical protection from people around them.

But the best-laid plans of mice and men often go awry. The very people who were supposed to help women "run a family" connected them to a range of organizations and actors who pushed them in a different direction: toward the law and toward "running a case." The organizations that transformed women's grievances into legal cases included women's NGOs, *mahila samiti*, political parties, and criminal gangs. Women's rights mobilizations against domestic violence had spawned a wider organizational field where all sorts of civil society groups weighed in on women's complaints. These organizations did not all promote women's rights, nor did they all believe that women were oppressed. What they shared was a strategic orientation toward women's legal engagements, where they brokered disputes for their own political and organizational purposes.

Women who had the kinds of complaints that served institutional interests were taken up and pushed forward by organizational personnel. Thus, despite their initial efforts to avoid the law, women ended up engaging with legal concepts and interacting with law enforcement personnel in some fashion or other. Their brokers helped articulate their grievances as instances of domestic violence. And these same brokers incentivized legal engagements by attaching material and social rewards to the law: providing medical care and financial help, job training, new social networks, and therapy. Brokers also provided the organizational resources and social networks women needed to become visible to law enforcement bent on ignoring them. Brokers helped women negotiate with criminal justice institutions, threatening and cajoling law enforcement to be somewhat responsive.

As a result, when women approached the criminal justice system, they did not interact with law enforcement as individuals with individual complaints. They brought collective claims visibly embedded in complex, unpredictable, and threatening organizational alliances. Law enforcement personnel who were only too happy to suppress individual women's complaints sang a different tune when women arrived with organized backing. They feared organized women might disrupt daily operations, threaten their job security, or unleash violence on their physical person.

Feeling disempowered, law enforcement adopted the path of least resistance. They did not complete the tasks necessary for case processing, but neither did they suppress charges. Instead, they "incorporated" organized women and their supporters into the regulation of violence. Law enforcement "incorporated" women in two ways: by reassigning casework and by telling them to replace a formal complaint with "parallel claim." They reassigned casework by telling women to complete paperwork, unearth evidence, and secure witnesses. At other times they told women to run "parallel claims," by threatening their perpetrators, extracting extralegal concessions, and carrying out extra-judicial punishments.

"Incorporation" resembles other forms of neoliberal governance where states govern from a distance, minimizing risk and work by encouraging civilians to manage social problems (Ferguson and Gupta 2002; Rose 2000). But "incorporation" is also specifically gendered. It is devised by state actors who are misogynist but feel compelled to appear minimally responsive when their authority is challenged. And it relies on the gendered notion that certain women are threatening and can fend for themselves.

In the process of becoming "incorporated" by the state, women learned to practice the art of "capability." Women with diverse complaints dreamed of acquiring money, political power, social influence, and independence by participating in the legal process. Instead of withdrawing, they remained embroiled in cases that dragged on for absurdly long periods. Like Rupa, many of them made a career out of helping other women get involved in a similar, seemingly never-ending dispute process. They remained engaged because legal ventures simultaneously helped them access otherwise inaccessible resources *and* produced a sensation of empowerment. They learned how to navigate the public sphere, negotiate with powerful state officials, forge social networks, access employment, threaten abusive husbands, and extract extralegal concessions.

Alongside these benefits, "capability" also entailed hard work, exposing women to the possibility of retaliatory violence, and sometimes leaving them socially isolated. Women found themselves struggling to complete many of the tasks law enforcement refused to perform. They were asked to confront the very people who had abused them. And many of them took these steps with very few financial resources and little by way of family support. As a result, not all women were able to be capable. Those who were lucky enough to have social, political, and financial capital had a significant leg up in the capability game, as did those who by dint of personality were fast learners and more courageous. Others fell behind, occasionally blaming themselves for their setbacks, arguing that if they had been more "capable" things would have turned out differently.

Moving Beyond State Protection and Victimhood

I did not anticipate finding what I found because the vast literature on gender, violence, and states had trained me to expect something else. Gender and legal scholars who analyze the effects of legal rights overwhelmingly argue that rights create protectionist governance regimes where state officials selectively award entitlements to "good victims": women who are docile, are passive, and fit hegemonic definitions of femininity (Bumiller 1987; Minow 1992). At the heart of these arguments lies a theory about how rights are or are not translated into practice: members of the criminal justice system decide how rights are realized, and they base their decisions on social bias. In the case of women, law enforcement personnel use gendered norms linked to class, race, sexuality, and other social categories to determine what kind of woman is actually recognized as a rights-bearing citizen (Collins 1998; Crenshaw 1991; Incite! 2007; Razack 1995).

This basic argument spans work on both post-welfare states like the United States and postcolonial, developing countries like India. In the post-welfare context, legal scholars highlight how state officials have co-opted women's rights in a broader project of expanding a "culture of control" and promoting carceral solutions (Bernstein 2012; Bumiller 2008; Garland 2012; Gelsthorpe 2004; Halley et al. 2006). In the realm of domestic violence, mandatory policies allow law enforcement personnel to prosecute cases without the consent of the victim and use protection orders to physically separate abusive men (Buzawa and Buzawa 2003; Coker 2001; Connelly and Cavanagh 2007; Corsilles 1994; Dixon 2008; Suk 2006). Culturally prevalent notions of women's vulnerability undergird this logic of masculinist protection: the notion that the state needs to protect certain kinds of women—read white, middle-class, straight, chaste—from certain kinds of men—read black, working-class, sexually perverse (Hollander 2001; Young 2003).

Scholars of India argue that, if anything, the dynamics of state protection and victimhood are heightened within the Indian criminal justice system. Protectionist legal measures span back to the colonial era. British responses to *sati* (widow immolation) and child marriage presupposed that Indian women needed to be protected from violent Indian men (Mani 1998; Sangari and Vaid 1999; Spivak 1988). After India gained independence, protectionist policies cropped up in numerous arenas related to violence against women: from skirmishes with Pakistan over "abducted women" to internal battles over minority rights within family law (Das 1996; Menon and Bhasin 2011; Pathak and Sunder Rajan 1989). This state of affairs has led some to argue that even the stories of infamous women outlaws, such as Phoolan Devi, who overpower and threaten law enforcement highlight the hegemonic gendered features of state power and the extent to which the Indian state is framed around "protecting" virtuous women (Sunder Rajan 2003).

Those who focus on domestic violence argue that the broader discourse of victimhood finds traction among activists, policy makers, and law enforcement. Many women's rights activists feel they have to establish their nationalist credentials by promoting an image of Indian women's exceptional innocence and vulnerability to violence (Kapur 2012). Similarly, legislators promote the language of victimhood, positioning themselves as guardians of women's modesty and virtue (Agnes 2005; Jaising 2005). Judges and police officers exhibit a great deal of paternalism toward female plaintiffs, treating them as incapacitated people who do not know what is best for them (Vatuk 2001). Paternalism goes hand in hand with demands for gendered merits, such as self-sacrifice and chastity, in exchange for entitlements (Basu 2015; Dave and Solanki 2000).

Complementing these political and discursive formations, the specific legal instruments that currently exist in India are similar to the ones criticized for expanding protectionism in post-welfare states. Section 498A, the criminal law against domestic violence, is a mandatory policy. In the language of the Indian Penal Code, 498A is a non-compoundable, cognizable, non-bailable offense. Once registered, cases cannot be withdrawn or settled out of court (non-compoundable). The police can initiate arrest proceedings and conduct investigations without a warrant (cognizable). Accused parties cannot negotiate bail without a court hearing (non-bailable). Similarly, the 2005 civil act against domestic abuse, PWDVA, creates a conduit between civil protection orders and criminal offenses. The PWDVA allows judges to issue interim protection orders before a trial. The violation of a protection order is a criminal offense that provides grounds for criminal prosecution.

Given this legal landscape and the theoretical expectations of other scholars, I should have found law enforcement responding to women's claims through their own selection mechanisms: namely, a set of criteria related to local definitions of virtuous femininity and aimed at protecting "good victims." Individual women, in turn, could have internalized these institutional demands by either identifying as victims or strategically performing victimhood: acting passive, demonstrating their innocence, sitting back and waiting for help. There was something to this expectation. A discourse of victimhood, alluded to through the term "women's oppression" (*nari nirjatana*), did float around police stations, courtrooms, and organizations that helped women make legal claims. Aggrieved women, in turn, did adopt this discourse from time to time.

But this was not the full story. There was also something else going on, something I had not anticipated. Even when the practices and discourses of victimhood were present, state officials urged women to be strangely proactive, rewarding those who gathered evidence and rounded up witnesses. Meanwhile, organizations that supported women's claims coached them not necessarily in how to appear passive and innocent but in how to take the law into their own hands and get what they could out of it. As a result, women facing violence did not necessarily wait for the state to protect them. Instead, they threatened and bargained with law enforcement, doing what they could to push their claims forward.

All of this meant that in my field site, legal rights against violence had not increased women's access to formal remedies. But neither had they created a protectionist governance regime for "good victims" as gender and legal scholars anticipated. To understand how and why these expectations remained unfulfilled, I consider how politics and enforcement capacity influence rights implementation, conditioning the terms through which women are recognized by the state.

Enforcement and Politics in Post-Colonial Developing States

Do all state officials pick and choose "good victims"? What if this process is context-specific, dependent on political and institutional conditions? After all, criminal justice institutions are not equally omnipotent. Enforcement capacity varies, rendering some law enforcement more vulnerable to political forces. Similarly, women are not as disorganized or as individualized as they were a few decades ago. The very process of legislative reform has provided new social and organizational resources to otherwise vulnerable women. Rights may involve negotiation between law enforcement personnel and women with disparate capacities, creating qualitatively different governance models.

First, law enforcement personnel are not always able to pick and choose who deserves entitlement. Their ability to control the selection process depends on the overall capacity of the criminal justice system within which they are embedded. Broadly defined, "sovereignty" refers to the state's ability to govern a given territory in the face of internal and external competition and resistance (Arendt 1976; Jackson 2007). In this way, sovereignty has to do with the state's monopoly over violence and its ability to define the rule of law (Agamben 1998; Schmitt 1985). The effectiveness of law consists not only in the underlying presence of a normative consensus, where citizens agree with what the law prescribes, but also in the "widely held expectation, borne out by exemplary evidence, that the law will be, if necessary, enforced by a central authority" (O'Donnell 1993: 1357). Not all states exercise a monopoly over violence, with developing, postcolonial states facing especially significant constraints (Hansen and Stepputat 2005).

Sovereignty is linked to institutional capacity. While much of the work on state capacity focuses on economic growth (Amsden 2001; Wade 1990), it also provides crucial insights on matters of law and criminal justice by highlighting the institutional foundations for effective legal regulation (Centeno 2002; Lange 2009). Capable states have cohesive bureaucracies: different departments coordinate with one another, and state officials are able to formulate rules, make decisions, and execute policies with relative autonomy from wider social forces, including special interest groups and mobilized citizens. These bureaucracies are embedded in citizen's groups, such as business conglomerates and unions, that help state officials steer programs and properly implement policies (Evans 1995; Evans et al. 1985).

Where state capacity and sovereignty are limited, we see a "decoupling" between law and practice (Meyer et al. 1997). In-depth studies of legal implementation indicate that state capacity is positively linked to human rights compliance (Risse et al. 2013). What this means for law enforcement overseeing rights implementation is the possibility that they are not always in charge: they may be unable to enforce the law, afraid of civilians who also command some form of violence, and overall insecure about their livelihoods and personal safety. In other words, law enforcement may not always be able to award rights to women they believe are "good victims" because women with political resources may force them to be responsive.

Second, and related to the last point, there is no need to assume that all women are unable to alter the outcomes of their rights claims. While law enforcement's ability to select good victims is conditioned by the institutions within which they operate, women's ability to influence law enforcement behavior depends on the political resources they have at their disposal. The state's limits shape the *kind* of political resources potentially available to women. Best theorized as "political society," limited states are populated by intermediaries who work with political parties and connect marginalized populations to otherwise inaccessible state-based rights and resources (Chatterjee 2004).

Members of political society mediate between civilians and the state partly by working within existing legal structures: using elections and demanding legal reforms. But they also deploy an array of extralegal tactics, circumventing legal procedure and mounting political challenges. Such "uncivil" tactics include clientelistic exchange networks (Auyero 2001); quiet, unobtrusive forms of encroachment (Bayat 2013); as well as violent confrontations (Paret 2015; von Holdt 2013). Members of political society reproduce themselves and acquire social credibility by liaising with state officials—but also through their abilities to threaten them. And demand for their services remains high among civilians exactly because the state does not guarantee rights through established legal channels (Mendez et al. 1999; O'Donnell and Schmitter 2013).

India currently houses both of the conditions that call existing theories of state protection and women's victimhood into question: the criminal justice system is of a limited nature, and women's access to political society is alive and growing. Indian law enforcement negotiate multiple and conflicting authorities that constrain and disempower them (Brass 1997; Jauregui 2013). In recent years, rising corruption and criminality among elected politicians have further hollowed out law enforcement autonomy and efficacy (Bardhan 2001; Vaishnav 2017).

Over this same time period, the activities of political society have arguably expanded. A host of new actors and social groups have confronted the state in what some have called the "second democratic upsurge" (Kohli 2012; Ruparelia 2013a; Yadav 2000). These groups see legal rights as a solution to social problems while simultaneously adopting a range of extralegal tactics to make the law work to their advantage (Jenkins 2013; Reddy 2005; Sundar 2011). The politics of domestic abuse is part and parcel of this broader trend in mobilization. Organized intervention was spectacularly visible in the massive protests that rocked the country after the Delhi gang rape of 2012 (Roychowdhury 2013). But political processes also influence mundane domestic disputes and routine prosecutions.

The Emergence of Capability

It is this book's central contention that within the kinds of conditions we find in India today, defined, on the one hand, by the criminal justice system's low enforcement capacity and, on the other hand, by women's access to organized help, legal reforms produce neither state protection nor women's victimhood. In this context, I find the rise of an alternative governmental strategy and gendered citizenship model: bureaucratic "incorporation" and women's "capability."

Borrowing from Nikolas Rose (1999), I define "governance" as patterns of power and regulation that direct social conduct. Recent work has theorized the rise of new forms of governance that work through devolution of risk onto private enterprises, civil and locally elected bodies, NGOs, and individual citizens (Barry et al. 1996; Burchell 1996; Cooke and Kothari 2001; Leve and Karim 2001).

For the purposes of this book, the most significant aspect of these broader transformations involves the particular way states use and deploy gender in new governmental initiatives. In key arenas from economic development to criminal justice, practices of inclusion and participation overwhelmingly target women (Alvarez 1999; Merry 2001). Even those women who are interned in correctional facilities are encouraged to be responsible citizens through discourses of therapy and self-management (Haney 2010; McCorkel 2013; McKim 2008).

These gendered realignments are apparent in diverse sectors in contemporary India. Developmental programs not only use the language of women's participation and empowerment but also put women to work to get things done (Corbridge et al. 2005; Sanyal 2009). Regional governments have increasingly addressed social problems, such as child malnutrition and rural credit, through women's self-help groups (Menon 2009; Rankin 2001; Tharu and Niranjana 1994). Where women's groups independently tackled governance issues related to violence and drugs, state officials extended public resources and attempted to imbricate themselves in movement successes (John 2005). Linkages between the Indian state and women, where state officials govern social problems through women, provide new insights on the transformations I observed in the realm of domestic violence.

"Incorporation" indexes a historically novel relationship between women and the Indian criminal justice system. In the past, law enforcement may have selectively protected a small group of idealized women, those who fit the criteria of virtuous victims. To everyone else, they could shut their doors, terrifying them into retreating or making them feel their problems were commonplace. In the present moment, these older strategies are no longer always politically feasible. The sheer increase in women's grievances propelled by the cultural dispersion of women's rights discourse and the growth of mediation services across the country has shifted the calculus for law enforcement personnel.

In the police stations and courtrooms I observed, ideological commitments jostled with other priorities, namely managing workload and containing popular unrest. Law enforcement felt compelled to consider women's organizational and political connections. Could the woman mobilize support, be disruptive, or threaten their livelihoods? Perceiving themselves to be disempowered relative to women who had organized support, law enforcement accommodated them in some way. Ceding authority, reassigning regulatory duties, encouraging women and their supporters to govern violence themselves, these strategies became the pathway of least resistance.

By incorporating organized women, law enforcement demanded "capability" rather than passivity and innocence. To engage the law and not be suppressed, women had to be cunning, socially connected, able to gather evidence, able to ferry documents, able to round up witnesses, aggressive, persuasive, and potentially violent both against the forces of law and against their own abusers. For women who got caught up in this process, the law provided new forms of social legibility and mobility, while also exposing them to new risks and dangers.

Amartya Sen's capabilities framework provides a strong moral argument for a positive definition of freedom: one that signaled people's abilities to attend school, to have a job, to participate in politics. Capabilities, in Sen's theory, are simultaneously a measure of well-being as well as a means to achieving more well-being. Our capabilities are the potential we have to convert primary goods (such as income, property, education) into a range of "functionings" (everything we may value doing or being).

For Sen, capabilities provide people with the freedom to achieve chosen lifestyles (Sen 1999). Being capable is better than simply being rich (a primary good), for it is our capabilities that allow us to transform that income into what we actually want to attain, be it living alone or learning to play a musical instrument or helping others. In Sen's theory, the conversion of primary goods into functionings is a product of active choice by the individual. But it requires the right context: a set of political, governmental, and social institutions that enable individual freedom in its most substantive and comprehensive form.

Sen's framework focuses on individuals and is relatively sanguine about institutions: with the right institutional support, individuals can gain capabilities. The main institutions, in his formulation, include a combination of markets and states. His vision of capabilities is missing the "social": other people and our relations to them. This is where the sociological literature on citizenship provides a much needed corrective to economistic understandings of rights. Individuals cannot rely on markets and states to ensure access to basic rights and freedoms; they need each other (Paschel 2016; Sanyal 2014). Relational and group-based phenomena shape and influence individual aspirations, capabilities, and social outcomes (Rao and Walton 2004). Associations mediate between individuals and the institutions that govern their lives, providing differential access to freedom and justice (Somers 2008).

The women I met acquired capabilities through organized groups. Access to and embeddedness in political society made them legible and worthy of attention to the state. Women "ran cases" in the way the urban poor in Brazil "run after their rights" (Holston 2008). The fight was not in their favor. The fight advantaged those who already commanded power: the people who abused them and the law enforcement personnel who could repress, ignore, and dismiss their allegations. It was because of this asymmetry that organizational connections mattered. Women's NGOs, *mahila samiti,* political parties, criminal gangs: these groups offered collective strengths essential to creating a slightly more even battlefield.

The stories that unfold on these pages underscore how women claim rights not as individuals but as members of organized groups. They make claims on the state through ceaseless negotiation, negotiation that demands courage, resourcefulness, and a good deal of dangerous, tiring, and uncompensated labor. Their endeavors rarely lead to rights: very few women receive state protection or compensation for the harms they have suffered. But women's ability to negotiate rights sometimes allows them to access something else: diverse capabilities that come with attendant risks.

Studying Rights Negotiations

The data in this book comes from the Indian state of West Bengal. For two years, I observed how women claimed rights from the criminal justice system, tracking allegations in West Bengal's capital city, Kolkata, and the villages and towns that lay to the south and north of the city. My observations led me into diverse arenas: women's homes, NGO offices, *mahila samiti* gatherings, public demonstrations, the headquarters of political parties, police stations, and courthouses. Alongside ethnography, I conducted interviews with the people who influenced and weighed in on domestic disputes, including activists, politicians, and law enforcement. Interview data allowed me to understand what had happened to the women I met in the decade prior to my ethnography as well as their trajectories after ethnography ended. All told, the book uses data spanning sixteen years.

Let me tell you a bit about West Bengal before I discuss the actors who traverse these pages. A map of West Bengal can be found in Figure 1.1. I chose West Bengal for two reasons. First, Bangla is my native tongue. I was born in Kolkata and spent the first seven years of my life there before moving to the United States with my parents. Ethnography requires immense command over language, especially the kind of ethnography that features in this book. Throughout the course of my research, there were rare moments when I, the ethnographer, was in a frame with just one or two other people. Most of my ethnographic observations took place in public arenas with numerous people in the same scene, talking over one another, arguing, and at times engaging in physical confrontations. Without a strong command over spoken Bangla, I would have had a difficult time comprehending the nuances and contradictions of these interactions.

Second, West Bengal provided an ideal site for understanding how women's rights are governed in India more broadly. The infrastructural constraints and political pressure endemic to domestic violence administration across India crystallize in West Bengal, making it a useful site for in-depth qualitative research. Key measures of criminal justice capacity, such as police strength, funding for protection officers, and judicial vacancy rates, indicate that West Bengal faces constraints that are similar to or slightly more severe than the all-India averages (Bureau of Police Research and Development 2015; Ghosh and Choudhuri 2011).

Meanwhile, the state is home to a growing number of organizations that supervise domestic violence law, including a high density of women's NGOs and feminist networks. Breaking with earlier traditions of women's organizing that focused exclusively on economic issues, these newer organizations attend to women's legal rights and gender-based violence (Basu 1994; Ray 1999). They exist in a crowded field with other organizations, including political parties such as the Communist Party of India (Marxist) and the Trinamul Party Congress, that have a record of intervening in domestic violence cases. Perhaps as a result of this organizational proliferation, since 2010, West Bengal has repeatedly registered one of the highest proportions of domestic violence cases in the country (Bhattacharya 2015). The latest numbers from the National Crime Records Bureau (2018) indicate that over 16 percent of criminal cases under Section 498A are registered in this state.

Now let me turn to the actors. I tracked seventy women who were experiencing domestic violence. These women came from different walks of life. A detailed breakdown of their social backgrounds can be found in Appendix A at the end of the book along with a lengthier methodological discussion and analysis of my position as a researcher within my field site.

The women I tracked varied by key social indicators that have been shown to influence women's access to legal rights in India: income, religion, caste, and residential location (rural or urban). Yet, despite their differences, they had one feature in common: they sought help. Help came from neighbors, family members, a women's association or NGO, political party representatives, a party affiliated thug, or a private individual who provided mediational services. While this feature of my sample may seem unusual, it is emblematic of how women make claims against violence in India. Qualitative studies as well as large-scale surveys indicate that women rarely approach the criminal justice system alone (Burton et al. 2002). Domestic violence allegations are rarely brought forward by individual claimants and instead involve a range of organizations and interest groups (Rao et al. 2000).

A number of the organizations that currently exist in West Bengal feature in this book. But the ones that crop up with regular frequency merit a degree of detailed attention. To ensure confidentiality, I have given each organization a pseudonym. I call them AIN ("the law" in Bengali), Andolan ("revolution"), and Shadheen ("free"). All three professed to "empower" women, using the English term "empowerment" to describe their goals. All three provided a mix of legal aid, counseling, and gender-training workshops for women and conducted community outreach. Yet, despite these similarities, these three organizations housed crucial differences.

Shadheen was located in the peri-urban area that linked south Kolkata to the villages of South-24 Parganas. It was an umbrella organization that housed numerous initiatives, from livelihood development to farming cooperatives to poultry production to microfinance. Parts of the organization were well funded through a combination of government and private grants; but its legal services unit grew cash-poor during the time I observed the organization, and many caseworkers operated on a partially volunteer basis. The second organization, AIN, was located in central Kolkata within a large, well-maintained office. It was well funded by transnational donors, and its professionalized staff were well educated and had personal connections with police officers, judges, lawyers, protection officers, and members of parliament. Like AIN, Andolan was also well funded, but its funding came from dues paid by its peasants' union. Andolan's caseworkers lived in a communal home, managed a communal farm together, and were provided a livable salary. With its headquarters in rural North-24 Parganas, Andolan also maintained branch offices in South-24 Parganas, Nadia, and East and West Midnapore. Andolan's union members linked the organization to a wide swath of villages throughout these districts, providing political clout and community resources. Together, AIN, Shadheen, and Andolan became key sites for my ethnography, providing a lens on how organizations mediated between women and the criminal justice system.

Last, but not least, the third set of actors in this book are law enforcement: police officers, protection officers, and court personnel. I conducted research with these three branches of the criminal justice system because they administer domestic violence law. The police and courts oversee criminal cases under Section 498A, ensuring case registration, investigation, trial proceedings, and enforcement. Meanwhile, protection officers oversee civil cases under PWDVA, and the police only get involved in these cases if a court order is violated. While women actively sought advice and interventions from brokers when they experienced violence, they were keen to avoid members of the criminal justice system. Simultaneously feared and reviled by ordinary citizens and the source of both antagonism and alliance on the part of brokers, law enforcement provided a surprising perspective on domestic violence cases. It was in the process of talking to and observing these individuals that I came to understand how and why the governance of gendered violence may take surprising pathways.

Book Overview

In the following chapters, I trace the emergence of incorporation as a governmental strategy on the part of an incapacitated and sexist criminal justice system and the evolution of capability as an identity and set of gendered practices among women experiencing intimate violence. Chapter 2 details the legal, social, political, and institutional history of domestic violence in India, highlighting its contradictions. On the one hand, rights activists have organized against domestic violence, helped initiate key legal reforms that promise women better and safer lives, and established institutional sources of legal aid and counseling. On the other hand, social stigma and limited access to housing and jobs constrain women's options outside of abusive relationships. And the criminal justice system, overburdened and sexist, does a poor job of ensuring women rights. This landscape shapes the negotiations that unfold through the rest of the book.

In the second section of the book, I trace how legal claims emerge and how they are contested. Chapter 3 focuses on women's initial attempts to manage violence. Using interview and observation data with women as they first seek help, I describe how the women I met did not want to pursue a legal complaint. Most of them did not even want to separate from their abusers. They hoped neighbors, political party members, and women's organizations would discipline their abusers and help them "run a family" (*sansar calano*). This chapter asks what it means to "run a family," why so many women remained committed to this practice despite experiencing violence, and how, despite their commitments, the very act of seeking help enmeshed them in organizations that pushed them toward legal engagements.

In Chapter 4 I examine the organizations that intervened in domestic disputes and ask why they did so. These organizations included women's associations, women's NGOs, political parties, and criminal gangs. These frequently antagonistic actors worked as brokers: they transformed private grievances into legal cases by mediating between women and the state. Violence brokers had distinct, and at times contradictory, understandings of domestic violence and gender inequality; and some were even ideologically opposed to legal claims and women's rights. Yet, all of them profited from intervening in domestic disputes. Disputes provided them access to financial, social, cultural, and political capital: opportunities to establish and expand their community presence, appear socially relevant, secure jobs and raise money, form personal relationships with state officials, and translate their new social credibility into pathways toward political office.

Invested in expanding women's engagement with the law for their own purposes, brokers still had to contend with the fact that most women wanted to "run a family." Before and during the actual work of mediation, brokers thus had to convince women to reorient their preferences. Chapter 5 shows how brokers negotiated with reluctant women, encouraging them to approach the criminal justice system for legal assistance. In addition to translating the law into local parlance, brokers provided therapy, embedded women in a group of other women who were pursuing legal cases, and helped them access key goods and services, including medical care, electricity, housing, and job training programs. These psychological, social, and material incentives lowered both the perceived and actual costs of legal cases for individual women while raising the potential benefits.

The state institutions that women turned to for assistance formed a juggernaut undergoing a slow yet perceptible transformation. With help from their brokers, women learned to navigate, confront, and form working relationships with law enforcement. Chapter 6 takes the reader into the halls of the Indian criminal justice system and into the lives of the police, protection officers, and court personnel who staff its offices. State officials simultaneously faced administrative constraints on their abilities to process cases *and* mounting organized pressure around domestic violence allegations. These conditions undermined their ability to exercise discretion, making it difficult for them to reject women they did not like and pick "good" victims they wished to protect. And it bred a sense of victimization, the notion that they were too overburdened and besieged to do their jobs. The main outcome of mounting political pressure for rights was thus twofold: law enforcement 's fear of alienating organized women and a concurrent discourse of disempowerment that rationalized poor performance.

Chapter 7 traces the tactics law enforcement developed to manage this contradiction. To balance political pressure against real and perceived capacity constraints, they neither suppressed women's claims nor did their jobs. Instead, they outsourced regulatory functions: reassigning casework and promoting "parallel claims." The governmental model that took shape was thus geared not around protection or outright suppression but around "incorporation." Law enforcement allowed women to pursue rights but only if they could take the law into their own hands.

In the last section of the book, I trace how women evolved in the process of claiming rights and came to exercise a limited form of citizenship. By incentivizing the law and by incorporating women into the daily work of regulation, both brokers and law enforcement encouraged women to run cases. Chapter 8 details what this entailed and the specific capabilities the practice of law engendered. To "run a case," women had to be able to risk estrangement, not only from husbands and in-laws but also from agnatic kin. Women had to confront and manage state officials: courageously demonstrating their social connections, overcoming insults and neglect, and resolutely pursuing rights despite delays. Finally, they had to be able to do the state's work: either completing case-processing duties or acquiring a semblance of justice outside formal legal procedures.

For women who "ran cases," the experience of confronting family and law enforcement and doing the work of the state created a subjective shift in how they perceived themselves and the law. Chapter 9 details this transformation in legal consciousness. Women who "ran cases" started believing they deserved what the law promised, a life free of violence where they could exercise a modicum of control over their bodies and material possessions. They began thinking of the law as a strategic field they could engage and manipulate. This "aspirational-strategic" subjectivity arose through their routine encounters with brokers and law enforcement. And it departed significantly from their initial orientations, which had included feeling disdainful of women who claimed rights and wishing to avoid the law at all costs.

Chapter 10 tracks what women actually got out of "running cases." For the vast majority of claimants, the outcome was illicit: not something guaranteed through a court order but rather something outside the law's environs. These illicit gains included lump-sum transfers of money, repossession of property and cash, regaining access to children, securing housing, finding jobs, making new friends, entering educational facilities, learning how to use public transport, feeling more confident talking to law enforcement, and using newfound knowledge of the law to become a caseworker. While these gains cannot be dismissed, this chapter also reveals that a mere handful of women actually received rights through the state.

Chapter 11 analyzes how the ideology and practice of women's "capability" stayed alive in the face of uncertainty and risk. The stalled institutional landscape, which promised everything but only meted out incremental gains, combined with feminist organizing and transnational discourses of women's empowerment, made "capability" a powerful ideal for ordinary women. At the same time, not everyone was able to successfully run a case or become "capable." Women with social, organizational, and financial resources were far more likely to flourish through this process. Even those who succeeded at becoming "capable" paid a price. Namely, they felt overworked, overwhelmed, lonely, and physically endangered. Trying to be capable had long-term negative effects on women's health, mental stability, and, for some, the very desire to survive.

The book concludes by considering the benefits and drawbacks of capability as a model of women's citizenship. I discuss how capability may create openings for underprivileged groups while simultaneously forcing women to take on new, dangerous burdens of labor. I end by theorizing the broader implications of my findings, both within India and outside. And I consider why rights continue to matter to people when states prove incapable of delivering justice.

‖ 2 ‖

Stalled

The Landscape of Domestic Violence

The social, political, and institutional environment surrounding domestic violence is riveted with contradictions. First, gender inequality remains pervasive, restricting women's exit options. Women who claim legal rights face social ostracism, physical reprisals, and financial destitution. Second, law enforcement personnel are incapacitated and sexist. They are neither able nor willing to enforce rights. But their limitations also make them vulnerable to political pressure, creating an avenue for women with organized support to make headway with their legal claims. Third, women have access to organized support. These organizations include women's groups and progressive NGOs, as well as political parties, labor unions, neighborhood associations, and even criminal gangs. Organized actors use a range of tactics, from bribery to threats, to pressure law enforcement and abusers.

Social Barriers to Legal Access

Before 1983, women experiencing violence in their homes enjoyed limited legal protections. Unmarried women had no legal recourse against domestic violence either from intimate partners or their natal families. Married women enjoyed limited remedies under religiously defined matrimonial law. And they could prosecute their husbands through general provisions under criminal law against hurt, grievous hurt, and wrongful confinement.[1]

This legal landscape changed in 1983 with the passage of Section 498A of the Indian Penal Code. Section 498A criminalizes "physical and mental cruelty" within marriage, allowing both men and women to register complaints against their spouses. Section 498A promises imprisonment and fines if violence is proven in court. In 2005, another set of legal reforms provided women with civil remedies. The Protection of Women from Domestic Violence Act (PWDVA) recognizes multiple forms of abuse, including physical, sexual,

Capable Women, Incapable States. Poulami Roychowdhury, Oxford University Press 2021. © Oxford University Press
DOI: 10.1093/oso/9780190881894.001.0001

financial, verbal, and emotional abuse. And it extends to women and girls in a range of domestic situations, including those who are unmarried. PWDVA provides orders of protection, residential rights, child custody, and financial compensation (Uma and Grover 2010). Appendix B presents a detailed discussion of both of these legal provisions as well as their procedural requirements.

Despite legal reforms, women still find it extraordinarily difficult to challenge violence and lodge legal complaints. First, gender inequality remains pervasive across class, caste, and religion. Gendered disadvantages structure everything from women's workforce participation and relative wages (Harriss-White 2003), to property ownership (Agarwal 1994), inheritance rates, literacy, nutritional intake, and life expectancy (Dreze and Sen 2002), and the gender ratio of live births (Oldenburg 1992).

Second, marriage continues to be a thoroughly hegemonic institution, configuring vast areas of cultural, social, and economic life (Chowdhry 2004; Uberoi 1994). According to the 2011 census, 49.9 percent of all women and girls were married. This number soared within certain age brackets: nearly 90 percent of women between twenty and forty years old were married (Government of India 2015). Divorce and separation rates remain low. Only 0.24 percent of married people get divorced, and another 0.61 percent are officially separated from their spouses (Jacob and Chattopadhyay 2016).

Marital practices across the country remain patriarchal, hierarchically organized around the authority of older male relatives (Uberoi 1994). Irrespective of their religious background and class status, women are expected to live with their husband's family and adjust to their in-laws' routines and expectations (Madan 1989). In addition, lower-middle- and low-income women who marry into houses without significant domestic help are expected to shoulder the brunt of domestic labor including cooking, laundry, and cleaning. Both Hindu and Muslim wives in rural areas continue to practice various degrees of *pardha,* refraining from conversing with unrelated men and veiling themselves in front of elder male relatives as a sign of respect and deference. In some cases, these norms break down in urban areas where wives live in tighter quarters with male relations. But in others, city life exacerbates gender segregation, forcing new brides to remain indoors and thoroughly isolated (Vatuk 1972).

Despite the hardships of marriage, leaving a marriage is financially and emotionally difficult for most women. Only a handful of the women I met earned a wage. These women came from opposite ends of the social spectrum: those who were well educated and had professional jobs and those who were poor and worked as itinerant agricultural workers and domestic servants. Women from lower-middle-class and middle-class backgrounds did not work outside the home. They were full-time homemakers who were financially dependent on their husbands and in-laws. Their financial dependence made challenging abuse an act that also challenged their subsistence.

In their lack of access to wage work and their concentration in low-wage temporary work, the women in this book mirrored broader patterns of gendered labor across the country. Women's labor force participation in India has steadily fallen since the mid-1990s. While roughly 35.4 percent of women worked outside the home in 1995, this number had fallen to 27.0 percent in 2013 (Andres et al. 2017). This drop is driven by trends in rural areas where women's labor force participation rates decreased from 33.1 percent to 25.3 percent. The nature of work has also shifted: women are more likely to be employed in marginal and temporary work now than they were in the 1990s. Concurrently, the number of women who say they "attend to domestic duties" has increased in both rural and urban areas. In 1994, 29 percent of rural women and 42 percent of urban women attended to domestic duties, whereas these rates had risen to 35.3 percent and 46.1 percent, respectively, in 2012 (Verick 2014).[2] While these trends have complicated and heavily debated causes, their impact on women's ability to escape violence is largely negative.

Women's financial options outside marriage are further limited by the fact that very few women in India own property of any kind. None of the women in this book, including those from relatively wealthy backgrounds, had a room of their own, literally speaking. Women's property ownership in the south Indian state of Kerala has been shown to serve as both a deterrent to violence and an exit option (Panda and Agarwal 2005). This dual mitigating function of property rendered women's lack of property even more tragic. Laws governing inheritance leave the vast majority of women propertyless in India. This outcome is the product of a peculiar disjuncture between legal rules and cultural practices.

Wives, irrespective of religious background, do not enjoy legal rights to marital property in India. Upon divorce, separation, or abandonment, a woman cannot make a legal claim on her husband's estate, even if she has contributed her own labor and financial assets to its upkeep (Singh 2017). While wives do not have property rights, daughters technically do. Under the 2015 Amendment to the Hindu Succession Act, a Hindu girl enjoys equal rights to ancestral property as her brother. Meanwhile, Muslim personal law grants daughters varying degrees of rights to ancestral property depending on the school of law (Hanafi or Shia) a family follows. While the law thus grants women property rights as daughters, social norms deem that a married woman is no longer a member of her father's household but rather a member of her husband's. In other words, most people, including women themselves, do not believe they *should* exercise a right over their father's property.

This India-wide problem takes on a particular form in West Bengal due to two sets of class-based localized practices. First, property-owning families of all religions tend to take and receive dowry and follow the customary *Dayabhaga* Hindu inheritance system, where sisters give away their rights to ancestral property to their brothers. Dowry, where a girl's family gives gold and other assets during a marriage, is traditionally a Hindu practice. But Muslims in West Bengal increasingly practice it, disavowing the Muslim tradition of *mehr*, where the husband pays the wife a certain amount of money that she is allowed to take with her upon divorce (Gupta and Chattopadhyay 2005). Dowry is integrally related to gender-based patterns of inheritance. Even though the dowry is given to her husband's family, it is interpreted as the woman's "share" of ancestral property. Thus, married women from both Hindu and Muslim families are expected not to make a claim on their father's property, the idea being that they already received "their" portion.

While dowry and *Dayabhaga* limit middle- and upper-class women's access to property, the gendered biases built into communist-inspired land reform initiatives set the terms of exclusion for poor women. By 1980, the Communist Party of India (Marxist)'s (CPI[M]'s) land reform initiatives, known as Operation Barga, granted the state's sharecroppers titles to land (Kohli 1990). Titles provided legal protection against arbitrary eviction from landlords as well as a set share of produce. Yet, at the time of the reforms, titles were exclusively registered under male "heads of household," even though over 50 percent of agricultural laborers were women (Mallick 2007). Since that time, the state government has attempted, with limited success, to grant women joint titles. But to date, very few women are registered as tenants with formal rights to the land they work (Gupta and Chattopadhyay 2005).

The financial costs of challenging abuse accompany a range of normative prescriptions. Domestic violence continues to be discursively constructed as commonplace, rather than something extraordinary requiring intervention (Kannabiran 2005). Terms such as *jhagra* (fight) and *mara-mari* (hitting) occlude the systemic and gendered character of domestic abuse. Meanwhile, traditional gender norms link women's virtue to their ability to sacrifice for their families. These norms consolidated in the nineteenth century, alongside a growing move toward monogamous marriage and extended families (Majumdar 2009). It was at this time that reformers moved away from definitions of Hindu conjugality as a terrain of pure love and reason to one of feminine self-sacrifice, pain, and discipline (Sarkar 2001).

Despite changes in women's status post-independence, culturally specific definitions of ideal femininity continue to impact women today. Women who wish to reconcile with their abusers are considered to be dutiful wives. Those who withstand abuse to provide care for family members, are patient, and refuse to assert their rights are deemed good women. When a woman decides to complain, she fails to live up to these culturally valued attributes. She risks being interpreted by friends and family as well as by law enforcement as uncaring, harsh, and impatient.

Meanwhile, the popular linkage between domestic violence cases and evil women remains ubiquitous. One finds it by opening any mainstream newspaper and by turning on the television. Conducting a simple Google search on Section 498A reveals pages of links providing help and advice to men accused of violence. Without providing any evidence, all of these sources broadcast the dubious notion that women make up false allegations. Conservative policy makers have used the trope of the manipulative wife to fight for a rollback in legal protections (Koshyari 2011). The Indian Supreme Court has gone so far as to issue directives encouraging police stations to suppress charges (Mahapatra 2014). And even putatively progressive activists have claimed that women "misuse" laws to torture their husbands (Kishwar 2003).

The notion that bad women protest violence is closely linked to the idea that only a bad woman would get hit in the first place. While there is no direct translation of "she was asking for it," the concept is commonplace. Inegalitarian gender norms are internalized, rather than subverted. Results from the National Family Health Survey of 2016 indicate that 52 percent of women respondents believed that husbands are "justified" in beating their wives under certain circumstances, for example, if they cook poorly or leave the house without their husband's permission. Men were *less* likely than women to say violence is ever justified. Compared to 52 percent of women, approximately 42 percent of men said that a husband can justifiably beat his wife under certain circumstances (International Institute for Population Sciences 2017).

All in all, the persistence of financial hurdles and moral prescriptions linking women to the institutions of marriage and family means that survivors have a very difficult time resisting violence within the home. Economically surviving on one's own remains difficult. Resisting social norms, some of which become internalized, and believing that one has the right not to suffer abuse is equally as difficult. Those women who are somehow able to overcome these massive social barriers must contend with the actual institutions of the law. These institutions are by no means hospitable to their legal claims.

Criminal Justice Bias and Incapacity

Women who claim rights must contend with the fact that their chances of success are very low. Law enforcement personnel systematically fail to enforce women's rights, especially when the rights involve domestic violence. Their failures are most visible in the realm of criminal law. Conviction rates under Section 498A fall every year and remain consistently at the bottom of all crimes prosecuted under the Indian Penal Code (National Crime Records Bureau 2008). By 2018, a mere 15.9 percent of tried cases resulted in a conviction. Meanwhile 10.9 percent of registered cases were illegally "compromised" in out-of-court settlements (National Crime Records Bureau 2018). While the Code of Criminal Procedure decrees it unlawful to withdraw a 498A complaint once it has been filed, "compromises" are officially recorded and actively encouraged by police and judges (Mahapatra 2014).

Falling conviction rates and illegal compromises accompany ever lengthier trials and massive delays at every step of the pretrial process. Some 30.5 percent of cases registered under 498A in 2017 still waited a police investigation by the end of the year, while 90.1 percent of cases awaited trial. Even more startling, 12,484 criminal cases have been pending trial for *over* ten years (National Crime Records Bureau 2018).

Once registered, PWDVA cases tend to fare better than 498A cases. By 2018, 47.3 percent of tried cases led to a court order. But, similar to the situation for 498A cases, law enforcement refuse to abide by mandatory time limits in PWDVA cases. By year end 2017, 23.8 percent of PWDVA cases remained pending investigation, while 81.6 percent awaited trial in court (National Crime Records Bureau 2018). Placing these hurdles aside, PWDVA's main problem remains usage. In 2017, only 616 cases were registered countrywide. Regionalized implementation studies indicate modest progress with case registration. But this progress has happened in select places, such as Andhra Pradesh, while other regions of the country continue to experience delays and negligence, including West Bengal where this study was conducted (Bhatia 2012; Ghosh and Choudhuri 2011). Low registration rates are due to a lack of awareness of the law and inadequate budgeting (Lawyers Collective Women's Rights Initiative 2013). Civilians, service providers, and even law enforcement are ignorant of the civil act; and state governments have refused to make allocations for protection officers (POs).

These official outcomes aggravate the already low levels of confidence women have in the criminal justice system. Ordinary women distrust the state and especially fear law enforcement. Partly, this distrust arises from a lack of familiarity with state institutions. Because private and public spheres are heavily gendered, political parties and civic associational life remain male-dominated realms. While ordinary men can become familiar with the state and with state officials through these channels, ordinary women are excluded from these venues. As a result, most women have limited knowledge of laws and legal institutions (Corbridge et al. 2005). And they do not imagine the criminal justice system to be a caring, gentle ally that provides shelter from the abuses of private life (Suneetha and Nagaraj 2010).

Women's antipathy towards law enforcement, while based in lack of familiarity, is nonetheless well founded. The Indian criminal justice system is both
sexist and incapacitated, making access to justice difficult and at times hazardous.
Bias against women operates at every level of legal institutions, from what Nancy
Fraser (1997) terms the "grammar of legal reasoning" to the physical threats law
enforcement pose to marginalized women. Existing research documents high
levels of hostility toward women who seek rights against violence (Agnes 2005).
Like their counterparts in other parts of the world, Indian law enforcement personnel make pointed remarks about women's attire, physical appearance, and
personal backgrounds (Basu 2015; Baxi 2010; Jaising 2005; Vatuk 2001). They
are openly disrespectful of marginalized women: those who are poor, Muslim,
tribal, and Dalit. And they are quick to dismiss violence when the victim engages
in sex outside marriage, sex work, homosexual activity, or non-monogamous sex
(Baxi 2005). Custodial rape and harassment are persistent threats, especially
for women who are underprivileged (Kannabiran and Menon 2007; Kapur and
Purewal 1990).

Judges, police officers, and POs express minimal interest in enforcing domestic violence law and openly express bias against women making legal claims,
calling them "monstrous" (Elizabeth 2000; Lodhia 2009; Rao et al. 2000). Many
encourage reconciliations because "good" wives are supposed to be dedicated to
their families, even if their family harms them (Burton et al. 2000; Dave and
Solanki 2000). Underlying these pronouncements is the idea that women are
"naturally" wives and mothers: obedient, self-sacrificing caregivers of husbands,
children, and extended family members (Kapur and Cossman 1996). This ideal
creates a range of contradictions for those looking to exit a violent domestic situation (Basu 2012). The very act of registering a complaint can render a woman
a bad victim under this framework, because she has dared to complain.

Gender bias coincides with significant capacity constraints that are visible at
multiple levels of the criminal justice bureaucracy. Both Section 498A and the
PWDVA mandate a long list of tasks for police, POs, and the judiciary.[3] Yet, none
of these administrative units are capable of fulfilling their duties in a comprehensive or timely fashion. Anyone who gains access to an Indian courthouse's
records room will immediately see the criminal justice system's capacity issues on display. Reams of paper, yellowed and brittle, provide evidence of the
massive backlog that plagues the country. As of November 2018, there were
over 28.5 million cases pending in India's district courts, the backbone of the
country's court system. Nearly 6.5 percent of these cases had been pending for
over ten years (National Judicial Grid 2018). There were another 56,320 cases
pending in the Supreme Court (Supreme Court of India 2018). This backlog
is a product of missing judges. By 2018, India's High Courts were functioning
with 676 out of an approved 1,079 judges, while district courts were missing an

additional 5,748 judges. Overall, this meant that India had nineteen judges for every million civilians (Gandhi 2018; Press Trust of India 2018a, 2018b).

Staffing issues coincide with inadequate administrative infrastructure and counterintuitive procedures. Forms remain unstandardized, and records are handwritten. Judges orally summarize testimony for court recorders, who are under no obligation to follow uniform recording procedures or classification systems. The schedule of cases is made available the day before or even early in the morning of the same day. As a result, witnesses routinely do not show up, leaving lawyers and judges waiting. The lack of out-of-court discovery processes means that court personnel are forced to wait even longer as evidence is filed in court. Finally, judges are rotated from bench to bench within a period of a few months, with little predictability in case assignments. Constant rotation prevents continuity in knowledge and creates perverse incentives. Since cases quickly become someone else's responsibility, judges do not feel a sense of ownership over their cases and thus have little incentive to dispose of them in a timely fashion (Mehta 2005).

The police have fared even worse than the judiciary. India has one of the lowest police to civilian ratios in the world, with one police officer for every 720 civilians. Acute staffing shortages and a series of organizational and infrastructural issues make the police one of the least cohesive and least embedded administrative units within the criminal justice system. These constraints span back to the foundation of the police in the late nineteenth century, when the British colonial government established policing units to prevent violence against the state (Arnold 1986). Little has changed post-independence. The institutional design of the police, from rules of recruitment to the location of constabularies, continues to focus on suppressing dissent rather than controlling crime (Bayley 1983; Verma 2005). Police stations are often in disrepair, have few vehicles, and lack adequate communication equipment such as wireless devices (Dubbudu 2015; Human Rights Watch 2009).

The police are organized into three separate tracks: the Indian Police Service (IPS), the Provincial Police Service (PPS), and the constabulary. Administered by the central government, the IPS comprises 1 percent of the total force and is highly trained and well compensated. The middle tier, the PPS, constitutes 14 percent of the force and is also relatively well educated and well compensated.[4] The last tier, constables, make up a massive 85 percent of the force. They are poorly paid, have minimal training, and have maximum exposure to civilians.[5] Required to pass only a tenth-grade exam and trained in simple drills and arms handling, they know little about conducting investigations, even though they are first on the scene when crimes occur and in charge of classifying incidents and processing complaints. They work in abysmal conditions: on call 24 hours a day, ill-fed, housed in poorly maintained barracks, and occasionally sleeping out in the open (Human Rights Watch 2009). Nearly 90 percent of them are on duty for more than eight hours at a time, with the majority doing eleven- to fourteen-hour shifts.[6] Approximately 74 percent of them receive less than one day off a month (Bureau of Police Research and Development 2015).

Rank hierarchies between IPS, PPS, and constables are completely unbridgeable and map on to strict social hierarchies. IPS officers come from politically connected, wealthy, upper-caste, urban families while constables come from poor, rural, lower-caste backgrounds (Verma 2005). This segmentation is further entrenched through formal rules about who sits down, who remains standing, and who eats together. Informal practices, where superior officers use constables as family servants, further the exploitation of subordinates. Because hierarchies are severe and unbridgeable, there is little information sharing between ranks. Upper-level officers consider information from lower ranks to be suspect, while constables feel compelled to produce "desirable" evidence for superior officers (Human Rights Watch 2009).

Similar constraints plague POs, who form the key administrative unit supervising civil cases against domestic violence. The number of POs continues to vary greatly from state to state. When I was conducting research, West Bengal had thirty-nine POs across its eighteen districts, covering a total population of 90.32 million residents. Like police officers, POs also had plenty of reasons to grumble about meager compensation. Advertisements for POs posted within the recruitment website of West Bengal's Women and Child Welfare Services agency in 2015 showed a monthly salary of RS 12,000. Support services for POs remain dismal across the country. By 2012, a full six years after the PWDVA went into effect, only fourteen out of India's thirty-three states and union territories had separate budgetary allocations for the law. POs lacked basic support, including staff to deliver notices, photocopying machines, mobile phones, and a daily travel allowance (Lawyers Collective Women's Rights Initiative 2013).

Problems across administrative units have a compounding effect. Backlog in courts adds to the burden of preserving evidence and keeps police and POs unproductively occupied in attending court hearings where their time is spent on procedural matters rather than deposing cases. Meanwhile, court cases stall because police and POs lack motivation to complete proper investigations (Saravade 2015).

Very little has been done to rectify any of these issues. The central government has repeatedly ignored calls for court and police reforms, making paltry financial provisions for infrastructure and personnel in its five-year economic plans (Commonwealth Human Rights Initiative 2007; Kapur and Vaishnav 2014). Where the central government has failed, state governments have done little better. On average, states currently spend 3–5 percent of their budgets on policing. West Bengal was among one of five states to request a further delay in salary increases recommended by the central government's Pay Commission (Srivastava and Verma 2015).

Politicians show little interest in institutional reform because keeping law enforcement on a tight leash poses key advantages (Tripathi 2016). Elected officials seek to limit law enforcement autonomy to cover up personal misconduct, conceal polling violations and interparty violence, and persecute political opponents (Subramanian 2007; Vaishnav 2017). Compared to other democracies, India has a highly politicized police force, with political parties influencing all aspects of police management (Bayley and Stenning 2016). State governments enjoy considerable authority over suspensions, promotions, transfers, and appointments of judges, police, and POs (Dhillon 2011; Raghavan 2003). Evidence of political party interference is easily observable in the ever-shortening tenure periods of district magistrates and senior police officers, the "transfer industry" that accompanies assembly elections, and the assignment of "punishment posts" to rebellious officials (Srivastava and Verma 2015; Verma 2005).

Law enforcement personnel know political parties control their livelihoods and realize they have to keep party members happy (Desai 2016; Subramanian 2007). Personalistic relationships between law enforcement and politicians have been documented to impede law and order functions in a range of places across India, including around major incidents of ethnic violence (Bayley 1983; Brass 2005; Hansen 2001). The judiciary routinely use internal lobbying networks to advocate for their position as well as those of family and friends (Tripathi 2016). Meanwhile, police officers report pressure to keep politicians happy by prosecuting certain crimes while overlooking others (Bureau of Police Research and Development 2015).

Fear of political parties coincides with fear of other kinds of organized groups. Police and court personnel have to contend with violent civilians surrounding their offices, throwing rocks at them, and burning government vehicles. Nowhere are the realities of physical danger more evident than in aggregate police injury and casualty rates. In 2017, a total of 840 state police died on duty, with another 2,684 officers injured. Casualties and injuries were highly concentrated among the lowest ranks of the police bureaucracy (constables, head constables, assistant sub-inspectors, and sub-inspectors), those officers who are directly involved in crime-control operations. Of those killed on duty, 92 percent were in these ranks; and it was also these ranks that accounted for 89 percent of injuries. Notably, violent civilians inflicted the majority of injuries, with "riotous mobs" causing 56.4 percent of injuries and "other criminals" another 22 percent (National Crime Records Bureau 2018).

Organized Support for Women

While social inequality and law enforcement bias and incapacity constrain women's abilities to claim rights, oppositional forces have fought to expand women's legal access. Neither Section 498A nor the PWDVA would exist without the massive organizing campaigns that preceded them. India saw the birth of an autonomous women's movement in the late 1970s, when women's rights activists split from male-dominated political associations and expanded their own independent base (Katzenstein 1991; Purkayastha et al. 2003).

The custodial rape of a sixteen-year-old tribal girl named Mathura provided the crucial political momentum the women's movement needed to focus on violence against women (Sharma 2019).[7] Activists took to the streets across the country and pushed for legislative reform. By the early 1980s, movement members were increasingly intent on domestic violence reform (Gandhi and Shah 1991; MacIntyre 1981). Nonprofit organizations and women's committees teamed up with feminist lawyers, staging direct action campaigns across the country, conducting petition drives, and working with friendly legislators to re-draft both criminal and civil law (Kannabiran and Menon 2007).

With the advent of economic liberalization and increased funding from the central government in the 1990s, parts of the women's movement became institutionalized within NGOs (Kamat 2003; Kudva 2005). But this institutionalization accompanied direct action campaigns and continued agitation at the grassroots. It also attended a growth in counseling and legal aid services. These services were not limited to the upper classes or women who lived in urban areas. The organizing that happened around violence included rural areas and housed a diversity of forms and approaches. Discourses of "women's empowerment" became visible in disparate spaces, from rural women's groups who talked of *stree-shakti* (women's power) to government-managed nonprofit organizations (Omvedt 1993; Sharma 2008).

Over time, movement expansion and institutionalization slowly made violence against women into what social movement scholars refer to as a "master frame" (Benford and Snow 2000). Developments within feminist circles encouraged a certain degree of isomorphism in related spaces (Powell and DiMaggio 1991). In the process of trying to help women facing violence, women's rights activists reached out to potential civil society allies. As a result, awareness of the issue grew among other kinds of organizations and among the general populace. Movement expansion lay the foundation for another important transformation in organizational practices. Organizations that used to address issues that had little to do with gender inequality started focusing on violence against women. Originally advanced by only the most dedicated of feminist activists, violence became a platform through which a wide sector of society articulated grievances and built livelihoods (Tarrow 2011).

Within West Bengal, this history took a specific form. Social movement organizing against violence took off under NNPM, the Nari Nirjatana Prathirodha Mancha (Forum Against the Oppression of Women). Founded in 1983, NNPM served as an umbrella organization for women's activism across the state.[8] Similar to what had happened at the national level, NNPM emerged in response to the Mathura rape case, when a sixteen-year-old tribal girl was raped in police custody in Maharashtra. NNPM continued to grow through the 1980s due to a series of incidents involving domestic and sexual violence in Kolkata.

In the early years, NNPM members worked on a voluntary basis and struggled to retain their independence from party politics. West Bengal's ruling CPI(M) dominated women's organizing in the state through its women's wing, the Paschim Banga Ganatantrik Mahila Samiti. Ideologically centered on class conflict, the CPI(M) tended to define "women's issues" as economic issues, sidelining questions of gender-based violence (Basu 1994; Ray 1999). By the 1990s, however, NNPM had established itself as an independent force to be reckoned with. NNPM members increasingly worked alongside Maitree, a women's rights network founded to specifically address state violence against women. At the same time, movement members began their own NGOs.

It was at this time that many of the organizations that feature in this book came into existence. AIN, for example, was specifically founded to address domestic violence; and this issue continues to be the NGO's raison d'être. Meanwhile, Shadheen and Andolan epitomized a second trend. As activists coalesced around domestic abuse, women's organizations that had previously focused on other aspects of gender inequality increasingly concentrated resources on violence.

Originally established to tackle various forms of economic inequality, Shadheen's casework team grew in the early 2000s as the organization spent less time on economic development and more time on legal services. Around the same time, Andolan created a women's wing from its original peasants' union, largely to address issues of domestic violence. Together, AIN's, Shadheen's, and Andolan's evolution underscored how women's rights against violence gained a certain hegemonic status in West Bengal, changing organizational practices within feminist circles and beyond (Roychowdhury 2016a).

Much like the story we see in West Bengal, women's rights activists and organizations in other parts of the country take a range of forms, from formal NGOs to informal women's organizations. And they use a range of tactics, from working closely with law enforcement to bribing them to threatening disruption. To achieve their goals, women's organizations form strategic alliances with political parties and criminal elements. And they embrace a complex stance toward the law, simultaneously working for rights while using illegality to advance legal claims.

The Gulabi Gang (Pink Gang) provides a case in point. Founded by Dalit women in Bundelkhand, Uttar Pradesh, the Gang has an estimated 400,000 members (Biswas 2007). The Gang uses a language of women's rights and empowerment, positioning itself as a mediator between women and law enforcement. Simultaneously, members are renowned not just for their pink uniforms but also for their characteristic *lathi* (a long stick). The Gang threatens abusive men as well as police with their martial arts tactics. They are known to bribe state officials to gain traction for women they represent and to cozy up to various political parties and underworld figures to shore up their prestige and threatening image (Biswas 2007).

Sampat Pal Devi, the Gulabi Gang's founder and erstwhile leader, publicly embraced illegality, welcoming media depictions of her group's vigilante justice (*Gulaab Gang 2014; Gulabi Gang 2012*). Sampat was deposed in March 2014, ostensibly because she was embezzling funds. But rumors indicate that she was either getting too cozy with the criminal underworld or insufficiently politically connected. Despite her removal, or perhaps because of it, Sampat continues to make public appearances and to portray herself and other Gang members as assertive, intelligent women who are capable of overcoming the abuses of useless men and doing what the criminal justice system cannot or will not do. The Gang's activities and discursive stances highlight an extreme example of how women's groups use vigilantism to advance legal claims.

The Stage Is Set

Together, pervasive gender inequality, criminal justice incapacity and negligence, and political pressure create an uneven legal landscape. The growing tide of legal cases accompanies a politicization of the legal process. An array of institutions and organizations provide legal assistance to women. Women's groups and NGOs intervene in domestic violence cases to be sure, but so do political parties, neighborhood associations, and even criminal gangs. In places like Maharashtra, for example, the women's wing of the Shiv Sena, a far-right Hindu paramilitary unit, routinely interferes in domestic violence cases (Bedi 2007; Hansen 2001). Meanwhile, in West Bengal, where this study was conducted, both the CPI(M) and the TMC take sides on mundane domestic disputes when the dispute touches the lives of party members and important constituents.

These diverse actors play a dual mediating role between state officials and citizens. First, they vernacularize legal rights into local parlance and articulate diverse grievances into legally recognizable cases (Levitt and Merry 2009). Second, they prove their worth to the communities they serve by mobilizing against what they identify as law enforcement negligence, pressuring criminal justice institutions to be more responsive. They frequently take opposing sides on any given conflict, with some taking the woman's side and others representing accused men. Intersecting affiliations enable rapid and unpredictable alliances between different groups, creating a constantly shifting terrain and multiple forms of political pressure bearing down on law enforcement.

Some of these organizations support survivors, while others help alleged perpetrators. They use a range of tactics to influence law enforcement decisions. They disrupt daily operations: showing up repeatedly at government offices, refusing to leave when told to do so, arguing. Disruptions occasionally involve ambitious projects such as *gherao*, surrounding an office so that people cannot enter or exit, and *dharna*, an act of civil disobedience involving fasting and camping peacefully outside a government building. Organized groups also physically threaten law enforcement: throwing rocks, chasing them from villages, breaking the windows on their vehicles, setting vehicles on fire, and beating them up. Finally, they use connections in the upper-level criminal justice bureaucracy and among elected politicians to threaten law enforcement's job security.

Organized claims hit a criminal justice system that is itself porous and vulnerable to political pressure. Together, resource and personnel constraints negatively impact criminal justice capacity along both dimensions of the term, by diminishing cohesiveness and embeddedness. It is not merely a question of how many cases law enforcement are able to process, though that is one very serious fallout of growing infrastructural constraints. Perhaps equally importantly, state officials end up less insulated from wider political forces and less capable of enforcing legal statutes. Incapacity disempowers them by robbing them of their monopoly over violence and hollowing out the esprit de corps so integral to bureaucratic autonomy (Evans 2012). They stop being able to pose a credible threat to civilians. And they become susceptible to corruption and political influence.

State officials' inability to maintain a strong monopoly over violence produces a vicious cycle of clientelistic alliances similar to practices documented in parts of Latin America (Caldiera 2000; O'Donnell and Schmitter 2013; Willis 2015) For law enforcement, keeping organized groups, upper-level bureaucrats, politicians, and the wealthy happy becomes a tactic to save their livelihoods and their lives in a context where it is very difficult to actually do one's job honestly or well. Keeping possibly threatening civilians happy in turn further fuels the cycle of incapacity. As a result, women with threatening organizational backers find an opening to make potential headway.

SECTION II

NEGOTIATIONS

Running a Family

Women's Reasons for Reconciliation

Brinda was adamant. She did not want to register a case. She wished to "run a family" (*sansar calano*). We were sitting cross-legged on a jute mat, huddled together for warmth in Shadheen's upstairs room. Rupa sat beside me, asking Brinda questions. Ten years ago, Rupa had been in Brinda's place, looking to Shadheen for help with her abusive husband. But since then, the nongovernmental organization (NGO) had become a place of work and second home. Located in the peri-urban area that links south Kolkata to the villages of South-24 Parganas, Shadheen housed a range of women's rights initiatives, from poultry and agriculture to a sewing unit to microfinance. Rupa worked within the anti-violence unit. She was the lead caseworker at the organization.

That morning Rupa spent a fair amount of time trying to understand Brinda's history. The cement floor numbed our legs as the wind sliced through the window shutters. Winters in the countryside could be hard. Rupa and I were appropriately bundled. Brinda, wrapped in a tattered shawl, was not. She had a hollow cough that rattled her thin frame, and her feet were cracked from the cheap rubber sandals that exposed them to the elements. Despite it all, she was beautiful: a bright flame of a woman with green eyes and golden skin. "It's hard to be poor and pretty," Rupa liked to say. "The pretty girls get into the worst situations."

An hour passed before we pieced together the extent of Brinda's problems. She still loved her husband. They had two children. Yes, he had hit her from time to time. No, she was not living with him now. She was living alone in Kolkata. Her children were in the village, with her parents. She worked in Kolkata, earning money to feed them. Where did she work? Oh, here and there. She lived in Kalighat. How had she gotten there? Her husband had left her there, in a house managed by a lady. She had left last week and returned to her parents. From these answers, we pieced together what Brinda refused to say outright. Kalighat is an area of Kolkata associated with sex work in the popular imagination. The "lady" Brinda mentioned possibly referred to a madam, someone who ran a brothel.

Capable Women, Incapable States. Poulami Roychowdhury, Oxford University Press 2021. © Oxford University Press
DOI: 10.1093/oso/9780190881894.001.0001

Her husband had not only "abandoned" her, he had possibly sold her into prostitution. She had managed to escape a few days back.

Despite these events, Brinda did not want a separation. Nor did she wish to register a legal case against her husband, not for domestic violence and definitely not for trafficking. What she wanted above all else was to reach "a harmonious agreement." Could Rupa arrange a meeting between them, she wondered? Her husband would listen to Rupa. He would learn to behave himself.

During the intake session, Rupa caught my eye. Later, she vented her frustrations. "You see what we are dealing with here?" Rupa was exasperated. "How can she want to go back to that husband of hers, after everything he has done to her and their children? 'Running a family, I want to run my family.' That's what all these girls want. They are getting beaten every day, or worse. And they still think running a family is a great privilege." Rupa threw up her hands in frustration.

Constantly hearing accounts of violence, Rupa's exasperation at women's desires to run a family was perhaps not all that surprising. Her own life, both at work and at home, appeared to challenge whatever ideological and practical commitments underlay this practice. As a caseworker, counseling women who wanted reconciliations, she was unyielding. "Running a family" would not do. Women had to stop capitulating to their abusers, patching things up, giving them another chance. She held herself up as an example: a woman who had escaped abuse by refusing to run a family. "I decided ten years ago I had enough of stirring a spatula around," she joked with a bit of bravado. The line helped her put on a brave face. She rarely let on that the decision to stop "running a family" had not been hers.

Her husband had abandoned her for another woman after years of sexual abuse. He was still with that woman, and the woman in question happened to be one of Rupa's distant cousins. Since that time, Rupa had built a new life for herself, fighting her own case against domestic violence and becoming Shadheen's lead caseworker. This trajectory, from an abandoned victim to a relatively powerful figure in a well-known women's NGO may have encouraged her to engage in a bit of historical reconstruction. "I never wanted to be like other girls and just run a family," she told me when I first met her. Later, once I had known her for almost a year, she let her guard down and confided that she had wished to keep her family together for her son's sake. She lamented that some women are fated to have "a life of happiness" with a husband and children. She was not one of them.

Rupa's occasional moments of empathy were clouded by the mission and overall ideology of the organization she worked for. Dolly, Shadheen's executive director, was adamant. Shadheen was not in the business of arranging reconciliations, she announced. In her mid-forties, born and educated in Kolkata in an upper-caste, middle-class family, Dolly had become Shadheen's executive director five years ago. Posters lined her office, instructing readers to "save money for a daughter's education, not her dowry!"

When faced with women like Brinda, women who wanted to run a family in the face of violence, Dolly grew depressed. "You know what our biggest problem is?" Dolly asked the question as if it was a statement. We were eating a leisurely lunch in her office. But Dolly was clearly agitated. By "our," she referred to the general category to which both she and I belonged: women. Perched at the edge of a less-than-sturdy plastic chair, one hand in my tiffin box, the other holding a small laptop on my knees, I must have looked confused by her allusion to women's "biggest problem."

Dolly answered her own question. "The main problem is within ourselves." She confessed she could not stop thinking about all the women who had approached Shadheen only to return to abusive men. Dolly regretted that "some women want to remain within their enclosures." Using the culturally loaded term *gondi* to signal enclosure, Dolly heralded an image of the Hindu goddess Sita standing within a circle drawn by her husband.[1] The circle promised protection as long as Sita did not stray beyond its borders. The *gondi*, a circumscribed space drawn by a patriarchal society, simultaneously enclosed women while enlisting their participation in such confinement. It provided a culturally resonant metaphor for the causes of women's victimization, an Indian version of Stockholm syndrome.

Dolly went on to flesh out these causes. Social, political, and economic constraints formed the first source of victimization: the prisons that lay outside and confined women's bodies. But this was not women's "biggest problem." For Dolly, the most challenging component of Shadheen's work involved women's desires, what she alluded to through the Bengali word *iccha* (intention, wish, pleasure, desire).

Dolly's explanation for why women sought reconciliations was condescending to be sure. But even if such condescension was based in some amount of truth, the metaphor of the *gondi* left much unexplained. What did it mean to "run a family?" What did it demand, and why did so many women want to do it, even while experiencing violence? And how, despite their commitment to keeping their families intact, did women like Brinda find themselves asking NGOs like Shadheen for help when that help threatened to dissolve the very institution they cherished?

The Logic of Reconciliation

Of the seventy women I talked to during the course of my research, only three sought help with the express purpose of pursuing a legal claim. Notably, these three women were the wealthiest and most highly educated in my sample. The vast majority (forty-eight women) wanted to "run a family": make the abuse stop; reconcile with their abusers; live under one roof with their children, husband, and in-laws; and work inside the home to provide care for the people under their roof. These women expressed a clear preference for remaining with the people who had abused them, be it their husbands or in-laws, embodying the desires Dolly found so problematic. Finally, a third group did not want to run a family but felt they had no other option (nineteen women). They could not imagine surviving on their own and were unwilling to entertain the idea that such a life might be feasible.

While pursuing a legal case was clearly something only the most elite women thought to do on their own, there was a great deal of diversity among the women who wished to run a family. The practice crossed income, caste, education, and religious boundaries. And in their initial attempts to hold on to their relationships, these women mirrored the vast majority of Indian women who have experienced intimate abuse. Women routinely reject legal cases because their adversarial nature threatens to break apart marriages and extended families (Das 1996; Sen 2010; Suneetha and Nagaraj 2010). "Marriage is everything," a longtime women's rights activist and lawyer acknowledged with sadness in her voice. Indira practiced in Kolkata's High Court, where she represented survivors of gender-based violence. She also served as a member of West Bengal's Legislative Assembly (MLA), affiliated with the Communist Party of India (Marxist, CPI). While Rupa and Madhavi felt frustrated by women's demands for reconciliation, Indira expressed sympathy for her clients' inclinations. "A woman has to suffer such indignities if she is unmarried. You will not be able to convince a common woman that she should not get married. The vermillion mark is everything."[2]

Being married and staying married, as Indira pointed out, was the norm. Wanting to "run a family" made a great deal of sense for most women. It made financial sense because very few of them owned property or had access to independent income. It made social sense because those who remained with their abusers received crucial forms of social support from family and neighbors, while those who challenged abuse faced social sanction. Finally, "running a family" made emotional and psychological sense because women who successfully kept their families intact were deemed to be virtuous, while those who failed were castigated as immoral and unfeminine.

Brinda understood these incentives. She had grown up in a village not far from Shadheen's office. She remembered going to the village school but could not remember how many years she had spent there. Her reading and writing skills were rudimentary. That morning at Shadheen, Madhavi wrote everything Brinda said down on a long piece of paper. When asked if she would like to read the statement herself, Brinda shook her head no, admitting she could not read very well. Madhavi read the statement aloud and then Brinda signed at the bottom in handwriting that resembled that of a child.

All of this meant that Brinda's employment opportunities were limited. A new factory had opened up not far from her house, where women were hired to make umbrellas; but those jobs were scarce, and she had heard that the factory had already filled its quota. Alternately, she could work as an agricultural worker, like her father. Or she could look for domestic work, cleaning people's homes and taking care of children. Or she could do what she had been forced into doing, sex work. Compared to these options, her husband had provided a certain amount of financial security. He worked as a security guard, wore a smart uniform, and received a relatively regular paycheck.

Brinda's residential options outside of marriage were even more limited than her financial opportunities. It is extremely difficult for women to live without a male relative in West Bengal. In urban areas, landlords refuse to rent apartments to single women. Women who attend universities or travel to the city for work manage this problem by living communally in dormitories and other establishments that cater exclusively to women. Relatively elite women who can afford to pay more for an apartment access housing through personal connections or an institutional guarantor. In villages, these options are nonexistent. Families linked by blood and marriage live together in extended family homes. Nobody is willing to take on a single woman and her children as tenants. If Brinda had been alone, she might have been able to find a position as a live-in domestic worker. But her two daughters made this option impossible.

She had temporarily solved her residential woes by moving back in with her parents. But her parents were unwilling to house her and her daughters indefinitely. Their refusal partly had to do with their poverty, which made life a zero-sum game. The house Brinda grew up in had a tiled roof and mud floors. There were two rooms and a small nook in the veranda that served as a kitchen. The bathroom was separated from the house, a small outhouse with a hole in the floor and space for a quick shower. The rooms were already occupied. Her parents slept in one, and her brother, his wife, and their son lived in the other.

"My parents would have kept me on if it wasn't for my brother's wife," Brinda complained. "She has always been jealous of me. She's saying that I shouldn't be there, that a decent married woman stays in her own home and doesn't take advantage of her brother." Brinda was outraged by the allegation that she was taking advantage of her brother. As frequently happened with the women I talked to, she blamed another woman for her problems. Brinda's sister-in-law happened to be the person who was in the most proximate position to her: another wife with limited financial or social opportunities outside marriage, responsible for childcare and household labor. Called on to expand her daily cooking and cleaning duties, it is very likely that Brinda's return placed the greatest physical burden on this woman. As a result, she may have complained the loudest.

Seen from a different angle, however, Brinda's sister-in-law was the weakest link in the cast of characters who determined Brinda's fate. She had as little legal right over the household in which she lived as Brinda had over her husband's. As wives, neither of them could lay a claim over their husband's house.[3] As daughters, they could technically claim rights over their father's property.[4] But here the irony of the situation reached tragic proportions, for it wasn't just her brother's wife who thought Brinda should go back to her "real" family. While Brinda enjoyed a legal right to the home she had been born in, she did not enjoy a social right to be there or to claim any of its benefits.

Brinda's father, who had worked his entire life as a sharecropper, would pass the land title to his son. Brinda's brother would inherit the right to farm the land, just as he would own the modest two-roomed house upon his father's death. There was no discussion on the subject. Everyone took it for granted. Not even Brinda thought to challenge this arrangement. Rather, she insisted over and over that she "was not there to claim a share" of what was not hers. She "loved" her brother and would never take "his" home from him. Brinda's pleas to her family may have been strategically motivated, an attempt to assuage her brother and sister-in-law's fears so that she could gain temporary shelter for herself and her children. But I believed her sentiments were heartfelt. She herself did not think of the house where she had grown up as her house. In Brinda's mind, her true home was the home she had made with her husband, the home she had no legal right to, the home from which she had been violently ejected.

The discursive construction of Brinda's husband's house as her real "home" and her own acceptance of this construction as legitimate underscored the degree to which Brinda's options outside marriage were restricted not merely by financial concerns but also by social arrangements and gendered norms. She felt the social incentives to "run a family" with her abusive husband acutely, through the daily slights of being back in her natal village and through the wear and tear of living with a hostile sister-in-law. Her return to her natal home strained her most intimate relationships. But she also felt social pressure indirectly, through the comments and questions neighbors leveled at her parents.

Neighbors questioned Brinda's parents about their absent son-in-law's whereabouts, asking pointedly if he missed his wife. Extended family members were just as unhelpful. An elderly aunt kept asking why Brinda still had not returned home. When I visited Brinda's house, her parents talked about the social slights they endured on their daughter's behalf. Brinda's father had taken to giving rote responses, while Brinda's mother was overly loquacious, trying to explain away people's curiosity. While some people asked questions because they were well meaning, trying to make conversation and check in on Brinda's family, others were less innocuous. Questions policed the boundaries of social behavior, serving as a form of communal surveillance against deviance. Repeatedly forced to account for their behavior to others, Brinda and her family lived in a Goffmanian groundhog's day (Goffman 1959).

The deviant thing to do, everyone intimated through their perpetual questions, was for a married woman to live with her parents. To keep up appearances, Brinda's parents explained that she was a temporary guest. "I told everyone she is staying here while our son-in-law lives in Kolkata because of a new job," her mother confessed having lied to the neighbors. This lie also conveniently provided an excuse for Brinda's husband's missing visits. Above all, the lies covered up what Brinda's parents did not want anyone to find out: that her husband had abandoned her and that she had worked in a brothel. The facts of her trafficking were not even discussed within the family. Her mother only obliquely referred to her work in Kalighat by telling me what would happen if people found out where Brinda had been. "We won't be able to show our face."

The idea that Brinda was a temporary guest could only be convincing if she returned to her husband at some point. Her parents' support was contingent on her continued desire and attempt at reconciliation. As long as she appeared to be trying to work things out, she attracted reinforcements. Family honor and the desire to save face worked alongside the financial burden of supporting a dependent daughter and her female children. Thus, Brinda's desire to "run a family" was strongly motivated by the fact that her parents would only allow her and her daughters to remain with them for a fixed period of time. She had to reconcile.

But shame was also a powerful motivator. The shame she felt came not from financial or social constraints but from her ideas about what it meant to be a good woman. A woman's virtue lay in her ability to keep her marriage intact, she told us that morning. Somehow, whatever had happened was her fault, not her husband's. Her return to her father's house marked her failure as a wife, not her husband's failure as a human being, she kept insisting. And it was because of this sneaking suspicion that she continued to insist that her husband was not a bad person.

This idea, that being beaten or trafficked meant that you deserved it, was relatively widespread. Brinda's mother summed up what Brinda was feeling in a succinct statement: "she couldn't make her husband love her." Brinda's mother was not the first or last person to say this about an abused woman. I heard this statement repeatedly throughout the course of my research. It revealed a set of attitudes about both violence and gender. The abuse Brinda had suffered was not violence per se; it was merely the opposite of love. And Brinda herself had incited it by failing to be the kind of wife a man would cherish. "Good girls" do not get beaten. When a man was violent, it must mean that his wife somehow deserved it. Violence, in other words, was a legitimate response to gender deviance.

Related to this notion was the idea that a "good" wife puts up with violence for the sake of her family. In this ostensibly contradictory viewpoint, a woman who was beaten was not bad per se. She was wronged, but the real testament of her virtue was her ability to withstand violence without budging. While this idealized wife stood slightly at odds with the notion that only "bad girls" get beaten, in people's everyday thoughts the two rationalizations coexisted without much conscious conflict. Among Hindu families like Brinda's, the ideal of the ever-sacrificing wife took on mythological significance. Sita, the goddess and wife of the god-king Rama, withstands countless tortures while remaining a devoted wife: she follows her husband into the jungle when he is banished from his kingdom, withstands abduction and possibly rape, and then, to prove her purity and devotion, voluntarily undergoes a trial by fire (Doniger 1999).

Brinda alluded to Sita at one point in our conversations, mentioning how Sita had endured so much pain on her husband's behalf. Her reference was not surprising. Young Hindu girls repeatedly hear Sita's story from their grandmothers and mothers. The story provides instruction on what is expected of them when they are older (Raheja and Gold 1994). Brinda's words lent a certain amount of credibility to Dolly's anxieties. It was Sita who was told to stay in her *gondi* and then punished when she strayed. Here was a woman who was using the epic as moral instruction for her own supposed sins. Dolly was on to something when she feared that women were socialized to like their patriarchal prisons.

Like Brinda, others who experienced violence extolled the ethics of women's patience. They argued that "running a family" took effort and demanded skill. One had to be tranquil and forgiving. Their in-laws deserved another chance. It was their duty to stand by their man, to wait and see if their husbands would change. Patience, tranquility, and forgiveness were gendered virtues. Women were supposed to endure, to put up with inconvenience, disregard, disdain, and mistreatment. A woman's tolerance (*sahya-sakti*) indexed her abilities, something she had achieved and for which she should be lauded. The word for tolerance tellingly contains the word for "power" (*sakti*). The ability to withstand violence, to keep the family together at all personal costs, demonstrated not weakness but rather its opposite: it showed a woman's ultimate strength.

The Dangers of Legal Action

Given the financial, social, and normative incentives of marriage, it was no surprise that Brinda wished to reconcile with her husband. But the costs involved in pursuing legal action did little to push women in the other direction. Legal cases came with a set of real and imagined dangers. Women's negative impressions of the state cemented whatever social pressure and socialization left to chance.

By registering a case, a woman not only challenged hegemonic gendered norms and exposed herself to retaliatory violence, she interacted with a set of state personnel known for their negligence to the needy and violence toward women.

Fear was something real and something every woman had to contend with when she decided to stop "running a family." Since women tend to be at greatest risk of being killed after they leave their abusers, they contended with the possibility of retaliatory violence (Kelly 2014; Pelley 2016). In addition to these life-threatening possibilities, most of the women I talked to felt terrified of talking directly to their abusers, far from trying to use the law to discipline them. Exposure to various forms of violence has the effect of eroding people's confidence, but none so much as violence within intimate relationships (Campbell 2002; Garcia-Moreno et al. 2005; Shepard and Pence 1999).

Against these possibilities, the law offered little in the form of safety. Legal cases were time-consuming and financially burdensome, and it was difficult to tell what would come of them. It was impossible to assess the potential trade-off between these various costs and rewards in advance. Since domestic violence cases rarely adhered to procedural guidelines, it was hard to know how long a case would last. Pending cases meant wasting energy on something that might not end in a favorable judgment. The financial burden of public transport alone, going back and forth between police stations, courtrooms, and NGOs, often over the course of months and years as a legal case dragged on, was prohibitive for low-income women. This did not account for all the other financial penalties: the cost of repeatedly missing work, the cost of photocopying documents, the cost of bribing the court clerk so that he would give you trial dates that were close together, the cost of a lawyer if you were running a civil case and did not qualify for government assistance.

Legal action demanded that women step into spaces they knew little about and whose protocols were unclear. State officials commanded a distant, formal power whose dimensions and extent were ambiguous and terrifying. Most of the women I talked to knew very little about the law or about legal procedure when they first came forward looking for help. Ten women, all of whom notably lived in Kolkata, had heard of Section 498A, the criminal law against domestic violence. Only three of those women knew of the Protection of Women from Domestic Violence Act (PWDVA), the more recent civil amendment. Lacking concrete knowledge of the law, they nonetheless sensed the potential threats that law enforcement personnel posed to vulnerable women. Media reports of police brutality and custodial rapes worked alongside popular distrust of law enforcement corruption and abusiveness (Brass 1997; Kapur and Vaishnav 2014).

These concrete hazards lent legitimacy to the false belief that the home was a safer space for women than the legal sphere. Despite incidents of horrific state violence against women, any given woman is far more likely to be physically and sexually assaulted at home, by someone she knows (Jaising 2007). Socialized to stay at home and indoctrinated to believe that state officials would violate their purity, women felt anxious about engaging the law. Those from socially disadvantaged backgrounds, those who were low-income, lower-caste, and Muslim, were especially likely to express fear at the thought of entering courtrooms and talking to police officers. Meanwhile, those who were relatively privileged associated legal institutions and law enforcement personnel with forms of indecency and incivility that threatened their own gendered and classed status.

Hema, a low-income, lower-caste Hindu woman who lived in a town not far from where Brinda had grown up, laughed when I asked her about registering a case against her husband. Short and fair, with a round face that communicated a lively wit, she laughed at the idea that the police would protect her. She summed up her opinion of police officers in the following pithy statement: "Faced with my husband or the police, I would run towards my husband every time. The police are worse than the thugs they lock up." Hema feared that the police either ignored or further violated women who asked for help. For Hema, the dangers, both real and imagined, of legal action made the dangers of the home seem relatively manageable by comparison. Intimate violence was familiar in a way that the potential violence of the state was not. The abuse she suffered occurred within the familiar confines of the domestic sphere, a space she understood and which she had been socialized to trust even though her actual experiences defied her ideals.

In addition to voicing fears about law enforcement personnel, as Hema had regarding the police, women talked about law enforcement partiality toward the wealthy and powerful. "They don't respect us," Najma, a young Muslim woman from a family of landless sharecroppers told me in the midst of a rights awareness workshop organized by Shadheen. She expressed a desire to seek help from the NGO's casework team but not to pursue legal action. The other workshop participants, women like Najma who were stepping into the NGO space for the first time, gathered around a blackboard on woven mats spread across the cement floor. They clamored to join in. "It's true what she says," one of them grabbed my hand to get my attention. "We could never go to the courthouse or police alone. They don't look us in the eye. But someone like you [pointing toward me], they will pay attention to."

While marginalized women like Hema and Najma expressed fear of law enforcement personnel, women who came from relatively more privileged backgrounds argued that state officials were incompetent or corrupt and that legal institutional spaces were inhospitable to "respectable" women. Some twenty kilometers north of where Najma and Hema lived, Koel routinely dropped by AIN's offices for counseling sessions. When I first met her, Koel had no intention of registering a case. She needed to talk through her experiences and figure out strategies for emotionally coping with the end of her marriage. Koel was upper-caste, middle-income, and Hindu. She had grown up in the city, was well educated, and worked as an accountant. She talked at length about the criminal justice system's poor performance in relation to not just domestic violence but all sorts of crimes. This complaint worked alongside the notion that a woman like herself should not spend time with the ordinary people who inhabited criminal justice institutions. "It's just not something girls from our backgrounds do," Koel remarked. "We weren't raised to be around street people. There are all sorts of loose characters." Linking the public spaces of the criminal justice system to a classed and gendered notion of the public as a sphere for low-income men, she was dismayed by the possibility of spending time in police stations and courtrooms. The very presence of poor people and of men in the public sphere, Koel intimated, would taint her reputation by association.

Koel's anxieties indexed the classed dimensions of women's anxieties. Legal action as well as the mere act of inhabiting legal institutional spaces threatened to contaminate their virtue as women of a certain class. Ashu, a middle-income Christian woman born and raised in North-24 Parganas, was staunchly set against pursuing a legal case when I first met her in Andolan's office. She had approached Andolan specifically because she had heard they helped women avoid the law. While she knew very little about her legal rights, what she knew for certain was that legal cases broke up families and ended the possibility for reconciliation. She had read news reports about how women "abused" the law to torture their husbands. "I'm not trying to do that," she rushed to reassure me, anxious that I was judging her. She wished to distance herself from the monstrous women of popular media, still at a point in her life where she believed virtuous women did not pursue legal remedies. She wished to retain some legitimacy as a good wife: someone who was working hard to forgive and make amends, someone who was set against a legal confrontation.

By registering a case, one took on the law and all its real and imagined travails. And one challenged deeply entrenched gender norms about what it meant to be a good wife and good woman. Case registration indicated that a woman did not wish to tolerate abuse, that she no longer had any patience, and that she chose her own individual well-being above and beyond the sanctity of the extended family. A legal claim threatened to make the claimant appear harsh, self-interested, and adversarial: everything in effect that a good woman stood against. Since these characteristics were interpreted as not just immoral but also unfeminine, a legal claim threatened a woman's femininity, masculinizing her and making her look inappropriately gendered.

Rupa was no stranger to assaults on a woman's femininity. In the process of fighting her own legal case, she routinely encountered disapproval of her gender performance. Rupa's husband's lawyer repeatedly accused her of being *jandrel* (stubborn, aggressive, authoritative) in court. When leveled at a woman, the term connotes not simply intransigence but also masculinity. By repeating the word over and over again, the lawyer hoped to paint a picture of Rupa as a bad wife, the kind of woman who did not know how to be appropriately feminine. A masculine woman, he intimated, could not be trusted. Not only might such a woman have provoked her husband into hitting her; she may have cooked up the whole story of abuse to extract concessions. There was not much evidence of Rupa's stubbornness or aggressiveness on display at court. She was unusually meek and silent during her trial, visibly worried about how others might perceive her. The only step she had taken that could be construed as *jandrel* was pursuing the case in the first place. Her very presence in the courtroom allowed her husband's lawyer to hurl accusations of gender impropriety in her direction.

Brinda quickly faced similar indictments. When she decided to register a 498A case against her husband, her mother-in-law retaliated by calling Brinda's femininity into question. Defending her son's actions and dismissing the idea that he had hit Brinda or trafficked her, she referred to Brinda through the derogatory term *meye-chele* (girl-boy). This term is not gender-neutral, nor does it refer to people of a third gender. Bengalis level it at women they deem immoral. The term communicates social disapproval by masculinizing the woman in question, highlighting how her flaws are not merely human frailties but violations of appropriate gendered behavior.

The Ties That Unbind

Given the normative and practical underpinnings of family life and given that Brinda seemed bent on avoiding the law, I wondered how she ended up at Shadheen. Here was a woman who wanted a reconciliation. Yet, there she sat, facing Rupa, a caseworker resolutely focused on legal measures. Brinda's situation was strangely commonplace. Hema, Najma, and Koel also found themselves in a similar predicament. Women routinely sought help from people who were either ideologically opposed to reconciliations or, for reasons that were not completely clear, bent on getting them to register legal cases.

It is impossible to understand women's movement toward the law without recognizing two facts. First, both the institution of the family and the act of "running a family" were far from private affairs. In their attempts to keep their families together, women sought help from a broad network of social relations. Second, members of this social network were able to intervene against violence because they commanded authority both within the family and in the public sphere. In the process of intervening, they frequently drew on their public connections, asking a range of political and civil organizations to help their cause. Together, the lack of privacy of family life and the nature of the authority required to inter-vene ensured that the woman experiencing violence rarely controled how that violence was resolved.

The domestic sphere that women inhabited was not a private space. It was a liminal and porous place linked to the public sphere through relations of work and kinship. For middle- and low-income women, the home was the center of family life as well as a space of work, involving an array of domestic workers (Ray and Qayum 2009). For women of all social backgrounds, the home in-cluded people bound by blood and marriage, as well as *atmiya sbajana,* what Bengalis refer to as "kin" or "relatives." *Atmiya sbajana* could be distant relations, neighbors, friends, co-workers, employers: people who became familial through long-term contact and relations of reciprocity (Fruzzetti and Östör 1976; Inden and Nicholas 2005).

In the daily course of managing their households and completing household obligations, women thus interacted with a wide range of people with whom they shared various forms of intimacy, from women who employed them as domestic help to women who they employed to cook and clean their homes to neighbors and a whole array of people who they considered kin. Women who experienced violence actively sought help from their social network. Poor women who did domestic work gained information about women's committees and self-help groups from the women who employed them. They asked *atmiya sbajana* to scold their husbands and reason with their in-laws. Women also had help foisted upon them. The structural weakness of married women as well as the fact that cultural norms defined women as vulnerable and helpless meant that *atmiya sbajana* believed it their duty to intervene when they witnessed violence.

A woman's natal kin network usually formed the first line of defense. Compared to their marital homes, women receive much greater care and support, are ex-pected to work less, and enjoy a greater range of movement and freedom in their natal neighborhoods and homes. As a result, these are the people women first look to for help. Survey responses from women experiencing domestic abuse show that 65 percent of those who sought help did so from their own family. But natal families can sometimes be distant and affinal kin more proximate: an-other 28 percent of survivors looked to their in-laws for assistance (International Institute for Population Sciences 2017).

Older men and some older women within the kin network were able to inter-cede because of the status and respect they received from their position within the family (Vatuk 1998). Hema, for instance, relied on her husband's eldest aunt for protection. "Whenever he [her abusive husband] gets in a bad mood, she tells me to go to her room. She is the only one he listens to." As the eldest woman in the extended family and the wife of the patriarch, Hema's aunt-in-law enjoyed a status that was very different from Hema's, the new bride. Her power relative to younger women in the household and relative to male heirs gave her the authority to shield Hema and demand behavioral change of her husband.

Status in the public sphere also gave *atmiya sbajana* the power to intervene. Before approaching AIN, where we met, Koel received help from her *kaku* (a term of endearment derived from the Bengali *kaka,* meaning paternal uncle). Koel's *kaku* had a successful medical practice in South Kolkata. And he was a long-standing family friend, someone who had attained the status of *atmiya sbajana. Kaku* arranged a meeting with her estranged husband and in-laws. Koel's in-laws likely agreed to the meeting because *kaku* was a well-respected doctor. *Kaku* was not someone who could be ignored: he was wealthy, was well known, and knew the right people. *Kaku's* cousin was an MLA and knew police officers and judges. *Kaku* was also good friends with a lawyer who managed a nonprofit organization. Koel's in-laws had doubtless heard of his influential connections. He had the authority to intervene because of his social and political connections.

Atmiya sbajana routinely called on these broader networks when their independent mediations did not bear fruit. Thus, when Koel's husband refused to seek therapy or admit any wrongdoing, her *kaku* contacted his cousin the MLA as well as a lawyer friend for advice. The MLA cousin promised to get in touch with the women's police cell in Lal Bazar. The lawyer told Koel to go to AIN. AIN is a pun on the Bengali word *aina,* which means "the law." The pseudonym fit the organization well because AIN, more so than any other women's NGO I encountered, was resolutely focused on helping women register and win legal cases. And thus, Koel, like Brinda, with whom she shared very little in common aside from their mutual desire for reconciliation, ended up receiving advice from caseworkers trained to guide women toward legal cases. Koel would eventually register a PWDVA case, but she would never in a million years have seen that coming when she first asked her *kaku* to intervene.

Koel's movement toward the law represented the course I found among other women. In essence, their attempts to "run a family" in the face of violence made them vulnerable to interventions that derailed reconciliations. Their trajectory toward the law was accidental but systematic. Since "running a family" was far from a private affair, women looked to *atmiya sbajana* for help with reconciliations. In the process of mediating reconciliations, *atmiya sbajana* in turn created spaces for further intervention. They called on their own social and political networks, expanding the range of actors who were involved in mediating any given conflict. While Koel's *kaku* relied on elite networks to help Koel, poorer women were not necessarily bereft of social connections. As more people became involved, the process spun out of women's control. A host of people and organizations got involved in their lives, and these actors had agendas of their own, agendas that led women toward the law.

4

The Business of Mediation

Why Organized Actors Intervene

Gouri was "looking for cases" that afternoon. Everyone else in the office was eating lunch and taking a much needed break. Gouri rarely rested. This was the only opportunity she had to do this work, she mentioned. Most of the day, she ran here and there and fielded a constant stream of phone calls. But "looking for cases" was an important part of her job at AIN. While Koel heard of AIN through a lawyer, most women did not have the money or social connections to approach the organization. "We get a lot of different kinds of girls here. They don't always know about us or have the ability to find us," Gouri explained. Sometimes, AIN had to find them. Sitting with the lights dimmed in the back room, surrounded by the morning newspapers, Gouri carefully cut clippings while looking at me through her large glasses.

As part of their training, caseworkers like Gouri learned how to cultivate relationships with local law enforcement and stay abreast of media developments. "I sometimes find cases through the TV," Gouri mentioned. Aside from the clippings that Gouri arranged before her, she made sure to watch the local news channels in the evenings. "Cases in the courts," I clarified? "Yes, some of them go to court. Sometimes, the police call us. They refer cases to us. But I like to do my own research, in case there is someone who needs help and doesn't know about us." I nodded, beginning to understand what "looking for cases" entailed. Gouri went above and beyond the call of duty. She did not simply counsel women who had made their way to an intake session. She unearthed reports of violence, situations where women might need legal assistance.

According to Gouri, the local government wanted nongovernmental organizations (NGOs) like AIN to help solve social problems. Without NGOs doing this work, the state would not function. While Gouri had a theory about why the police might refer cases to her, what she left unexplained was her NGO's participation in these governmental initiatives. She assumed it was quite natural for her, an NGO staff member, to do what she was doing. But as an outsider, I was struck by the entire arrangement. Instead of waiting for women to approach her

Capable Women, Incapable States. Poulami Roychowdhury, Oxford University Press 2021. © Oxford University Press
DOI: 10.1093/oso/9780190881894.001.0001

for help, here was a caseworker who was proactively searching for incidents that could then become legal cases. While Gouri framed her work of "looking" as a simple act of discovery, legal cases did not exist without her active intervention. "Looking for cases" involved a process of construction. AIN's caseworkers brought legal cases into existence.

Gouri's interventions differed in one crucial way from the intervention Koel's *kaku* offered. *Kaku* interceded on Koel's behalf because she was the daughter of a good friend. He did not make this kind of act a routine part of his life, nor would he have stepped in to help a woman he did not know well. *Atmiya sbajana* mediated domestic violence sporadically and randomly. Their involvement in any given woman's life depended on their membership in her kin network. Gouri was beholden to no such social constraints. She played a role in a large number of conflicts and worked on behalf of women she had never met. Mediation was Gouri's job. And the services she provided were part of a nonprofit organization that stayed alive by ensuring that women engaged the law.

In this way, Gouri's daily quest for cases was neither idiosyncratic nor uncommon. She had a specific way of going about it: scouring the news, waiting for calls from police officers. But "looking for cases" provided a metaphor for a kind of work that was happening in diverse circles. Gouri worked within one of the many organizations that provided mediation services to women experiencing domestic abuse. By "looking for cases," these organizations provided a counterweight against women's desires for reconciliation and the bureaucratic negligence of the criminal justice system. For the fact was that women's rights was no longer just a social cause: it was also a business. The profit involved was sometimes, but not always, financial in nature. Mediation provided access to social, cultural, symbolic, as well as economic capital: social networks, expertise, reputation, and money.

Violence Brokers

Opportunities for brokerage arise whenever there is a gap in social structure. Unevenly distributed information and spatial, political, economic, or social isolation between two or more social groups fuel social gaps (Burt 2005; Obstfeld et al. 2014; Stovel and Shaw 2012). The environment surrounding domestic violence housed both of these conditions. Women experiencing violence needed help. New laws promised protection, but very few people knew about them or felt confident about making rights claims. The criminal justice system did little to help them. The stage was set for a new set of characters to emerge on the scene: people who could mediate between women and the criminal justice system.

Brokers were neither parties to the conflict nor related to the parties through kin networks. They were also not members of the criminal justice system. They were intermediaries, those who provided an important service in the rights market, mediating between women, extended families, and the criminal justice system. They filled the gaps that rampant social inequality and state failure created. Women's rights activists like Gouri were only one section, albeit an important one, of the larger set of people who provided these services.

Brokers comprised a motley crew. They came from multiple walks of life, espoused conflicting worldviews, and provided disparate mediational services. They differed in social background and age. Some of them were wealthy, well educated, and embedded in transnational networks. They lived in Kolkata, and traveled within India and overseas. Others were poor, minimally educated, lived and worked in villages, and had never left West Bengal.

Women referred to brokers through two common nouns: *dada* (elder brother) and *didi* (elder sister). "Elder brother brought me to the police station," one survivor mentioned. "I came here [to the NGO] with elder sister," another stated. Notably, Bengalis use these terms to address blood and marital relations, *atmiya sbajana*, as well as members of the public sphere who are either older than them, wealthier than them, or in a position of relative authority. A *didi* can be an elder sister, an elderly woman on the bus, a rich neighbor, or a nurse at the hospital. Similarly, a *dada* can be an elder brother, the bus driver, your supervisor, or a thug.

In the context of domestic violence mediation, *didi*s tended to be women who were connected to a women's organization or NGO, members of microfinance self-help groups, women who worked outside the home in a well-respected profession such as a schoolteacher, women who had been elected to public office in the past, and those who had a record of voluntary public service. Like *didi*s, *dada*s tended to be men who had served in public office or had a history of public works. But many of them were men who did "party work": they were card-carrying members of political parties, those who campaigned on their party's behalf, and those who represented the party at the neighborhood or village level by occupying public spaces known as clubs. *Dada*s were also men of more dubious credentials, reputed to have connections to the underworld or well recognized as gang leaders and petty criminals.

A survivor's kin network influenced which of these figures she approached for help. Women who had support from their natal families, and especially those who had men in their natal families connected to political parties, tended to receive help from a *dada*. Norms governing gender segregation meant that women felt uncomfortable directly petitioning men for assistance. And *dada*s were unlikely to help a woman who did not come to them via a male relation. Political parties in India are men's domains, with leadership positions and membership bases dominated by men (Sandhu and Ravi 2014). By 2019, women held a mere 11.85 percent of all seats in India's upper and lower houses of parliament (Inter-Parliamentary Union 2019). Help from a party member followed a series of clientelistic exchanges between men who had social and political relations with one another.

Women tended to approach *didi*s either on their own or through female relations, friends, and neighbors. There was a certain respectability to the notion that one was getting help from a woman who helped other women. Women who lacked male family members with political connections or whose male kin did not support them thus tended to rely on *didi*s for help. Women told other women about *didi*s. Employers shared information about women's NGOs with domestic workers. Women who had experienced violence told other women experiencing violence about a *didi* who lived in such and such a village. A woman would be introduced to a *didi* by a mutual acquaintance, recount her story, and wait for advice and instruction. Those who were able to, of course, contacted both *dada*s and *didi*s and multiple ones at that. At all times, women attempted to diversify the potential sources of help to which they had access.

*Dada*s and *didi*s often held radically different attitudes about women's rights and espoused widely disparate visions of social justice. Some had witnessed the desperation of women experiencing abuse and wished to help. They embraced a language of women's empowerment and were concerned about protecting the vulnerable. Others did not appear to be motivated by issues of inequality or injustice at all. They simply saw a service that needed to be provided and realized there was something to be gained by providing it. A third group was openly hostile to discussions of women's rights, decreeing them "foreign" transplants and lamenting the end of the Indian extended family and traditions of tolerance and compassion.

*Dada*s and *didi*s even differed in their purported methods. Some believed that legal cases would ensure women's well-being. Others found the law to be a waste of time: they tried to negotiate separations and financial settlements through community-based arbitration (*shalishi*). A third group believed that the best thing for everyone, including women experiencing violence, was to keep families intact. They aimed to mend broken families, counseling abusers, chalking out compromises, and mediating reconciliations. To a certain extent, gendered ideologies overlapped with methods. Those who espoused a language of women's rights and empowerment tended to align more closely with legal measures. Those who either did not use this language or believed it to be "foreign" tried to arrange reconciliations.

But ideology and method did not always neatly overlap. Some of the strongest methodological disputes erupted between organizations based on feminist principles. AIN, Andolan, and Shadheen—three women's NGOs that appeared in the previous chapter—housed significant differences in their approach to violence. AIN provided counseling and legal aid services and raised public awareness about women's rights. Having played an important role in the mobilization for civil reforms that led to passage of the Protection of Women from Domestic Violence Act (PWDVA), AIN continued to monitor the law's effects and encourage women to make use of it.

On the other end of the spectrum, Andolan registered legal cases to "threaten" abusive men into negotiating or as a last resort when all other interventions failed. Andolan routinely led *shalishi* to help women secure financial settlements and housing. Originally established in the 1970s as a peasants' union, by the 1990s Andolan had begun informally intervening in domestic disputes after a number of peasant women approached the organization for help. Over time, Andolan's work in this area grew, and it established a women's wing that eventually outstripped its union base. Neelu, Andolan's leader, scoffed when I brought up legal reforms, claiming "horses had laid eggs" (a proverb signaling an absurd or futile venture).

Meanwhile, Dolly, Shadheen's executive director, was dead set against *shalishi*. Once well funded and well regarded in the area, Shadheen became financially burdened and increasingly alienated from local communities and law enforcement through the course of my study. Convinced that community arbitration was a shoo-in for reconciliations, Dolly believed anybody who conducted one was undermining the women's movement. Shadheen pursued a combination of legal and therapeutic tactics against violence, coaching women to leave violent relationships while training them in employable skills, in the hope that financial options would lower barriers to legal access.

Given their social, organizational, ideological, and methodological differences, how and why did brokers end up pushing women toward the law? This question is especially puzzling given that some brokers dismissed legal cases, embraced reconciliations, and shunned discourses of women's rights. The answer is to be found in the tightrope act all brokers had to perform in order to do what they did. On the one hand, brokers thrived within the social gaps opened up by a limited criminal justice system. They had an interest in widening those gaps to make more room for themselves. By further calling the capacities of the state into question and actively trying to do what the state was supposed to do, they could more effectively convince women to turn to them for assistance.

On the other hand, brokers thrived from their proximity to the very institution they were trying to supplement. Brokers convinced women of their mediation skills through their relationship with the site of "meta capital": the state (Bourdieu 1994). As the culmination of processes whereby various forms of capital became concentrated, the state was unavoidable even if its powers were limited. Contact with the state, an intimate knowledge of its operations and personnel, no matter how much one wished to avoid it, provided the authority and social credibility one needed to be a mediator between civilians. This simple fact drove brokers of all stripes and persuasions to become entangled with domestic violence law, even when they ostensibly despised legal measures and were unsympathetic to a rights framework.

Networks

Brinda reached Shadheen via a *didi*. Everyone called her Sila *di*, with *di* being the shortened form of *didi*. She was in her fifties, wiry, with frizzy hair that escaped the bun she tied to the nape of her neck. Her tongue was as sharp as her wit, and she displayed both with unbridled satisfaction. Sila's motivations for doing the work she did largely centered on the social networks she gained from her services. She boasted about the "saris and countless boxes of sweets" she had received from grateful women she had helped. While there may have been a financial dimension to these transactions that Sila hid from me, the women Sila worked with never mentioned giving her money. And after knowing Sila for several months, I sensed that whatever monetary remuneration she may have received in the form of material goods was secondary to the honor such gifts bestowed. She was proud to be someone people trusted. By acting as a broker, Sila established herself as a person other people appealed to for help.

Sila lived in a village a few kilometers west of Shadheen's office. Her house was large, brick, and surrounded by an expansive garden. Born into a middle-class Christian family, Sila's father had been a police officer, and she herself had attended college and worked as a secretary before getting married. The family she married into was also middle-class and relatively progressive. Her husband worked with a UNICEF-affiliated NGO, and Sila's mother-in-law was a teacher. Once her children were in school, Sila dedicated herself to public service. Having completed her *panchayat*'s volunteer training program, she became a fixture in various community improvement projects.

Sila clearly viewed the mediation she provided to be an extension of her services to the public. And in her mind, the service she provided was mending broken families and creating a "healthy society." Unlike Rupa and Dolly, who took a firm stance against reconciliations, Sila believed that abusive men could change. "What could be better than a husband and wife living in mutual agreement," she retorted incredulously when I questioned her position. Criticizing Shadheen's leadership, Sila complained "they are always starting cases. 'Get a case going! Let's do a case.' Tell me, where has that ever gotten a girl? None of these girls want their marriages to break up." For Sila, legal cases led nowhere, and men were not beyond reform. If abuse could be mitigated, family life provided financial security, social belonging, and emotional fulfillment for women.

Given her professed antagonism toward legal measures, her constant presence at Shadheen was quite perplexing. She always attended their public events, routinely sat in on intake sessions, and accompanied caseworkers on their daily rounds. Sila claimed that she "worked with," rather than "worked at," Shadheen. Dolly claimed she was a volunteer. Whatever her official or unofficial status, Sila ensured women experiencing violence made their way to Shadheen and that Shadheen's casework team remained busy. Nearly half the women I met at the NGO mentioned that Sila had directed them to Shadheen.

The fact was, Sila needed Shadheen as much as Shadheen needed her. In many ways, Sila was a prototypical *didi*: confident, energetic, resourceful. Sila was able to do the work she did partly because of her personality and partly because of her social class. But neither of those factors would have mattered very much without her connections to the state. Sila was a credible mediator because she was familiar with the institution that monopolized juridical capital (Bourdieu 1994). From her father, who was a police officer, she had gained a lifelong comfort with the police and personally knew officers in the upper ranks. Her own volunteer work with the local *panchayat* had expanded her contacts among elected officials. Her collaboration with Shadheen ensured ongoing relations with the state. She accompanied caseworkers to police stations, bustled around the court complex, and had memorized the protection officer's phone number. As if by osmosis, the authority of the state rubbed off on Sila. And this halo in turn allowed her to meet more people and to accumulate status within her village.

Expertise

Rupa remained Sila's main confidante and partner in crime at Shadheen during my entire time at the organization. The two women were inseparable. Sila notified Rupa whenever she heard from a woman in distress. In turn, Rupa immediately called Sila whenever she was working on a new case. The partnership was an unlikely one. They had very little in common. Sila led a comfortable middle-class existence, was ideologically opposed to legal measures, believed in the power of abusive men to reform, was well educated, and had been loved and respected by her husband whose death had left her bereft. Rupa financially struggled to make ends meet, was a single mother without a high school diploma, and worked hard to help women register legal cases. She distrusted men, believed that abusers never changed, and had herself been abused and abandoned. Despite their differences, the work Sila and Rupa did brought them together. Brokerage benefited both of them in different ways.

Even more so than Sila, Rupa could attest to the immense status change she had experienced by becoming known as someone who mediates between women and the state. Rupa had been a social pariah when her husband abandoned her. "The people in our neighborhood did not even talk to me when I returned to my parents' house," she recalled. When I visited her home, she made a point of bringing me to her neighbor's house after lunch. By introducing me, an outside researcher from the United States, she further cemented a growing image of herself in the area as someone with power and connections.

But the real turnaround in her status, according to Rupa, had happened a few years back, when a police officer she knew had visited the village. Conducting an investigation on a separate issue, the constable ran into Rupa in the village and then accompanied her home to say hello to her parents. Rupa glowed when recounting the visit. This social call from an officer of the law demonstrated in a very public fashion that she was someone worthy of acknowledgment and attention. "Everyone addressed me differently after that [visit]," Rupa recalled with satisfaction.

The benefit that Rupa accrued through her mediation services was deeply entwined with her ability to know and be close to the state. This proximity to the state helped Rupa, who had once been a social outcast, become someone others respected. Yet, if I had to place my finger on the reason Rupa valued her work above all else, it would have to do with the way her mediation services provided access to cultural capital. The cultural capital she acquired came in the form of expertise: proficiency in law and legal procedure, competence in navigating police stations and courts, knowledge about women's organizations, familiarity with women's lives and travails, and an awareness of how to conduct oneself and communicate with all these different people without being ignored.

The information she had at her fingertips was both valuable and scarce. Very few people knew how to fill out a First Incident Report (FIR), how to talk to a lawyer, or how to dress for court. Rupa's expertise came from the training sessions she completed at Shadheen and through years of on-the-job experience. For a woman of Rupa's social background, someone from a lower-caste family who had grown up in a village and never finished high school, the skills she acquired helped her secure a foothold in a culture where educational attainment was highly prized and socially applauded.

She wore her expertise like armor, protecting herself and the women she represented by reeling off obscure statutes. Rupa's very demeanor, the way she held herself and moved through social space, seemed calculated to communicate her skills. She always sat very upright and moved swiftly, without hesitation. Since I did not know Rupa before she became a caseworker, I cannot say with certainty that her bodily comportment was an artifact of the cultural capital she had acquired. But I would hazard a guess that it was. When I slouched on a court bench after hours of waiting, she would tap me on the shoulder, point to nearby police officers, and gesture that we were being watched. Meanwhile, when I met her at her home, she spent most of the time lounging on her bed. She had put aside the Rupa she presented to the world and seemed to be taking a much needed holiday.

The expertise Rupa acquired through her mediations eventually opened an avenue to the more formalized halls of knowledge that she so idealized. More so than other people I interacted with during my research, she was curious about the book I was writing and wanted to know what my life would be like when I became a professor. Her delight was hard to capture when she was invited to speak at Jadavpur University, a prestigious university located in South Kolkata. Unable to attend the event myself, I garnered from Rupa that she had been part of a panel of speakers who talked about violence against women. According to Rupa, however, she was one of the only people on stage who actually helped women register legal cases. "Everyone was asking how we do our work," she beamed with pride. She had taught all those fancy people, with their fancy degrees, about the nitty-gritty of the criminal justice system.

Reputation

Proximity to the state simultaneously enabled brokerage and was one of its ultimate rewards. And this proximity came via multiple avenues, some more ironic than others. While Rupa's and Sila's credentials were respectable, it was not unheard of for brokers to use their own disrepute as a launching pad to enter the mediation business and then use mediation to become intimately attached to state power. Perversely, having a bad reputation, especially in relation to the criminal justice system, indicated that one had the ability to challenge and overpower law enforcement.

On one of the many cases that Rupa oversaw at Shadheen, she ended up running into a character named Pora Khokhon ("Burnt Boy" in Bengali). At best, Pora Khokhon was what one could call a fixer, someone who helped people access electricity and ration cards through his political connections. At worst, he was a *goonda* (a criminal) for hire, paid to rough up the opposition in and around elections. He had worked hard to acquire his moniker and displayed the burn mark on his arm with great bravado to anyone who cared to see it. The mark was ostensibly the product of a street fight between his gang and the police. He had thrown a bomb at the police, but the bomb had accidentally exploded in his hand instead. To what degree the details of his story were true was hard to say.

More importantly, everybody who lived in the area seemed to believe it. Here was a man who had challenged law enforcement personnel and had the scar to prove it.

In person, Pora Khokhon was charismatic and mercurial, friendly one moment and angry and disgruntled the next. On one of our routine visits to the local police station, Rupa and I ran into him while he was in custody, charged with assault. The station was small and Pora Khokhon's holding cell visible to passersby. When he saw Rupa, he called out a friendly hello and struck up a conversation. Having learned that we were following up on a 498A case where the abusive husband had eluded arrest, he shook his head in dismay. Addressing Rupa, he lamented "I have done a lot of bad things in my life *didi*, but wife beating, that's something I cannot abide."

Taken on its own, Pora Khokhon's statement indicated a certain level of sympathy for women's plight. He was against domestic violence and seemed to feel bad for those who were targeted. But in reality, his sentiments about women were largely negative. He believed that "some girls are ill mannered" and confessed that he would readily support men who had been "falsely" accused by dastardly wives. During most of our conversation, Pora Khokhon engaged in a long-winded tirade about one "good" boy he knew who was wrongly accused of wife beating by his mendacious, adulterous wife.

Far from being a proponent of women's rights, Pora Khokhon seemed to believe that women were more likely to make up false accusations than men were to beat them. But despite his ideological distrust of women in general, he promised to help the particular woman we were representing. Clearly disinterested if the police heard him or not, Pora Khokhon promised to pay the abuser a visit as soon as he was released. "You'll see, I'll root him out and give him a good beating. He will voluntarily walk through those doors once I'm done with him."

The irony of the situation did not escape us. Charged with assault, locked up in a police cell, Pora Khokhon was publicly promising to help the same officers who had arrested him arrest another man. And he would help them by assaulting the perp. Once we were back in Shadheen's office, Rupa told everyone about Pora Khokhon's antics, sending other caseworkers into hysterics. Pora Khokhon, widely known as a thug, wished to establish himself as a champion of women.

While it is entirely possible that he was motivated to help women in distress due to the largesse of his own heart, rooting out an abuser and turning him over to the police benefited Pora Khokhon in a number of other, hidden ways. "He has his eye on a *panchayat* seat," Sila remarked astutely while everyone else was laughing. "Mark my words, he is planning to run. He is creating a space for himself." The West Bengal *panchayat* elections were scheduled in two years. And

Pora Khokhon had recently switched party affiliations from the once dominant Communist Party of India (Marxist) (CPI[M]) to the Trinamul Congress Party (TMC). Sila believed that he had long held political ambitions and had simply been biding his time for the right moment.

Sila's suspicions about Pora Khokhon's motivations did not emerge from thin air. Criminality is arguably an electoral asset in India (Michelutti 2010). The number of members of parliament in the Lok Sabha (lower house of parliament) with criminal records has steadily risen over the past decade, reaching 34 percent in 2014. The accepted thinking on this curious development is that criminality allows politicians to deliver much needed goods to voters (Vaishnav 2017). Building schools, paving roads, distributing subsidies: a thuggish official can more effectively use threats and coercion to secure these services for his constituents. With his particular set of skills, Pora Khokhon was an ideal candidate.

By wading into the mediation business, Pora Khokhon was in some ways simply extending the kind of work he already did at the village level. Getting . people ration cards and Below Poverty Line cards, acquiring electrical connections: all of these initiatives made him a broker who mediated between citizens and various government and private institutions. But intervening in domestic violence had some special perks. First, the legitimacy factor was high: a *goonda* who helped vulnerable women fit the age-old trope of the gangster who was Robin Hood in disguise. Second, the potential to expand social networks, a necessary asset in any political campaign, was even higher.

The particular woman involved in this case was politically useful. Pora Khokhon knew her brother because he was affiliated with the political party Pora Khokhon worked for, the TMC. Here was a woman whose male kin were affiliated with the party he hoped to run under. Assisting her was a clever way to cement his social relationships to male party cadre. But the political implications of intervention extended far beyond the party cadre who might be immediately touched by the case. Shadheen on its own had some 19,000 self-help group members spread throughout the upper areas of the district. The organization was also connected to a number of other NGOs and *mahila samiti* in the district. By helping Rupa on her case, Pora Khokhon established himself as a figure on this wider landscape.

Once it became known that he might be a willing ally, his name would spread to a much broader swathe of civil society groups (and the associated publics they worked with). When it came to election time, the connections he forged with women's groups might pay off in the form of a widely recognized name connected to good works. Time and the vote count would tell, but for now Pora Khokhon could use "women's rights" to rebrand his public image.

Money

None of the brokers I met voiced their social, cultural, or symbolic objectives directly. And it is possible that they did not consciously realize that it was through their relationship to the state that they acquired such resources. Those who broke this code of silence were denounced and reviled, labeled as vulgar and opportunistic. Special ire was reserved for anyone who provided mediation services for overtly financial reasons.

In the peri-urban fringes that bordered South Kolkata, a character named Girish routinely cropped up in women's stories as someone who mediated conflict for payment. Rupa, who had come across him from time to time on her rounds, could not stand him. "He is taking money from these poor girls and what does he get for them? Nothing." In person, Girish was a relatively ordinary-looking man in his fifties, short and overweight. A number of years back, he had established himself as a homeopathic doctor, which involved tacking a sign with his name on his front door and distributing placebo pills. But through that business, he met and formed close relationships with a wide number of people, some of whom lived in surrounding villages and others in Kolkata. His list of patients included lawyers, social service workers, police officers, block development officers, and *panchayat* representatives. It was also through his homeopathic business that Girish met his first clients, women who came to him with injuries from the violence they suffered at home.

"I couldn't keep giving them pills," he confessed when I asked him about the evolution of his business. Already well networked among people who might be able to help abused women, Girish decided to expand his operations and become a mediator. He professed to be non-partisan in his commitments. "I don't do politics," he assured me when I asked if he had contacts within any of the major political parties. "Healing the body and the mind, you have to have a different mentality to do this work." But everyone who knew him or had heard of his work claimed that he was a CPI(M) crony. "How else would he get anything done," snorted Rupa suspiciously?

The women Girish worked with confirmed Rupa's suspicions. "His family is with the party," claimed Hema, who had used Girish's services while also seeking help from Shadheen. Hema, who lived in Behala, had heard of Girish through her cousin who bought homeopathic drugs from him. "The elder sisters here [at Shadheen] don't have those contacts. Girish *da* does." In Hema's case, Girish provided a link to the CPI(M) that Shadheen could not. And the surveillance offered by his political connections put a temporary stop to the abuse Hema suffered.

To what extent Girish believed that reconciliations were good for women was difficult to say. Unlike Sila and Rupa, who were visibly motivated by women's suffering, and unlike Pora Khokhon, who sided with particular women while denouncing women in general, Girish's ideological commitments remained elusive. He did not appear to care all that much about women's plight. Nor was he passionately inspired by women's deceitfulness. One thing, however, was clear. He was interested in making money and in expanding his Rolodex of influential contacts. I sensed the two objectives were integrally connected. When Hema came to him for help, he could have simply run an arbitration with her husband. Instead, he suggested that she contact a lawyer he knew, go see her neighborhood political representative, and visit the police station where he had friends. From Girish's perspective, pushing Hema toward these people was simply part of a quid pro quo. They in turn oriented women in his direction ensuring his pockets remained brimming.

For Girish, helping women with violence was very similar to setting up a homeopathic business: he saw an opportunity to make money, and he seized it. And he expanded his potential market of clients by retaining close contacts with people who were mixed up with the state and its operations: lawyers, social service workers, police officers, elected and non-elected officials. Regarding the money itself, he was casually dismissive. "I tell them to just give me what they can. I have to feed my family, what can I do." He folded his hands in a display of resignation, signaling that it would be financially difficult for him to provide these services for free. While he avoided telling me how much money he made, he appeared to be doing well. He had recently renovated his house and wore expensive leather shoes. Each of his fingers was adorned with an amulet ring, what Bengalis refer to as *maduli*: semi-precious stones that protected him from evil spirits.

Even though Rupa dismissed Girish as an opportunistic crook, the two of them were not as dissimilar as she would have liked to believe. They both secured a livelihood by interfacing with the law. While Girish did it directly, by taking money from women, Rupa did it indirectly, by receiving a salary from an organization funded to represent women. More than Girish, however, Rupa was dependent on the income her brokerage services brought in. As a well-known homeopathic doctor, Girish could probably have done just fine dropping his brokering activities. Rupa did not have a fallback plan.

Before joining the casework team, she had earned a third of her current salary by running a sewing business out of her home. But stitching women's blouses and children's clothes was intermittent work with a fair amount of competition from other women who also worked out of their homes. Casework had allowed Rupa to gain a slightly more secure footing. She no longer had to worry about scrounging together the fees for her son's tuition and books. She was able to replace the outhouse she had used with a *paka* bathroom, one with a cement floor and tin roof. She financially supported her aging parents, a contribution that allowed her to remain in their home and without which she was convinced her brother would boot her out.

While brokerage provided access to symbolic, cultural, and social capital, ultimately, all of these various forms of capital translated into financial resources (Bourdieu 2011). For people like Rupa, those who existed at the margins, brokerage provided a secure livelihood. For people like Girish, those who existed in the middle ranks, brokerage enhanced an already comfortable lifestyle. Ten kilometers north of where Girish had set up shop at the edges of Kolkata, Gouri also did what she did to make sure she stayed employed. She scoured the news during her lunch break, going above and beyond the call of duty by "looking for cases," because her financial fate was linked to her ability to steer women toward the law.

From what I could tell, "looking for cases" was not part of Gouri's formal duties at AIN. But she was taking it upon herself to look proactive, showing initiative. Partly, she hoped to rise within the ranks at AIN. Partly, her prospects outside AIN were less rosy than one might have imagined. Armed with a degree in English, Gouri would have been hard placed to find a job if she failed to be a good caseworker. And a job like the one she had was difficult to find. Nonprofit work was scarce and highly coveted, especially by women who had families, because the hours were reasonable, the pay was decent, and the work conditions were humane.

Taking a bird's eye view of the situation, it was not just Rupa or Gouri or Girish whose economic lives were linked to women's engagement with legal institutions. There were much bigger concerns at stake. The economic incentives of brokerage spanned class and geography and linked individual social mobility to the survival of larger institutions. Entire organizations were built and survived around women's legal engagements. AIN, Shadheen, and even Andolan profited from their involvement in the business of mediation. AIN's fate was, of course, the most tightly linked to the legal fate of women. Founded exclusively to address domestic violence and integral to the civil reform initiatives that culminated in the passage of the PWDVA, AIN had no other potential area of work to expand into if its legal mediations failed.

Shadheen housed a range of empowerment initiatives, from poultry and agriculture to microfinance. And the organization would have survived without its casework team. But it had received a large grant to expand its anti-violence work. And in order to secure the grant again, Dolly had to demonstrate effectiveness. The more women Shadheen could report to have represented in official legal cases, the more likely the casework team was to look like they were changing women's lives. Registered FIRs and Domestic Incident Reports provided an easily quantifiable index of organizational efficacy.

Even Andolan was far more integrated with the state than I initially imagined. Neelu, Andolan's founder and leader, snorted when I mentioned legal reforms. To her, the effects of legal reforms were as illusory as horse's eggs. But the fact was that Andolan had a distinctly strategic relationship to case registration. A few minutes after telling me that laws were a waste of time, Neelu explained what Andolan did. When a woman came to the organization seeking help, caseworkers first tried to resolve her issues through a woman-oriented community arbitration, calling in different parties to the conflict and involving local community leaders to seek a resolution that would be most helpful to the woman in question. But the threat of the law provided ammunition for their arbitrations.

For men who refused to sit down to an arbitration, Andolan used the law as a threat. If they did not negotiate, Andonal threatened to register a formal case. They also used the law as a disciplinary measure of last resort: when an abuser violated the agreement from an arbitration. The law gave Andolan's arbitrations additional force, lending teeth to its joint compromises. Underlying this everyday reliance on the law was Andolan's working relations with transnational legal initiatives. I came to know about Andolan through its work with the International Center for Research on Women (ICRW), an organization based in Washington DC and funded by USAID. The ICRW worked with Andolan and a range of other women's organizations throughout India over the course of several years to understand how violence affected women's lives and how laws and legal initiatives could better serve women.

Andolan's story demonstrates how the resources brokerage provided were difficult to acquire without a certain level of engagement with the state. An organization which at first glance seemed to be overtly hostile to legal measures could not ultimately avoid these attractions. It was through their proximity with the criminal justice system and the promise of rights that brokers did the work they did and were able to make a name for themselves. To acquire economic, social, symbolic, and cultural capital, they had to continually demonstrate and renew their relationship to the state, and especially to its legal environs. Gouri, Sila, Rupa, Pora Khokhon, and Girish all worked hard to cultivate relationships with law enforcement and remain visible and active within government offices. The organizations they associated with did the same. It was in a broker's interest to propel women toward the criminal justice system, even if the meeting did not lead to an official legal complaint.

|| 5 ||

Incentivizing the Law

How Organized Actors Change Women's Preferences

Brokers faced a problem. In order to be a broker, they had to mediate between women and the criminal justice system. But most women wanted nothing to do with the law or with law enforcement. As I have already mentioned, within the sample of seventy women with whom I conducted research, forty-eight initially wanted a reconciliation, and another nineteen wished to avoid the law due to a host of financial and social barriers. Their reluctance mirrored wider patterns of legal avoidance. Women experiencing domestic violence rarely seek help from the state and repeatedly voice concerns about registering legal cases (International Institute for Population Sciences 2017).

Before and during the actual work of mediation, brokers had to negotiate with women. They somehow had to convince them to stop "running a family" by reorienting their preferences and perceptions. This reorientation took some work. Brokers sometimes pursued a tactic of "vernacularization," what Peggy Levitt and Sally Merry (2009) have identified as a process of translating and transforming the discourse of rights into local parlance. In my research, I noticed that vernacularization rarely happened on its own. Brokers encouraged women to pursue rights by incentivizing legal engagements: they lowered both the perceived and the actual costs of legal cases while raising the potential benefits by providing therapy, embedding women in new collectives, and helping them access key goods and services.

*Didi*s like Sila, Gouri, and Rupa incentivized the law through therapy and community. Because of the rules of gender segregation that governed both private and public life, women could only hope to become part of a community with other women. They had little chance of entering political parties or criminal syndicates. Therapeutic services also tended to be offered by women's groups and nongovernmental organizations (NGOs), partly because of the feminist-inspired ideologies that permeated these sites and partly because these organizations

Capable Women, Incapable States. Poulami Roychowdhury, Oxford University Press 2021. © Oxford University Press
DOI: 10.1093/oso/9780190881894.001.0001

received funding to undertake counseling and lead training sessions. But *dada*s like Girish and Pora Khokhon had other tricks up their sleeves. Their connections to political parties and criminal networks gave them access to resources that *didi*s and women's groups had in short supply: namely the ability to help women secure key private and public services such as ration cards, Below Poverty Line cards, electricity, and tanks of cooking gas off the black market.

Therapy

Brokers used therapy to challenge women's devotion to marriage and family. They promoted alternate goals, such as financial freedom and sexual liberation, sentiments that were supposedly less aligned with running a family and more conducive to legal rights. Therapeutic interventions abounded at Shadheen, where Dolly believed that women's "biggest problems" were their desires to remain within a patriarchal *gondi* (enclosure in Bengali). Two key sites provided a lens on how the organization used therapy to orient women toward the law: gender workshops and intake sessions.

Gender workshops attracted participants from Shadheen's self-help groups as well as women who lived in the surrounding area. They always took place at an off-site destination, usually a hotel far away from Shadheen's office. It was not that hotels were not available nearby. But by traveling a certain distance, Shadheen removed women from their regular lives so that they could have a vacation and discover what they "really wanted." The vacation frame had the added benefit of attracting a large number of applicants: women who were too poor to travel or stay in a hotel.

The workshops were designed and led by Mona, an indomitable woman in her early sixties and a well-known member of the local women's movement. Mona made her livelihood by working with a number of women's rights organizations in and around Kolkata. Through the workshops, she hoped to educate not only women who attended but also their friends and acquaintances. "We get a lot of cases through referrals," Mona pointed out. The idea was that once workshop participants learned what freedom and independence actually looked like, they would be able to identify its opposite: confinement and violation. They would go back to their regular life and look at it with new eyes, identifying abuse in their own homes and in the homes of others.

During the first workshop I attended, Dolly encouraged participants to cut loose by turning on Bollywood music during the bus ride to the hotel. The environment became quite riotous when the pulse of *Munni badnaam hui* ("Girl's Got a Bad Reputation" in Hindi), a recent chart-topper featuring a scantily clad actress joyously bemoaning her sexual escapades, hit the waves. Radha, a self-help group member, suddenly jumped into the middle of the aisle. Hiking her sari over her calves, she mimicked Munni's well-known gyrations as the rest of the bus exploded in shouts and whistles. When Radha regained her seat, Mona felt vicariously exhilarated: "She could never do that at home," Mona explained triumphantly. Within the confines of her family and community, Radha would have been censured for dancing provocatively. But the gender workshop was already doing its work: it was helping Radha challenge the norms of regular life and express what she "really wanted."

Radha's inspirational dance set the stage for a number of group exercises. The exercises encouraged participants to envision a life where they were financially independent and not bogged down by familial commitments. In one exercise, participants were asked to draw a picture of who "they really wanted to be." Jahanara, a young Muslim woman who depicted herself wearing pants and working as an engineer, received the loudest commendations. Engineering remains a heavily male-dominated field in India. Jahanara's picture demonstrated her aspiration for financial independence in a heterodox field. Meanwhile, an older Hindu woman named Kali, who drew herself pretty much as she was, a wife and mother of five children, elicited laughter and consternation. Kali had failed to envision a life beyond the confines of her family. "You wouldn't change a thing about yourself?" joked Mona, genuinely puzzled.

At the end of the workshop, Dolly asked participants to gather in a circle and consecutively remove various articles of clothing. The exercise was meant to embody the process whereby women freed themselves from bondage. In the context of South Asia, removing one's clothes in public marks a special kind of transgression for women. When they realized what was about to happen, several participants tried to run out of the room, only to be dragged back shrieking hysterically. They grasped the ends of their unraveling *saris* in a futile attempt to hide their emerging nakedness. But their nakedness was central to Shadheen's project. Radha's dance, Jahanara's picture, the enforced disrobing: each incident highlighted the possibility of an alternate existence organized outside the boundaries of patriarchal family life.

The literal stripping down of the female body provided the most daring example of this alternate world: the disrobing forced women to envision a society where their bodies did not inspire shame. Ironically, the fact that this vision was realized under coercive circumstances was lost on Shadheen's trainers. If women did not want to step outside their *gondi*, Shadheen took upon itself the task of making sure they did. Gender workshops proved to be rites of passage that initiated women into future participation in a range of legally oriented activities. For some, it was the beginning of more training, including workshops that concentrated on legal rights: relatively staid affairs where women were introduced to the ins and outs of legal statutes and legal procedure. For others, it laid the groundwork for their own legal case.

While gender workshops drew a wide net, intake sessions attracted a preselected group of women: women who might be seeking reconciliations. Caseworkers used counseling and surveillance to orient women toward the law during these sessions. Madhura's intake session provided an intense example of how caseworkers achieved these results. In her early twenties, Madhura arrived at Shadheen bloodied and shaken. Her lover, Ashok, had hired thugs to beat her up after she broke off their relationship.

Ashok was something of a broker himself. His domain was party politics. He worked closely with the Trinamul Congress (TMC), the ascendant political party in the region, helping local residents build houses, access water, and acquire fertilizer and other agricultural supplies in exchange for electoral support. And perhaps because of his political clout, he was able to maintain both a wife and a mistress, setting up two households on opposite sides of the same village. The mistress was Madhura: pretty, poor, and two decades his junior. After six years, however, Madhura had had enough. She gave him an ultimatum: divorce your wife and marry me, or I am leaving. Apparently, Ashok did not like the choices presented him. When Madhura broke things off, he retaliated, hiring men to break into the house he shared with Madhura and assault her and her elderly mother.

A legal case was the last thing on Madhura's mind when she arrived at Shadheen. She dreaded both Ashok and the police. The police, she kept insisting, were in Ashok's pocket. They were his friends, and he paid to keep them content. If she registered a legal case, not only would the police not protect her but Ashok would come after her family. But in addition to expressing fear of Ashok, Madhura also declared her abiding affection for him. He did love her, after all, she kept repeating. Why else would he have gone to the trouble of orchestrating the attack? Perhaps he was hurt that she had left, and all would be well if she patched things up.

Namita and Jhinuk, the caseworkers first on the scene that morning, exchanged knowing glances. They took turns rebuking and encouraging Madhura, who did not appear to know their names and simply referred to them as *didi*. In the fashion of elder sisters, they instructed Madhura to think of herself, not of Ashok. Namita instructed Madhura not to "worry" about how her family or neighbors would perceive her. Jhinuk repeatedly urged Madhura to focus on what "she wanted."

The caseworkers intervened when Ashok began calling Madhura. Jhinuk wrenched the phone from Madhura's hands, reminding her that she was not the first woman to have faced a powerful man. "We help girls like you all the time. Listen to me when I say that you have the strength to do this." Madhura needed to envision a life outside the shadow of an abusive lover. Namita, meanwhile, stroked Madhura's hair in a maternal fashion. "Look at what he has done to you. Where is the love you have for yourself?" Namita wondered why Madhura was not angry with Ashok for setting his thugs on her and instructed her "to think of herself." She linked cultural notions of feminine respectability to self-care and independence, reminding Madhura that a happier, more joyful future was possible if she registered a report. It was only through the law that Madhura stood a reasonable chance of achieving any of these objectives.

For Shadheen's caseworkers, Madhura had to overcome the fear that paralyzed her, as well as the love and attachment she felt. Their therapeutic interventions attempted to change Madhura's desire to stay away from the law by questioning her sentimental commitments. Part of the reason Madhura hesitated in moving forward was that she still held out some hope that Ashok would marry her. Jhinuk and Namita aimed to question this desire in ways that mirrored the workshop modules of the gender workshop. They did this not only through their institutional credentials as caseworkers at a well-recognized NGO but also through notions of familial care and authority associated with the term *didi*.

Thus, while workshops and intake sessions attempted to reorient women's perceptions of legal claims, hidden within Shadheen's therapeutic initiatives lay another form of legal incentivization. In the process of urging Madhura to overcome her attachment to her actual family, Shadheen incorporated her into a new family, replete with elder sisters and the "other women" Namita referenced who had also pursued legal cases. These invocations were far from accidental. Namita wanted Madhura to know that by pursuing a legal case, she would become part of a new community, a new family of sorts.

Community

Domestic violence produces social isolation: cutting off access to friends and family is one of the tactics abusers use to control and inflict harm. Challenging abuse also produces social isolation. Given the hegemony of marriage and dominant cultural expectations that women will sacrifice themselves for their husbands and children, those who speak out or seek help risk being ostracized by those they know. Meeting people who sympathized with their situation or those who had gone through similar experiences helped women overcome isolation. Even the possibility of attending community events, such as theater productions or NGO-organized workshops, provided respite and an occasion to meet new people and enjoy oneself.

Mindful of these background conditions, brokers encouraged individual women to approach the law by embedding those who registered legal cases in new social networks and by linking legal engagements to the possibility of attending social activities. Brokers were able to forge community because they did not work alone. Like Rupa and Gouri, many held official positions within organizations that mediated conflicts. Others, like Sila, Girish, and Pora Khokhon, lacked official credentials but did the work they did through the organizations with which they were affiliated. Sila volunteered at Shadheen. Pora Khokhon ran a criminal network with connections to the TMC. Girish was connected to the Communist Party of India (Marxist) (CPI[M]). These organizational affiliations were not coincidental. They allowed brokers to do what they did. Without organized support, it was difficult to approach the state or confront abusive men. The structural underpinnings of mediation allowed brokers to connect women to institutional spaces where groups of people came together, discussed problems, provided support, and shared resources. By approaching a broker for help, women accessed a new social network.

AIN's leadership dedicated organizational resources to promoting a community among the women they helped. The NGO ran a theater troupe, reserved one afternoon every week for tea for their "survivors' network," and encouraged network members to attend and participate in community outreach events. Mina, AIN's executive director, viewed these activities as opportunities for social bonding. "It is important for the girls to get together and enjoy themselves." She went on to say how rights activists "don't pay enough attention to that side of things."

On a mild, sunny day in early March, I experienced AIN's social initiatives firsthand. It was the annual Fortnight Campaign for International Women's Day. AIN had teamed up with other organizations to inform the general public about women's rights against violence. The mood was boisterous. Members of the NGO's survivors' network ran across the field, laughing and shouting to get each other's attention. Food vendors lined the peripheries of the crowd, selling cane juice and fried snacks. Large, colorful posters with detailed information about Section 498A and the Protection of Women from Domestic Violence Act (PWDVA) lined the bottom of the stage while music blared from microphones installed on each side of the dais.

With introductory remarks out of the way, AIN's theater troupe filed on stage. Wearing bright blue and red *salwaar kameez*, the troupe included eight women who self-identified as survivors and were members of AIN. Onstage, troupe members danced and sang a song they had co-written named *Esheche Ekti Notun Aina* ("A New Law Has Arrived" in Bengali). The song referred to the PWDVA and through its lyrics spelled out each provision of the law, its benefits over previous legal provisions, and the necessary steps for registering a case. Their performance evoked hearty applause from the crowd, many of whom knew troupe members personally. The performers marched off elated, not simply from the applause but because public performances of this kinds, in front of so many people, created a heady sense of achievement and collective effervescence.

The next phase of the outreach event further cemented social bonds, producing a collective identity geared around breaking free of violence and claiming legal rights. As the stage was rearranged for another round of performances, the television screen positioned in front of the crowd crackled with action. I turned around to hear the beat of *Mann ke Manjeere* ("My Mind Has Begun to Play" in Hindi) rolling across the field. Originally produced by the transnational organization Breakthrough, the music video was a popular feature of AIN's awareness-building campaigns.

Mann ke Manjeere narrated the real-life story of Shameem Pathan, a domestic violence survivor who left her husband and became a truck driver. The music video depicted Pathan's nighttime escape from abuse and then showed her driving her truck across the desert to pick up other women experiencing violence. Together, these women sang as they drove across the desert, stopping at a *dhaba* (truck stop) to dance and drink *chai*. In an age where transnational institutions link the promise of development and progress to women's rights, *Mann ke Manjeere* had global appeal and held specific local significance. Women almost never drive trucks in India. They are not supposed to dance or sing in public spaces. And they are definitely not supposed to be loud, boisterous, and lounging at truck stops: public spaces associated with working-class men and sex work.

Behind me, AIN members broke into enthusiastic applause, some of them going so far as to bring their fingers to their lips to let out loud whistles. They loved the video. And like its protagonist, the iconoclastic Shameem Pathan, they exuberantly demonstrated their own abilities to break gender norms by doing what men are normally allowed to do: whistling in public. Pathan, who gathered a collective of women on screen, served as a symbol for a concrete collective of women off screen. Both the music video and the theater production that came before it helped orient the women in the audience toward the law not simply by invoking legal statutes but by creating a new common sense. Individual women in the audience became part of a social group whose norms and ideals embraced women's empowerment and legal rights. It was by hearing these ideas echoed back at them from the faces and mouths that surrounded them that the law grew more acceptable.

Jhumpa, a member of AIN's survivors' network who I had gotten to know well, sat next to me and grasped my hand in delight when the video ended. She was the one who pointed out the broader significance of the video for her and all her friends. The experience was not merely about individual pleasure: it was a moment of collective effervescence. AIN's survivors' network had stood by her when she had nobody else. Without their presence in her life, she doubted if she would have had the emotional resilience to keep pursuing a legal claim. "One of us always accompanies each other to court. Wherever a girl needs to be, we try to send someone with her," Jhumpa mentioned. AIN's network ensured that individual women had the support they needed to engage the law. And it was through collective experiences like watching an empowering video together that members of the network forged collective bonds.

Jhumpa's words intimated, however, that she received more than emotional and social support from the survivors' network. Collectives provide associational power, which can be translated into political might. Historically, people have accessed citizenship rights by staking claims on the state through their membership in peasant associations and urban guilds. Civil rights to liberty, in essence, presupposed the achievement of a prior right to community and social attachments (Somers 2008). Recent work in other developing countries confirms this general point. Community organizations provide the means through which marginalized groups learn to use the law to advance collective as well as individual interests (Caldiera 2000; Holston 2008). And in the case of the women I met, community helped them claim rights by connecting them not simply to people in the same situation (other women experiencing violence) but to people who were more powerful than them: caseworkers, lawyers, rights activists, politicians, thugs, and friendly law enforcement personnel who might back their claim and threaten their abusers.

Social networks were instrumental to making rights claims. The brokers I talked to, from individuals like Girish to caseworkers at established women's NGOs, would immediately announce who they knew and how quickly they could draw on their contacts to help women in need. If you did not know powerful people or enough people, there was no way you could convince law enforcement to take you seriously. Networks became especially important when a case stalled.

Lata, an upper-caste, middle-income Hindu woman, was experiencing ongoing verbal and physical abuse at her in-laws'. An orphan who had grown up with her uncles, Lata felt unwelcome back in her natal home. She asked AIN to help her claim residential rights in her matrimonial home. The Domestic Incident Report (the first step of a PWDVA case) had already been filed and forwarded to the court, but the judge was either negligent or reluctant to grant an interim order.

It was at this point that AIN mobilized its social network to push the case toward completion. Mina called the district magistrate, a man she personally knew and met with from time to time. He promised to get a hold of the local judge. Meanwhile, AIN's caseworkers worked their contacts within the Kolkata police, who then mobilized support with the inspector of police who supervised Lata's precinct. The inspector sent one of his constables to pay Lata's in-laws a visit, to "keep them in line," so to speak, so that she would not get kicked out before the judgment was passed. Together, these various legal networks and connections allowed AIN to secure a temporary legal solution for Lata, one that entitled her access to a private room and bathroom within her marital home and use of the common area and kitchen.

The importance of community membership surfaced even at Shadheen, where caseworkers at first glance appeared intent on psychological manipulation. During Madhura's intake session, Namita and Jhinuk did more than rebuke her for her inappropriate attachments. They also accompanied her to the police station, bringing other members of Shadheen with them to show the police that Madhura was not socially isolated. These collective resources were especially important given the status of Madhura's abuser, Ashok, who had significant organizational capabilities of his own. Madhura could not effectively challenge him on her own, and Shadheen's caseworkers knew it.

Recalling other women she had helped, Namita assured Madhura of Shadheen's political and social clout. "You have the ability to take on a legal case now," Namita informed her. "So what if he [Ashok] knows the police? We also have contacts in high places. He thinks his thugs can threaten us? We have our own gang!" Namita used the flexible term *dol* (group, party, crew, family, gang, mob) to describe what Shadheen and its sister organization Jagori provided for women. Even if the police were in Ashok's pocket at the moment, Jagori and Shadheen could pressure them to switch affiliations.

Even Shadheen's gender workshop linked therapy to membership in a broader community of women. On the bus back to South-24 Parganas after the workshop, I came across workshop participants giggling. The disrobing, which they had resisted, had become a collective secret that marked them. Shared transgression forged an emotional bond, eliciting laughter and excitement and separating participants from society in a very concrete, physical way. It was through this initiation into an alternate social group, with its own sentiments and ethical commitments, that women were encouraged to reframe their desires. And it was the collective that provided the associational power women needed to become legible to the state as rights-bearing citizens. Community fostered expertise and knowledge and provided social connections, muscle power, and protection.

Services

But women experiencing violence also needed concrete, material goods if they were to leave abusive situations: money, employment, housing, electricity, access to schools for their children. *Didis* could sometimes provide these services. *Dadas* like Girish and Pora Khokhon, with their connections to political parties and underworld networks, had these resources at their fingertips. Uma, a middle-aged Hindu woman who lived in South Kolkata, understood the significance of material incentives before she came under Girish's tutelage.

The apartment complex where Uma lived was set back from the main road, gated, and patrolled by a security guard. Well-constructed, spacious apartments lined a central courtyard; and from the outside, residents looked middle-class and comfortable. But within the complex, Uma's apartment lacked electricity. Her teenage daughter had recently stopped attending school because they no longer had the money to pay tuition. Uma's husband, a well-paid civil servant, had abandoned the family after years of sexually abusing Uma. Living in the dark and unable to pay her daughter's school fees, Uma was at her wits end when a neighbor introduced her to Girish.

Girish agreed to help Uma, waving his usual fees and telling her she could pay him what she wanted once she had the money. Though I cannot speak with certainty about his motivations (in his usual fashion he refused to directly answer my questions), I believe he waved the fee for two reasons. First, Girish realized that he would be paid if his interventions were successful and Uma received a financial award: her husband was a well-paid government employee. If Uma received a financial settlement, she would pass on some of the money to Girish. Second, Girish was motivated by politics: Uma's husband was supposedly friendly with the TMC. Girish's party, the CPI(M), was fighting an uphill battle to retain seats in the state legislature.

One of the first things Girish did for Uma was help reinstate her electricity. Girish called someone he knew at the Calcutta Electric Supply Corporation (CESC), the company that provides electricity to Kolkata. Someone from CESC's corporate social responsibility unit then put Uma in touch with one of CESC's NGO partners. The NGO in question provides relief services for children living in poverty. Since Uma had a daughter who could be considered to fall under their mandate, the NGO contributed money toward Uma's electricity account. The rest of the money came from Girish's friends at the CPI(M).

In addition to contacting CESC, Girish contacted his friends in the neighborhood club that oversaw Uma's area. At the time, the club was controlled by men aligned with the CPI(M). The club *dadas* agreed to watch over Uma. But more concretely, they raised donation money to help Uma pay for electricity and her daughter's tuition. For Uma, Girish's interventions, no matter how pecuniary or politically motivated, made life bearable. Perhaps unsurprisingly, it was only after her lights were back on and her daughter returned to school that Uma considered moving forward with a legal complaint. From long experience, Girish probably knew that by offering goods and services that were seemingly unrelated to a legal claim, he had moved one step closer to his ultimate goal: collecting the money he was owed by giving Uma the physical ability to pursue a financial settlement.

While *didi*s and the women's organizations they worked with had a harder time procuring the kinds of goods and services *dada*s traded in, they did offer important material resources. At Shadheen, women who agreed to follow caseworkers' advice were introduced to other units within the NGO. Shadheen was after all an umbrella organization, housing diverse streams, many of which were devoted to income generation. Women who sought help from Shadheen's casework team tended to crop up with regularity in the NGO's microfinance self-help groups, job training programs, and livelihood development initiatives. Najma, the landless Muslim sharecropper who wished to steer clear of the law, entered Shadheen's poultry production business. Meanwhile, Hema, the low-income Hindu woman who joked that she would rather run toward her husband than face the police, became a self-help group member.

It was through the promise of a sustainable livelihood that Shadheen hoped to steer women away from their desires for reconciliation. "Once they have a way to feed themselves and their children, everything changes," Mona explained. Dolly, who was sitting next to us, agreed, pointing to what the organization had done for Brinda. "Remember how that girl wanted to go back to her husband? Think how desperate she must have been to head down that path."

While Brinda's desires to reconcile with her husband were probably more complicated than Dolly's summarization, financial survival was a key issue. She had to find a way to support her daughters and contribute to her parent's household finances. Brinda entered Shadheen's sewing unit soon after I met her and within a few months had started taking piece work at home: patching torn blouses, kurtas, and underskirts, attaching linings to the bottoms of *saris*. Piecework generated a modest income, providing a few hundred rupees a month on average. But the money went a long way for a woman without any other options: it helped Brinda secure a more stable footing within her parents' house by demonstrating her financial contributions.

Shadheen and AIN also provided medical assistance. Both private and public medical facilities sometimes denied survivors medical care. Those who lacked money faced special challenges in this regard. But there was also a stigma associated with being a victim of violence that made medical professionals refuse treatment. In the face of this institutionalized neglect, caseworkers had connections with doctors and were able to get women appointments quickly and negotiate reduced rates. They accompanied women to hospitals, ensuring that they received proper medical care and were not ignored or overcharged. In Madhura's case, for instance, Rupa and Jhinuk confronted resistance at the local hospital where a doctor demanded to know why the NGO always sent them "dirty" cases. It was by threatening to round up more supporters that Rupa was able to get Madhura admitted.

In North-24 Parganas, Andolan incentivized legal engagement through material incentives. They ran a shelter where women could stay on a temporary basis. Given women's lack of property rights (lack of legal rights to marital property and lack of cultural rights to paternal property), the shelter provided a crucial landing place for those who needed a safe place to stay. Second, Andolan used its political connections with *panchayat* representatives and politicians to help women access the kinds of resources Girish and Pora Khokhon provided, including water, gasoline, and electricity. Andolan's membership base was so large, the organization also had the capacity to raise seed funds for women who needed immediate financial assistance.

Brokers' Effects

By providing therapy, community, and services, brokers pivoted women toward the law. They met women who faced violence and hoped to run a family, and they pushed them toward a more antagonistic approach involving some kind of engagement with the criminal justice system. By challenging women's perceptions of what a good life looked like, by embedding them in associations that supported legal claims, and by extending material goods that made their lives more secure, brokers aimed to change women's preferences.

Basic needs like electricity, children's school fees, shelter, and medical care were important incentives for low-income women as well as women like Uma, those who had been affluent as long as their abusive husbands financially supported them. Goods and services such as these provided women with livable options outside family and marriage. They not only spelled the difference between extreme deprivation and a tolerable life but lowered the financial costs women had to incur when they chose to extricate themselves from an abusive situation. And they raised the potential benefits, benefits that did not necessarily have anything to do with what 498A or the PWDVA promised but which women nonetheless acquired circuitously by registering cases.

But lowering costs and raising benefits meant nothing if the survivor in question wanted a reconciliation. Therapy aimed to change women's attitudes and desires by promoting the law as an aspirational ideal. Caseworkers encouraged women to desire financial and social independence and sexual liberation. They questioned gendered norms of deference, self-sacrifice, and tolerance and urged women to value freedom and women's empowerment. In one sense, therapeutic interventions individualized women, promoting the dubious notion that they stayed in abusive situations because they wanted to. But, on the other hand, therapy brought women together. Shadheen's gender workshops addressed groups of women, encouraging them to envision an alternate life in league with other women. Even the education women encountered within supposedly "closed" intake sessions were rarely cordoned off from a broader collective. As in Madhura's case, multiple caseworkers attended intake sessions, invoking the trajectories of other women they had represented to convince the survivor who sat in front of them that she was not the first or only woman to sever her sentimental attachments.

Some brokers were explicit and conscious of the need for associational power. At some level, they recognized that even while the law grants rights to individual citizens, citizens do not claim rights on their own. During the Fortnight Campaign I attended on the Kolkata maidan, AIN brought women together in an environment geared to promote collective effervescence. The theater troupe embodied the collective promise of the law. *Mann ke Manjeere* provided female role models women could look up to and emulate. Meanwhile, the public nature of the Fortnight Campaign pitted participants against *samaj* (society): the public that they were striving to change. They emulated their alternative group ethics by whistling, by engaging in a public performance, and by declaring themselves as legal claimants.

In some ways, brokerage made women into clients and reproduced social inequality between the woman and her broker (Stovel and Shaw 2012). All three of the tactics brokers used to push women toward the law partially worked by inculcating a sense of obligation among women and by establishing the authority of the broker as someone to be respected. Uma expressed it best. Referencing Girish's advice that she should register a PWDVA case against her husband, Uma explained why she had decided to follow his advice. "*Dada* has done so much for us [her and her daughter]. How can I disregard his wishes?" Uma herself did not know much about the PWDVA. Girish told her what to do, and she did it.

Uma was not alone in making an uninformed decision. Many women did not know what they were getting into when they "decided" to move ahead with a legal case. The law happened to them, and they attempted to adapt themselves to the undertaking. Many women did not understand the nature of the broker they had approached, what they did, or what motivated them. Uma did not know Girish's name the first few times I talked to her. Madhura did not seem to know what Shadheen was or why she was there. A neighbor had brought her to that office, and that is all she could tell me. Nor did she seem to know how to respond to Jhinuk and Namita's instructions. She vacillated back and forth, expressing contradictory intentions, and ended up registering a case out of what seemed to me to be pure confusion.

Simultaneously, brokerage did have certain positive effects: it bridged social gaps that women would never have been able to breach on their own (Stovel and Shaw 2012). It lowered the costs of legal participation, gave women access to much needed goods and services, and provided new social networks that provided an alternative to family and marital life. And while I have highlighted how brokers went out of their way to find women and offered them certain incentives in exchange for legal action, the story was not always so one-sided. As recent work on political brokerage in India indicates, citizens are not always passive recipients of brokerage services; they do a fair amount of selecting (Auerbach and Thachil 2018). The market for brokers is competitive, and brokers must demonstrate efficacy and that they are capable of distributing favors across the population.

The women I met ended up doing a fair amount of shopping around. Once they met one broker, they frequently came to know the names of other people and organizations and ended up approaching them for assistance. Uma, for instance, at first sought help from Girish and then learned about Rupa. In the end, it was Shadheen that helped her register a case for alimony, which she ended up winning. This diversification afforded certain advantages. As Hema pointed out, *dadas* were able to procure certain benefits and *didis* others. Uma ended up getting electricity and her daughter back in school because of Girish *da*, while Rupa *di* provided casework support and introduced her to the company of other women in a similar situation.

Ultimately, one of the key effects brokers had was to push women who would otherwise never have interacted with the state toward that institution. Caught up in the incentives brokers provided, women who were originally dead set against legal claims found themselves approaching the state with some kind of claim for assistance. And the wing of the state that they approached, the criminal justice system, was a juggernaut populated by people with particular biases and objectives.

6

Under Pressure

Law Enforcement's Sense of Victimization

Borobabu regularly complained of "pressure." A heavyset man in his late fifties, Borobabu was the Inspector in Charge (IC) of a police station in South-24 Parganas district of West Bengal. From March to September, he was remained safely ensconced in his office, a large, bare room with a wheezy air conditioning unit that provided a modicum of relief from the incessant heat. A modest brick building surrounded by a less than sturdy-looking fence, the station he presided over was perched halfway between the exhaust-filled thoroughfares of South Kolkata and the tiger-stalked mangroves of the Sunderbans. The station's physical location, between the metropolis and its hinterland, symbolized the many contradictions Borobabu was forced to manage. The district was poor, was prone to political conflict, and housed a diverse and rapidly growing population.[1]

Perpetually anxious, Borobabu was given to sudden sweats and a redness of the neck. At these times, the office peon would retrieve a tattered hand-fan from a nearby cupboard and wave it furiously around his supervisor's face. Borobabu's "pressure" came directly from his job, which involved managing the station's performance. But he also suffered from the "pressure" that signaled a ubiquitous Bengali health condition, hypertension. At times, it was difficult to tell which kind of pressure Borobabu was referring to or if, in a psychological and physical alchemy, the two had become synonymous.

Aside from his wife, who let Borobabu know exactly how displeased she was to live in the backwaters of Kolkata, his stress boiled down to two things. The station had limited resources for case processing. Yet, it fielded a growing number of politicized complaints. Allegations of domestic violence involved not only individual victims and perpetrators but a whole set of organized groups: NGOs, women's committees, labor unions, political parties, and even criminal gangs. Usually, these various factions were at war with one another, but occasionally, they formed sudden and unexpected alliances. As the IC of the station, Borobabu had a simple mandate: resolve as many complaints as possible without wasting too many personnel hours or spending too much money, and don't piss anyone off.

Capable Women, Incapable States. Poulami Roychowdhury, Oxford University Press 2021. © Oxford University Press
DOI: 10.1093/oso/9780190881894.001.0001

In the good old days, Borobabu had managed the challenges of his office in the style of a benevolent yet firm patriarch. Even his moniker, "Borobabu," had an overtly paternalistic ring to it. His real name was documented on a plaque behind his desk, but nobody seemed to know what it was, and nobody referred to him by his name. His moniker combined two words: *boro*, meaning "big" or "elder," and *babu*, the term for a bureaucrat or a man of power and prestige. Loosely speaking, Borobabu meant something akin to "eldest man with power" or "most important bureaucrat." But because the moniker combined the word "elder" with "bureaucrat," it signaled something intimate and familial. The name marshaled the power of extended families populated with elder brothers and uncles. Borobabu embraced the identity and all it culturally connoted.

His paternalistic tendencies were especially on display around women, including myself. He regularly admonished me for being too skinny and urged me to eat a constant stream of fresh fruit, salted crackers, and heavily sweetened *chai*. When women in his precinct asked for help, he liked to size up their character, disapproving of women who appeared "lazy" or "quarrelsome." If a woman had what he deemed to be minor injuries or negotiable conflicts, he thought she should calm down and think things over before rushing into a case. After all, he reasoned out loud, legal cases robbed women of what was good for them: running a family with their husband and children. As an official who was responsible for governing civilians, he believed he should help families stick together.

But the problem was, women no longer behaved the way Borobabu expected. The number of complaints grew every year. Those who were told to go home came back, bringing groups of supporters with them. These supporters yielded various threats. Some were disruptive, crowding his station, shouting, and making a general nuisance of themselves in ways that obstructed daily operations. Others were potentially violent, accompanied by shadowy underworld figures with connections to organized crime. And then there were those with political connections to Members of Parliament who threatened his job. Faced with these contending forces, Borobabu felt disempowered. How could his officers be expected to work under these conditions? he grumbled angrily.

To sociologists and legal scholars who think at length about gender and law, certain aspects of Borobabu's ideology will sound familiar. His belief that women should tolerate violence to maintain family life, that their personal interests were best served by remaining within a patriarchal institution, mirrored existing studies of domestic violence where state officials fail to see women as individuals and encourage reconciliations (Basu 2012; Lazarus-Black 2007). His discursive construction of legal rights as rewards for the "truly" victimized marked another common theme in law enforcement responses to gender-based violence (Baxi 2014; Burton & Duvvury 2000).

Yet, there was something surprising about Borobabu's confessions, parts of his narrative that did not fit accepted knowledge. He claimed that he could not always apply his normative framework to the problem at hand. He complained that women had changed: they were less likely to back away from legal cases and more likely to approach the station with organized support. He linked his present troubles to a series of infrastructural and political constraints he felt ill equipped to handle.

I have to admit, I felt fairly unsympathetic listening to his complaints, interpreting them as barely veiled attempts to shirk work and rationalize state neglect. But I was also intrigued, puzzled by this older man's willingness to admit vulnerability, by his visible uncertainty regarding the best course of action. Was Borobabu unique, or did other law enforcement personnel feel similarly? What kinds of social and political circumstances engendered such anxieties? And how did these circumstances allow state law officials to excuse their own poor performance?

After spending time with police, protection officers, judges, and court clerks across West Bengal, I realized that the discourse of "good" and "bad" women was rampant. And like Borobabu, the majority of law enforcement personnel I talked to worried more about the preservation and sanctity of the Indian family than they did about helping women in distress. Yet, alongside these in-egalitarian attitudes and ideological commitments rested another equally powerful set of perceptions. Administratively incapacitated and wary of mounting political conflict around domestic violence allegations, law enforcement felt disempowered. They did not feel up to the task of enforcing rights, and neither did they feel equipped to silence women who approached them through organized intermediaries. Their gendered biases about women's mendaciousness and putative ability to undermine family life morphed into the notion that certain women could and would threaten their own safety and employment.

Ideological Commitments

Borobabu utilized a common heuristic to distinguish good from bad women. Those who were *bhadra* (genteel, civil) merited assistance. Meanwhile, those who were *jandrel* (stubborn, aggressive, authoritative) needed to be disciplined. Borobabu's favorite adjectives housed significant classed and gendered connotations. *Bhadra*, when attached to the word *mahila* (woman), becomes *bhadramahila*, a term that simultaneously signals a woman who conducts herself properly and demarcates class and caste boundaries. The *bhadramahila* is a middle- or upper-class, Hindu, upper-caste feminine subject defined in opposition to working-class, lower-caste, non-Hindu, "unchaste" women (Banerjee

1999; Ghosh 2008; Ray and Qayum 2009).[2] Meanwhile, *jandrel* connotes a woman who is not just bossy and forceful but masculine. Borobabu used this term to disqualify women he deemed unworthy of state assistance. The notion that inappropriate femininity justifies disciplinary actions on the part of husbands and family members, and that discipline does not constitute abuse, provides a pervasive logic of adjudication for law enforcement (Basu 2006; Lodhia 2009).

The *bhadramahila* is one of a handful of feminine subjects deemed worthy of state protection in West Bengal. Poverty, old age, and other forms of structural or culturally recognized vulnerability also elicited sympathy from law enforcement. A district judge who worked in North-24 Parganas expressed special concern for poor, Muslim women. Women from these social backgrounds were more vulnerable to violence than others, she contended, and had fewer exit options.

In a telling slippage, the Judge referred to Muslim men through the term *duskriti* (miscreant). Much in the way African American men are associated with violence in the American context, minority men are connected to terrorism, incivility, and criminality in India (Hansen 2001; Kapila 2008; Rao 2009; Skaria 1997; Varshney 2003). The judge, herself part of the upper-caste Hindu majority, had internalized these widespread sentiments. As a self-described upholder of law and order and a guardian of society, she believed it was her official duty to protect Muslim women from abusive Muslim men.

Law enforcement wished to safeguard a society where certain women receive protection, while others were kept in their place. The protection officer (PO) of Hooghly district grumbled about all the "false" cases she fielded: complaints where women were manipulating legal statutes because they wished to abuse their husbands. She claimed that only "sixty-five percent of cases are legitimate." Variations of the ratio she quoted floated around other arenas of the criminal justice system, with judges, POs, and the police using a range of numbers to illustrate the putative prevalence of illegitimate allegations. While the PO believed the ratio was 60/40, a judge in Howrah claimed that 82 percent of cases were concocted to harass men. He was so convinced of his numbers that he repeatedly asked me why I was studying domestic violence, since such violence "did not exist."

The fact that a district judge in North-24 Parganas voiced concerns about poor, Muslim women while her compatriot in neighboring Howrah believed 82 percent of women had false allegations is far from a random inconsistency. Their statements made up two sides of the same ideological coin. As public officials, they believed they were responsible for protecting the weaker sex *and* for watching over "abused" men. They took the mandate to safeguard society seriously, linking social order to appropriate social relations: one where innocent men were safe from manipulative women and innocent women from "miscreant" Muslim men.

If state officials' ideological commitments had been the only salient feature of the criminal justice landscape, their lives would have been relatively easy. As Borobabu had conducted himself in what he thought of fondly as the good old days, law enforcement would simply have suppressed most allegations while selectively rewarding rights to a handful of virtuous victims. In reality, they confronted a rapidly changing environment. And this environment did not always allow them to weed out the "manipulative" and selectively protect the "virtuous."

Perceptions of Threat

While law enforcement held strong opinions about who was or was not a "good" victim and how they should be treated, they had to balance their ideological commitments with other pertinent factors: namely, their own capacity constraints and the political threats posed by organized civilians. Women used organized groups to mobilize various threats. They rarely approached law enforcement on their own, but rather through organized groups. Even in court, they were flanked by organizational representatives. They behaved this way because they were afraid they would be neglected or face sexualized violence on their own. Having an organization back their claim made them feel safer and raised their chances of being taken seriously. And that is exactly the effect organized groups had on law enforcement.

Madhura's case showcased the crucial nature of organized connections. This was the same Madhura who inadvertently became the target of Shadheen's sentimental education. Her trajectory starkly highlights how the social and institutional environment surrounding domestic violence compelled law enforcement to help women they did *not* necessarily identify as virtuous.

By all accounts, Madhura was not a good woman. She had been carrying on a long-term sexual relationship with Ashok, an older man. Ashok was married. Independent of his relationship to Madhura, he was considered something of a bad character, engaging in the "dirty" world of politics (Ruud 2001). "Party *bazi kore*," people liked to say of him, which was a snobby way of saying that Ashok was good for nothing aside from politics. On top of all of that, neither of them had the decency to try and keep the relationship a secret. It was all out in the open. A neighbor spat with disgust on the ground, saying Madhura was little better than a prostitute. "She used to walk around as if she was the queen of the village because she had that man in her house," the neighbor observed.

The neighbor intimated that Madhura had clearly financially profited from the relationship.

The police shared Madhura's neighbor's character assessment. When I accompanied Madhura and Shadheen's caseworkers to the police station after the attack, the general atmosphere in the station was polite but tense. For the entire duration of our stay, the officer in charge (OC) exclusively addressed Shadheen's caseworkers, ignoring Madhura completely. He did not seem overly eager to acknowledge her existence, far from helping her secure redress. He even went so far as to ask why the nongovernmental organization (NGO) did not help the "truly oppressed," referring to Madhura as a "kept" woman. "Kept" is a derogatory term used for women who provide sex in exchange for long-term financial assistance. How did the NGO know that a woman of such character was not lying, he demanded? Rupa, who had led the entrance into the OC's office, immediately caught his meaning and was incensed. "How dare he say she is a 'kept' woman?" she grumbled to me later. "You see the kind of attitudes we have to deal with here?"

Unfortunately, the OC's questions reflected a general attitude among officers at the station. With the registration completed, I accompanied two constables back to Madhura's house, observing them as they began a criminal investigation. The house was in disarray, with clothes, furniture, and food strewn all over the floor. Surveying the contents of what must have once been Madhura's refrigerator, the constables conferred in a contemptuous undertone. "See that? He's [Ashok] been feeding that girl [Madhura] shrimp all this time. No wonder he got upset." For the constables, the evidence in the house incriminated not Ashok but rather Madhura. It was not just any kind of shrimp, after all, but *galda chingri*, the largest and most expensive shrimp on the market. In their eyes, any unmarried woman who accepted such expensive favors from a man deserved what was coming her way.

If the police officers' opinions of Madhura's character had been the only factors under consideration, the case would never have been registered. But her virtue, or lack thereof, was only one part of their calculus. From its very inception, Madhura's case involved a complex constellation of organized interests. The violence she experienced came through the orders of a controlling and abusive man with political connections. The actual act of violence was carried out by a well-known criminal syndicate with links to a political party. The neighbor Madhura contacted, Soma, was known in the area as a *didi* because she led a successful self-help group. Soma's self-help group was affiliated with Jagori, which in turn was affiliated with Shadheen. These two organizations together claimed to have over 19,000 members, some of whom could be mobilized both around elections and in direct face-offs with the police.

Once Shadheen's caseworkers were able to convince Madhura to register a report, Dolly mobilized her political connections to place downward pressure on the local police. She called the additional district magistrate's (ADM) office. "We won't be able to register this case without his help," Dolly informed the caseworkers in a separate room. She knew she had to enlist the ADM's support because Ashok's political and criminal connections would make the police reluctant to register a case against him. Shadheen would have to up the ante and get someone even more politically connected to weigh in on Madhura's behalf. And in this initiative, fate, or rather politics, was on Dolly's side.

The ADM had been appointed to his office by a government controlled by the Communist Party of India (Marxist) (CPI[M]). The CPI(M) not only saw the Trinamul Congress Party (TMC) as a general political threat but was at that very moment engaged in a tooth-and-nail fight with TMC workers over the legislative assembly elections scheduled to begin just one month away, in April 2011. The particular area where Ashok and Madhura lived happened to be one of the more heavily disputed electoral blocks in the state. And, as such, Ashok's affiliation with the TMC and its underworld networks made him a perfect target for a CPI(M)-appointed bureaucrat looking to highlight the criminality of his political opponents. While the ADM would never have voiced these calculations out loud, Dolly knew how things worked. Just as the police were vulnerable to direct threats to their livelihood and lives posed by organized groups, the ADM was vulnerable to electoral calculations. He did not disappoint. He promised that a criminal report would be lodged against Ashok without delay, calling the OC of the police station in Madhura's precinct to ensure that the First Incident Report (FIR) was registered.

By the time Madhura reached the police station, her "case" thus involved not only a personal conflict between her and her ex-lover but also a conflict between two political parties, appointees of the ruling party, a criminal gang, a women's microfinance network, and a women's NGO. The OC and his officers reacted with appropriate caution. Madhura was by no means a "good" victim in the traditional sense of the term. The OC and his constables clearly did not identify her as such. In their eyes, she was a "kept" woman who had materially profited from an extramarital affair and thus did not merit sympathy or assistance. Despite their assessments, they worried about alienating the organizations and politicians involved in the dispute. It was unclear which political party would win the upcoming elections. And Madhura's story could evolve, and her alliances might shift.

The OC who refused to acknowledge Madhura's presence later explained to me that "in situations like this the girl always gets back together with the man." In a few weeks Madhura will return to Ashok, and then "the two of them will say he [Ashok] wasn't behind it, you see," he reasoned. "Then they will turn it on us. They'll say the girl was beaten by goons and we didn't help." According to the OC, "anything was possible" in the villages where his officers worked. To protect them, he had to consider all the possible angles, present and future included. The best idea was to register a Domestic Incident Report (DIR) under the Protection of Women from Domestic Violence Act (PWDVA) and an FIR for aggravated assault.[3] The DIR could always be resolved through mediation, he pointed out, and the FIR rewritten to exclude Ashok's name.

Feeling Victimized

Cases like Madhura's gave law enforcement the excuse they needed to feel disempowered. Prosecuting crimes takes time and money and poses physical risks. They pointed out they were short-staffed, used outdated infrastructure, and suffered from resource shortages. They feared angry civilians might disrupt operations or beat them up. This discourse of disempowerment was Janus-faced. It was simultaneously real, in the sense that it responded to concrete institutional constraints, and a narrative law enforcement told themselves to excuse poor performance. State officials were administratively overburdened and did confront disruptive, violent civilians (Express News Service 2016; Roychowdhury 2016b). But they also used these challenges to cast themselves as victims of insurmountable circumstances.

I sensed both the reality of disempowerment and its strategic utility working in tandem when I interviewed the PO of North-24 Parganas. Like Borobabu's station, perched precariously in the midst of fields covered in a dull coat of paint, the PO's office represented the challenges she personally faced. It was not really an office at all but rather a section of a hallway. Seated behind a pony wall, the PO looked irritated when I approached her desk. The conversation quickly spiraled south once I asked about processing delays with PWDVA cases. "Do you know how many complaints I receive every week?" she snapped. "I couldn't tell you because there are so many." Because there were so many complaints, she did not keep track of the number of applicants. Neither did she register each complaint as a DIR.

Undercompensated, understaffed, and lacking basic forms of support, the PO felt justified in falling behind on her duties. In rationalizing her failures, the PO blamed the state government. "What have they [the state government] given me to work with? I don't have paper or envelopes to send notices. I buy my own stamps." Throughout our conversation, the PO looked both annoyed and injured. She seemed to want me to simultaneously fear her and feel sorry for her. This dual stance, one that combined state authority with victimhood, pervaded every corner of the criminal justice bureaucracy.

Law enforcement indexed their disempowerment not only through the administrative constraints the PO highlighted but also through their vulnerability to disruptive civilians. "In the old days, girls did not behave this way," Borobabu peevishly summed up the multidirectional nature of his anxieties. "We only had to worry about boys." Other officials expounded on this sentiment: civilians were both a nuisance and a menace. The ADM of South-24 Parganas explained how women's organizations infiltrated his office and disrupted daily operations: "I don't need a bunch of girls sitting on my head," he commiserated. The expression "sitting on one's head" indicates an act of compulsion whereby an individual or a group of people pressure someone to do something, either by nagging them or by making their life more difficult in some way.

Meanwhile, a judge from Hooghly district recalled a time when his courthouse had been "surrounded" by protestors. "We were afraid to leave our houses, far from going to court," he reminisced. From this story of the blockade, he reasoned that both men and women have "a gang behind them these days." As a result, domestic violence cases posed special perils. The judge's narration of his own disempowerment combined key kernels of reality with large doses of extrapolation. Blockades do happen, but they are rare occurrences. The one the judge described had nothing to do with a domestic violence case. Yet, he used this experience to claim that he felt too overwhelmed and fearful to help women in need. Such spectacular instances of citizen resistance, however infrequent and unrelated to intimate abuse, became embedded within law enforcement personnel's imaginations as the "realities" that rationalized their own negligence.

Those who worked in the field conducting investigations highlighted yet another reason they felt disempowered: the threat of violence. The PO who rebuked me for asking about PWDVA processing delays also expressed concerns about personal safety.

> We [POs] are always getting threatened when we serve notices. I don't have access to a car so I go into these villages on a cycle. Who respects a person on a cycle? Nobody helps me if the boy's [the alleged perpetrator's] friends show up and start threatening. But then everyone gets upset if I side with the boy. The girl's family gets together, and the neighbors get involved and start yelling and harassing me. And the only thing I have is that old cycle [to get out of the situation].

A single woman, unarmed, and lacking a government vehicle, she feared conducting the investigations she was mandated to complete. Her lack of access to a car not only rendered her physically vulnerable to assaults; it symbolized a broader sense of disempowerment. It made her the kind of person who rode a bike, not a person culturally deemed worthy of respect. No matter what she wrote down in her report, if it was in favor of the woman with a complaint or in favor of the alleged perpetrator, she invoked ire. And she could never quite anticipate which side, the girl's or the boy's, posed a greater threat.

Constables, who did have access to vehicles and weapons (batons), expressed similar fears. A constable who worked in Borobabu's station detailed how he and a fellow officer were forced to run across the field with a group of angry villagers on their trail. The villagers had pelted the officers with stones when they attempted to conduct an investigation in the Muslim neighborhood of a nearby village. "The Muslims in that village have powerful friends," he concluded, alluding to political connections between that neighborhood and the TMC. It was difficult for me to verify the constable's story. Borobabu's precinct did lie in a region where political parties had violent underworld connections. But the image of police officers fleeing for their lives also mobilized broader discourses of Muslim criminality that made me suspicious. The story mirrored concrete ground-level realities while simultaneously using those realities to excuse a failed investigation.

Like the constable, who was quick to link the threats emanating from the Muslim neighborhood to politically connected criminal gangs, law enforcement frequently alluded to the workings of political party power on their lives. A lady constable who worked in the Women's Police Cell in Kolkata complained that she could not do her job because she lacked cooperation from POs.[4] According to her, POs were all "political appointments." She pressed her lips in disapproval. "A lot of people want these jobs, you understand? You have to know the right people. . . . If they anger the party boys, that's the end of the job for them." Arguing that POs knew which side their bread was buttered on, the lady constable fleshed out how the politicization of appointments shaped case processing.

Meanwhile, a sub-inspector who had been transferred from Kolkata to a remote location on the India–Bangladesh border in North-24 Parganas blamed his "punishment post" on a politically connected woman. He had failed to register a 498A case against a man whose wife was a distant relation of their local member of the Legislative Assembly. He adamantly believed that he would still be at his old job if he had helped the woman in question. Like the constable who worked in Borobabu's station, the sub-inspector had a narrative about his professional difficulties that was hard for me to corroborate. He may have been transferred for the reasons he pointed out, but it is also possible that the linkage was completely ad hoc. Notably, earlier in the conversation he had claimed that "girls make up false allegations." The specter of a manipulative, politically powerful woman destroying his career may have provided a tidy solution to whatever feelings of shame he experienced from his relocation.

Avoid and Delegate

Law Enforcement's Responses to Women's Claims

Feeling disempowered, law enforcement personnel reasoned that they simply could not do their jobs. They were not in control. Civilians and political parties had all the power, not them. They were overworked, were undercompensated, and lacked autonomy from political forces. Within this landscape of constraints, both real and imagined, the woman that became legible—the kind of woman they felt they had to recognize and pay attention to—was not necessarily the demure, middle-class, Hindu "good victim." It was a different kind of woman altogether, someone like Madhura, someone who might be lower caste and "kept" but who had the potential to create a disturbance.

Borobabu said as much in my second interview with him. The girls he worried about were those with "connections." The more organized support a woman had, the more likely Borobabu was to identify her as a potential disturbance. Suppressing or attempting to silence a woman of this kind was a bad idea. Suppression was reserved for women who were socially isolated and did not pose a visible threat. But a woman with "connections" could not easily be told to go away. If silenced, she might come back and hold up daily operations, undermine an officer's job security, and even threaten their physical safety.

Instead of telling these women to go away, he told them to move ahead. The woman could "stake a claim" but had to be "assiduous" and "able to work" to get the case moving. After registering a case, they could use their organized supporters to help his officers complete the investigation. Alternately, they could avoid a formal case all together while extracting concessions outside the criminal justice system. There was no need to wait for a court order to regain custody of your child or retrieve your possessions, he explained. "They can get what they need without the hassle [of case registration]. We are willing to help on the side," he reasoned. All in all, Borobabu assured me, these arrangements were in everyone's interests.

Suppressing women's claims is nothing new. Both within India and outside, gender and legal scholars have documented how law enforcement personnel

Capable Women, Incapable States. Poulami Roychowdhury, Oxford University Press 2021. © Oxford University Press
DOI: 10.1093/oso/9780190881894.001.0001

systematically silence allegations of gendered violence and tell women to reconcile with abusers. But we know less about the alternate strategies Borobabu
described, those he reserved for women he found threatening and disruptive,
those who had organized support. In these instances, Borobabu allowed women
to register a case and then complete casework. Or he encouraged them to extract
extralegal concessions with some level of informal oversight from his officers.

These two strategies are part and parcel of a governmental model I call "incorporation." Law enforcement personnel incorporated organized women into
regulatory duties in two ways, one that was quasi-legal and another that was completely extralegal. In the quasi-legal form, law enforcement reassigned casework.
They allowed women to register criminal and civil reports but refused to do any of
the work needed to process the complaint. Instead, it was women and their organized supporters who were told to fill out First Incident Reports (FIRs, for criminal
cases) and Domestic Incident Reports (DIRs, for civil cases), help conduct criminal and civil investigations, locate witnesses and take statements, photocopy and
ferry documents between administrative units, deliver subpoenas, and ensure that
witnesses showed up to court.

In its second iteration, incorporation involved a more complete outsourcing
of regulatory duties. Here, law enforcement personnel promoted what I call "parallel claims." A formal case was never registered. Instead, the police or the protection officer (PO) would urge a woman to acquire what the law promised through
illicit means. This included negotiating legally non-binding financial agreements,
engaging in illegal seizures of property and children, and carrying out extrajudicial punishments such as public shaming and beatings. The woman, along with
whatever organization supported her, would directly carry out these tasks while
law enforcement personnel offered assistance and supervision from a distance.

Borobabu's decision-making criteria around what kind of woman should be
treated in which way is worth noting. Social background characteristics (class,
caste, religion) did not determine the sorting mechanism, and neither did
appearing demure and innocent. Rather, it was a woman's ability to round up
social support and yield credible political threats that lay the grounds for her incorporation. Women who lacked organized support were silenced. Women who
had organized backing were "incorporated."

Meanwhile, in deciding which form of incorporation to adopt, state officials
were influenced by a confluence of factors: their localized capacity constraints,
the particular proclivities and political influence of the organized group backing
a woman, and the nature of the opposition (who was supporting the perpetrator
and how powerful they were). If the woman's broker favored legal cases, as was
the case when Shadheen or AIN brought a case to the state, state officials would
lean toward the quasi-legal form. If the broker disdained legal measures, as was
the case for Andolan, law enforcement proceeded toward a parallel claim.

Suppressing Individual Claims

While law enforcement personnel talked at length about their ideological commitments to protecting certain women and punishing others, when push came to shove, their ideologies alone did not guide their actions. Borobabu may have believed that a *bhadramahila* deserved special consideration, and the PO of Hooghly district may have genuinely thought that 60 percent of women were making false claims. But the political and infrastructural constraints that surrounded them, as well as their interpretation of how these conditions threatened them personally, led law enforcement personnel to base their responses to women's claims around a different metric.

Women who lacked organized support could be ignored. They could check all the right social boxes (middle class, upper caste, Hindu) and still be left out in the cold. They could self-present in all the appropriate ways (soft-spoken, modestly dressed, shy) and still be told to go home and work things out. Fitting the ideal of the "good victim" did not ensure legal assistance, just as being a bad victim did not prevent women like Madhura from registering a complaint.

Uma, who had been living without electricity, unable to pay her daughter's tuition fees, found this out the hard way on her first trip to the Alipore police station. She had yet to meet Girish, the homeopathic doctor. And it would take another few months for her to find Shadheen. I myself would not meet Uma until her entrance at Shadheen, so the events I relay are based on her own recollections of what happened.

It had been several weeks since Uma's husband had moved in with another woman and cut off all communication. Uma did not work, and she was isolated, estranged from her natal family. They had disapproved of Uma's marriage: she was Brahmin, her husband was tribal and from a poorer family. Lacking a support system and the financial means to provide for herself and her daughter, Uma sought help from a neighbor, a retired teacher who accompanied her to the police station. Together the two women waited for several hours. Finally, a lady constable ushered them inside and asked what had happened.

With the help of her neighbor, who relayed parts of the story Uma felt too embarrassed to communicate, Uma told the lady constable her story. She recounted how for years her husband had sexually abused her, forcing her to have sex five to six times a day. He had not only insisted on having sex "naturally" (vaginal sex) but also forced her to perform oral and anal sex. He had done all of this after convincing her to run away from her upper-caste family. When she could no longer fulfill his demands, he had found someone else and abandoned her and their teenage daughter.

Uma recalled that as she had spoken, she had felt uncomfortable. The constable had made little effort to be approachable. She neither smiled nor made eye contact with Uma. And at times, Uma thought she sneered and seemed disgusted at her for detailing what she had suffered. When Uma finally stopped talking, the constable confirmed Uma's suspicions by scoffing. In a condescending voice, she demanded to know how the police could prosecute a man because his wife had "failed to satisfy him." Instructing Uma to be "thankful" for all the years her husband had comfortably fed and housed her on his government salary, she dismissed the case as unmeritorious.

A quiet and unassuming woman in her early forties, Uma dressed modestly and stood hunched over as if trying not to take up too much space. While I was not present at her first meeting with the police, I very much doubt her comportment differed radically from what I observed months later. Uma did not just act *bhadra* (genteel), she was a *bhadramahila* (a middle-class woman). She was Brahmin and came from a middle-class family. And she was abused by a tribal man, someone who fit the social background law enforcement personnel associate with "miscreants." Her self-presentation, her class and caste background, and her social status relative to her abuser should have positioned Uma as the perfect victim. Despite her profile, however, Uma was ridiculed and denied the opportunity to register a case. The police officer laughed off abuse as an index of Uma's failure as a wife, refusing to proceed with either a 498A case or a claim for maintenance under Section 125A.

The situation could not have been more different once Uma gained organized support. Three months after her initial attempt to access rights, Uma returned to the same police station and spoke to the same lady constable. But this time, Uma was under Girish's wing. Girish had already connected her to her neighborhood Communist Party of India (Marxist) (CPI[M]) cadre and to the Calcutta Electric Supply Corporation (CESC). Uma was also receiving help from Shadheen. She had met Rupa, who had taken a special interest in her case. Rupa urged Uma to return to the police, arguing that Uma's husband owed her financial support. Thus, on her second attempt to register a case, Uma was accompanied by Rupa, myself, and two members of Shadheen. Meanwhile, Girish had called the station before our arrival, mentioning Uma's name and the problem she faced. This time, the police were expecting Uma and knew she was organizationally supported.

Uma's second attempt to access rights went dramatically differently from her first. We waited about fifteen minutes and then were ushered in with a degree of politeness. Uma proceeded to retell her story, this time with Rupa's help. The Lady Constable's reaction to Uma's second visit was telling. She expressed shock at the frequency of sexual encounters, and then moved toward visible disgust when Uma discussed anal and vaginal sex. Clucking sympathetically, she announced loudly to the general public that Uma was truly "oppressed." Noting physical evidence of her oppression, the constable referenced how Uma's "face and eyes have dried out," a popular way of saying someone looks ill. The constable allowed Uma to register an FIR under 498A and then went above and beyond her duties, advising Uma to demand alimony directly through her husband's employer.

Notably, the constable's reidentification of Uma as "oppressed" hinged on Uma's ability to demonstrate her organizational connections. Uma had relayed much the same information the first time they talked. She was demure and unassuming in both encounters. She was the same Hindu, upper-caste subject she had been all her life. Yet in the second iteration, holding all these factors constant, Uma was allowed to move forward. Uma now had Girish and Shadheen's combined presence backing her claim. Both brokers could make the Alipore police's life uncomfortable: Girish through his contacts at the CPI(M) and Shadheen through its caseworkers who could crowd the station and cause a headache. Uma was no longer a woman easily ignored. She had become a woman who could be disruptive and, as such, someone to whom law enforcement personnel owed attention and accommodation.

Reassigning Casework

The kind of attention and accommodation organized women received was not necessarily what the law promised. Women with organized help received a different kind of treatment from those without, but this treatment was a compromise that allowed law enforcement personnel to juggle their various constraints, including overwork and potential threats from perpetrators. The proceedings of a community-building workshop that took place in Nodakhali, in South-24 Parganas district, illuminate how law enforcement personnel achieved this balance.

The Nodakhali workshop brought together Shadheen's caseworkers, women experiencing violence, police officers, and the district's PO in a daylong community-building initiative. I arrived to find everyone gathered in a circle in the front courtyard of the station. There were a number of familiar faces in the crowd: Rupa and Jhinuk, caseworkers at Shadheen, and Hema and Najma, women experiencing violence who had turned to Shadheen for assistance. They were all gathered around four law enforcement personnel. It was a pleasant day, warm and sunny with a cool breeze that ruffled the leaves of the trees that shaded the courtyard. The mood was as congenial as the weather.

The workshop's intended purpose was to create dialogue between state and nonstate actors around new legal reforms. But in the process, the workshop did something much more. It rationalized direct transfers of responsibility and work from law enforcement personnel to civilians. When I arrived, the PO of South-24 Parganas was in the midst of discussing what her office could and could not handle. The PO spent a good deal of time lamenting her working conditions, laments that almost verbatim mirrored the excuses another PO had hurled at me when I had asked about processing delays with Protection of Women from Domestic Violence Act (PWDVA) cases. Like the PO of North-24 Parganas, this PO also detailed her administrative constraints. She did not have the authority to use a government vehicle and thus had to conduct all her investigations on foot. She did not have her own office; she had to share a large room with secretaries and court clerks. She did not have a budget for paper, envelopes, or stamps. The audience shook their heads in commiseration.

Given these infrastructural constraints, the PO noted how cases proceeded more quickly when women took initiative. Some girls "sit back" and wait for others to do everything. What are they expecting? It was the "active" girls who were getting places, the ones who made sure the right people signed off on the DIR, the ones who helped her gather evidence for her initial report for the magistrate. The PO even used the English word "active" to describe these exemplary individuals. The English word added a certain emphasis and subtly connected "active" girls to everything the English language implied in a postcolonial setting: modernity, progress.

It was really not that hard to get the case moving when everyone chipped in, the PO continued. "Times are changing and we [women] have to change with it. Those days are gone, the days of our grandmothers, where girls sat at home and let boys do the work." Audience members enthusiastically nodded in agreement, hearing the language of empowerment that percolated through the nongovernmental sector repeated back to them from a relatively authoritative member of the state. One audience member went so far as to call out excitedly that she was living proof of what the PO was saying: she was the "active" girl the PO promised would move forward. She beamed with self-satisfaction.

While the PO encouraged women to become "active" and get involved in their own cases by detailing her own infrastructural limitations and alluding to Indian women's modernization, the police officer who followed her highlighted a set of social constraints. An assistant sub-inspector at the station where we sat, he discussed the way gendered norms constrained his ability to help women in distress. Even though the law says one thing, family disputes were beyond police jurisdiction because ordinary people considered it improper for male police officers to question or be alone with female victims.

"If we walk into a girl's house without anyone else around, people say we have done something improper, that we've insulted her honor, insulted her family." He explained calmly and I noticed many audience members nodding in affirmation. Because domestic violence was a woman's issue, these matters were best dealt with by women themselves, he reasoned. It was only through a partnership between the aggrieved woman and a women's organization that an abusive situation could really be resolved. He was young and sincere. His starched shirt and perfectly combed hair indicated that he respected social norms. His appeals seemed genuine. A few of the women sitting next to me whispered how his invocations seemed to be in women's best interest.

At this point, a second police officer cut in. He was the inspector in charge (IC) of this particular precinct. Tall and muscular, he towered over the women by a good ten inches. What he said after he stood up seemed additionally significant given his visible physical prowess. He wished to discuss a third reason the police had difficulties regulating domestic violence. It had to do not with resources or social norms but with West Bengal's political landscape. He reminisced about a particular case that had become politicized. The abuser did "party work" for the CPI(M), rounding up votes and ensuring that loyal supporters had the necessary services. The minute his wife tried to register an FIR, the CPI(M) party honchos came and camped out in the station, pressuring the IC to suppress the case. The IC lamented that he had really wanted to help the poor girl, but those "thugs" had tied his hands, crowding his office day and night and spreading rumors about him in the surrounding villages. The IC sighed and hung his head in defeat and shame.

The women in the audience clucked sympathetically as if to reassure him that it had not been his fault. The case would have gone differently if this particular person had worked closely with a women's group. Nobody accuses women's groups of having political motivations. Both the IC and the workshop participants agreed that women, be it a caseworker or a survivor of violence, had the moral strength and social credibility to confront political party thugs. Spreading his hands in a sign of deference as if he was indebted to the very women he was paid to protect, the IC took a bow and regained his seat. Everyone clapped in appreciation.

Together, the IC, the assistant sub-inspector, and the PO accomplished a hat trick. In three strokes, they outlined various constraints they faced in their work, used those constraints to create a foundation for women's involvement, and absolved themselves of responsibility and blame for the shortcomings of their offices. Work reassignments relied on and reaffirmed the discourses of state disempowerment I found throughout my interviews with law enforcement personnel. The PO detailed her administrative constraints and then told women to be "active." The police narrated political party pressure and then reminded women that they were morally and socially more capable of managing party interference.

The Nodakhali workshop figuratively reassigned work, encouraging audience members to behave in certain ways in the future. In the context of a particular allegation, however, work reassignments were concrete and immediate. It was in these moments, when women experiencing violence, brokers, and law enforcement personnel confronted each other and negotiated how to move forward, that law enforcement personnel were most effectively able to reassign tasks.

Work reassignment occurred at multiple levels of the criminal justice bureaucracy. Faced with a complaint, the PO of Hooghly district told a woman who wished to register a DIR to complete the investigatory report herself. It was the woman experiencing abuse along with representatives of a local *mahila samiti* who contacted the necessary witnesses, transcribed their statements, and completed an assessment of household assets.

Meanwhile, the officer in charge (OC) of Howrah police station admitted that the stations in his district registered cases that involved either life-threatening injuries or women who had the "resources" to see a case through. By women with resources, he was not talking about women who could hire lawyers. He referred to women who were able to help complete case-processing tasks. These were women who, in his words, could unearth evidence, round up witnesses, and make the criminal investigation less arduous for his constables.

Even court officials, long identified as the bastion of conservative demands for women's victimhood in the Indian context, argued that women needed to be proactive. A retired member of the Kolkata High Court reasoned that the court system was too overburdened to assist women who quietly waited for relief. The judge spent his afternoons counseling women experiencing violence, caseworkers, and members of nearby women's organizations. He encouraged them to be "restless" if they wanted to make a case work. If something's not getting done, she has to step in and provide a helping hand.

Meanwhile, an upper division clerk in the Howrah court had a standing agreement with particular NGO caseworkers to expedite "their cases." He would hand over confidential documents, including the PO's investigatory report, the police charge sheet, and evidence. The woman who had registered a complaint would then work with a caseworker or *mahila samiti* member or political party *dada* to ensure that these documents were photocopied and transcribed. Civilians oversaw discovery, guaranteeing that evidence was appropriately filed.

Promoting Parallel Claims

Encouraging women to assume responsibility over case-processing duties was one way to incorporate women into the work of regulating violence. Another tactic involved replacing a formal case with an informal process. In this alternate mode, law enforcement personnel promoted extralegal punishments and encouraged women to illegally extract concessions. Parallel claims did not have official standing within the law, but they mimicked the law. Women used a parallel claim to secure what existing legal statutes promised, using a range of coercive practices to access their demands. For law enforcement personnel, parallel claims housed several advantages. First, since there was no legal case, they were not accountable or responsible for what happened. Second, not recording a crime kept crime rates low, and this is what elected officials wanted.

Because the character of a woman's support network influenced criminal justice responses, parallel claims tended to emerge in contexts where law enforcement personnel interacted with organizations that were willing and ready to embrace extralegal actions. Nodakhali, it must be pointed out, brought state officials face to face with Shadheen, an organization known to support legal reforms and case registration. The public nature of the event as well as officers' knowledge of their audience influenced their decision to focus on work reassignment.

While quasi-legal reassignments were openly celebrated at workshops, parallel claims were not publicly broadcast. Nor was any element of these "claims" documented. Frequently, state officials did not acknowledge parallel claims even while they were happening. A collective denial by all parties involved allowed this form of incorporation to function as an open secret.

Payel's extralegal property repossession provided a lens on how these arrangements came about and proceeded. When I first met Payel, she had run away from her husband and was living with her parents. She sat cross-legged on the floor of Andolan's back room, flanked by Bani and the Andolan union member who had brought her there for help. It was some weeks since she had run away from her husband's house, she reminisced. I wondered if she had waited for her wounds to heal, one of which was still visible on the left side of her face where her husband had burned her with a hot metal spatula. Bani was writing notes in Bengali in her notebook, while Payel's infant son crawled on the floor next to us.

Payel had a ninth-grade education and did not work. Her parents owned a small amount of land and survived largely on the pension her father received from his job in the Indian railways. As one of two daughters, without a brother who would inherit the family home, Payel felt assured that she could stay with her parents indefinitely. But the family income was small, hardly leaving enough to support two more people. Payel was intent on retrieving her belongings from her husband's house, including what she had been given as dowry: a modest amount of gold, kitchen utensils, clothing, a bicycle for her husband, and a pack of ducks. She did not think she could get the bicycle back, but everything else she felt should be returned to her.

"Well we don't like to do 498 unless we have to, and it won't help you with this anyway," Bani explained, indicating the organization's distaste for legal cases. In fact, neither 498A nor PWDVA had provisions for regaining possessions or dowry-related payments. After some back and forth, during which Bani suggested a *shalishi* that Payel rejected, they decided to approach the local police to see what could be done. "Let's see if they do a 406," Bani stated, referencing Section 406 of the Indian Penal Code. Section 406 allows married women to regain possession of *stridhan*, legally defined as gifts bestowed on a Hindu bride at the time of her wedding.[1] In Bani's experience, 406 cases tended to take less time and led to more favorable rulings than 498A cases. And thus, despite her general hostility toward legal measures, she was willing to entertain the possibility of registering one for Payel.

A week later, I accompanied Bani and Payel to the local police station where Andolan had "friends": police officers who worked with them on cases. When we finally met a sub-inspector at the station, he politely told us he did not have men to spare for a full investigation. "It's a very busy time," he lamented, pointing to the extra work that was piled on the police around local elections. All his men were supervising polling booths, and he hardly had anyone left to man the station. He encouraged Payel to return after the elections; he would make sure the case was registered then.

Payel mentioned that she was afraid that her husband would sell everything and pocket the money by then. Bani agreed, asking the sub-inspector if there was any other option. The sub-inspector spread his hands on the table. He noted that Andolan had a large membership base. "Can't you folks do something for her? Go talk to the boy," he recommended. Bani nodded as if they had agreed on something. "Yes, we can talk to the boy, but we need your help." The sub-inspector remained silent, seemingly thinking things over. All Andolan needed, Bani continued, was one constable to "supervise" their progress. With a constable nearby, they could "take care of the rest," she assured him. He hemmed and hawed for a moment and then nodded his head in agreement. "If you can handle it, it is fine with us," he said amiably. Without spelling out details, they had come to an agreement.

Nobody had to articulate the terms of the agreement because this was not the first time this officer had brokered such a deal with Andolan and the women they represented. What was left unsaid was that Payel would pursue a parallel claim, Andolan would assist her, and a police officer would provide some modicum of protection from a distance. In essence, when Bani asked for a constable to "supervise" while they did the rest, she proposed that Andolan would assist Payel in an act of extralegal repossession. Payel and Bani would enter the house and forcibly carry out whatever they could get their hands on. Andolan's union members would accompany them, ensuring a sizeable presence of supporters guarding against any possible reprisals. The officer would ensure that Payel and Andolan posed a credible threat, communicating to Payel's husband and any onlookers that they had the blessing of the state.

The sub-inspector understood the merits of this arrangement. He looked helpful and thus minimized the risk of alienating Andolan, an organization with a large base that had a proven track record of disruption. At the same time, he avoided the ordeal of an official case by decentralizing authority and redistributing the state's monopoly over violence. His constables would not have to conduct an investigation or put in all the work of showing up to court. One officer could just take a few hours during an afternoon and make sure that Payel's venture went smoothly.

Payel's extralegal repossession was not the only one of its kind that I observed. And Andolan was not the only organization to aide women in these efforts. Sobha, a young, low-income, Christian woman who had spent her life in a small village close to Shadheen's offices, used Rupa's services to regain her possessions. The words exchanged between Rupa and the OC in South-24 Parganas sounded eerily similar to those that transpired between Bani and the sub-inspector in North-24 Parganas. The OC also claimed he did not have "men to spare," to which Rupa also asked for one constable to "supervise" their progress from a distance. Like Bani, Rupa also claimed they could "do the rest."

Among the parallel claims I witnessed, extralegal repossessions and gaining custody of children were the most popular initiatives. One reason for this might have been the anxiety Payel expressed. Women who had been kicked out of their homes wanted to repossess their property as quickly as possible before it was sold off. They wished to bring their children back under their custody both because they missed them and because they feared for their safety in violent homes.

Another reason was the relative ease with which women could grab possessions, relative to hidden assets such as cash stored in a bank. Finally, repossession and regaining children enjoyed a level of social validity. Brokers of all varieties, women themselves, their families, and even law enforcement personnel seemed to think that women should be able to just go and get what was theirs. Everyone I talked to thought children, especially young children, belonged with their mothers. The social consensus on these matters was such that women had the legitimacy they needed to act swiftly outside the law.

The Gendered Logic of Incorporation

By doing the work of the state, women became a wing of the criminal justice system, participating in its daily operations. Their incorporation was gendered in two distinct ways. First, it largely targeted women, be it women experiencing violence or the large number of organized actors who helped them, many of whom were also women. Second, in the process of incorporating these women, law enforcement personnel mobilized a gendered discourse. They claimed that women were uniquely suited to carry out the work of the state because of their special capabilities.

In the process of reassigning work and encouraging parallel claims, law enforcement promoted a particular image of women. Women needed to be "active" and "restless." They could no longer afford to "sit back" or wait for someone to take care of them. This gendered logic differentiated contemporary women from women of the past. Contrasting the current generation of women to their mothers and grandmothers, the PO at Nodakhali argued that *this* generation was capable and active. Law enforcement also distinguished women from men: the violent men who abused women, the corrupt men who populated political parties, and the incapacitated men who manned the criminal justice system. Through these direct and indirect comparisons, state officials used notions of gendered differences to rationalize why women should help them, instead of the other way around.

The additional district magistrate (ADM) who had ensured Madhura's case was registered later fleshed out the gendered nature of women's capabilities to a large audience. He was a guest of honor at Shadheen's annual festivities for International Women's Day. Every year, women's organizations throughout West Bengal organize demonstrations and rallies around the first week of March in what is known as the "Fortnight Campaign" against violence. In front of the ADM, hundreds of women crowded into a giant meeting space, some of whom were part of Shadheen's microfinance networks and some of whom had outstanding domestic violence cases overseen by Shadheen.

When the ADM began speaking, he recalled how Shadheen's caseworkers helped his office by bringing women in need directly to his doorstep. He then went on to congratulate caseworkers and the women they represented. Women are not just "oppressed," he asserted. Using the Bengali term *khomota* (capability, ability, power), he argued that women have the "capability" to challenge violence. It was because he felt inspired by women that he was able to do the work he did, he reasoned. His office felt that they could take on cases because they were serving a population that knew how to work hard and help themselves.

In the end, the ADM's Fortnight address relied on the same rhetoric as the state officials who sought to forge alliances with women at the Nodakhali workshop. They claimed that women were able to do things law enforcement personnel were not. The state needed women's help, not the other way around. Without fail, law enforcement personnel rationalized their incorporative practices by asserting women's unique moral strengths, ability to work hard, and courage to withstand danger.

Thus, a PO urged a PWDVA applicant, a poor woman from a village, to finish her report for her. She joked that the woman was "braver" than her. Meanwhile, a court clerk in Kolkata's Alipore courthouse chuckled that "girls these days are very dynamic," energetically moving around in the heat while he was on the verge of collapse. The OC of Howrah station mentioned how state officials had forged joint ventures with women all over the countryside because women were more "enterprising" than men. He even roped me into his commendations. "Look at you madam, living so far away, but here you are, doing your research. Very impressive!"

Putting a theoretical spin on these diverse practices, the retired High Court judge who counseled women to be "restless" discussed how women had become central to the state government's developmental initiatives.

> You see the KMC [Kolkata Municipal Corporation] doing so many things with women, with poor women even in the slums. It is the woman who is responsible, you see. She takes care of the children, the old people. So she does what is necessary to maintain the household. Same for these social issues. . . . Women can be very feisty. They have strength. You have heard of strī śakti [women's power]? This is what I am saying.

The retired judge seemed to be quoting a page from some long-forgotten handbook on women in development. Speaking in English with me, he used the Sanskritic term strī śakti as a vernacular term for women's empowerment. The ghosts of Mohammed Yunus and the World Bank glimmered somewhere in the shadows as he called forth the vision of women's unique developmental promises. Cecile Jackson and Katherine Rankin, who so astutely pointed out these connections years back, could not have wished for a better synthesis (Jackson 1996; Rankin 2001).

Tellingly, the retired judge referenced the KMC as an organization that was "doing so much with women." The KMC is a local government body that oversees public services such as roads, electricity, education, and health for the residents of Kolkata. It also houses an entire department that focuses on women's empowerment. Its Social Welfare & Urban Poverty Alleviation Department channels resources to local NGOs that do domestic violence work. KMC-funded projects are managed by NGOs that use government money to provide legal aide, counseling, medical care, housing, and financial support to women experiencing violence.

The KMC is not alone in pursuing joint ventures. At the national level, one of the more established government schemes of this type involves a partnership between women's NGOs and the Integrated Child Development Services (ICDS).

The ICDS, which is managed by the Indian government's Ministry of Women and Child Development, funds NGOs to run domestic violence trainings for state employees. The KMC and ICDS came together in a number of women's organizations where I conducted interviews. These organizations used KMC grants to conduct casework and worked with ICDS to train *anganwadi* workers who staffed rural health centers.[2]

Partnerships between nonprofit organizations and various institutions of the national and local state provide the broader context within which incorporation has emerged and gained traction. After all, the practices I observed within the criminal justice system did not magically appear out of thin air. They responded to changing social and political conditions, namely limited state capacity and women's growing organizational strength. But they also fundamentally made sense to law enforcement personnel and organized actors, and even to the women who had turned to these people for assistance.

Incorporation was a response to the moment. It was structurally conditioned by law enforcement personnel's exposure to political pressure and infrastructural constraints. And it was discursively defined by a transnational focus on women's participation and empowerment. Gender sensitivity, inclusion, capabilities: all of these were buzzwords that infiltrated various state bureaucracies and the development sector. But the judge, the OC, the court clerk, and the PO added their own unique twist. Women were no longer simply a developmental panacea but also a solution for law-and-order problems. Their gendered "capabilities" solved the incapability of a politically besieged, sexist, and neglectful criminal justice system.

SECTION III

CITIZENS

Running a Case

The Praxis of Law

Hameeda's case had run into a roadblock. She had filed a Domestic Incident Report (DIR) over a month ago. The protection officer (PO) should have forwarded her application for relief to the district magistrate by now. Instead, the PO kept stalling and refusing to complete the necessary report. Hameeda was poor, Muslim, and uneducated: factors that contributed to her marginality and made it difficult for her to move ahead. It was her caseworker, Samoli, who told her what to do. Hameeda needed to "drive her case forward." She could not just sit back and wait for the PO to do her job. She would have to get involved, propel her claim forward through her own efforts.

Like Hameeda, Samoli had once been in a violent situation. Her husband had never hit her, but her in-laws had been verbally and physically abusive, starving her and working her to exhaustion. These days, she was a member of Shadheen's casework team and a member of the organization's self-help groups. She lived twenty minutes from Shadheen's office with her husband and son in a mud house with a new brick extension. The extension attested to the family's upward trajectory: financed by her earnings and her son's job tutoring schoolchildren. In addition to her income-generating activities, Samoli organized a *mahila samiti* in her village. It was through this *mahila samiti* that Samoli had encountered Hameeda. Samoli knew the tricks of the trade and could help Hameeda learn how to make law enforcement responsive to her claim.

The particular PO Hameeda sought was well known for avoiding work and was notoriously difficult to locate. I myself spent a good two months trying to get a hold of her via phone and impromptu visits to her office. When I finally did run into her, her eyes darted back and forth over her tortoiseshell glasses like a cornered animal looking for escape.

Like me, Hameeda and Samoli spent nearly three weeks trying to register the DIR. But the DIR was just the beginning of a much longer waiting period. After the registration, the PO told Hameeda to check back in a week. She needed to

Capable Women, Incapable States. Poulami Roychowdhury, Oxford University Press 2021. © Oxford University Press
DOI: 10.1093/oso/9780190881894.001.0001

draw up her report: she would have to visit Hameeda's husband's house, talk to neighbors and family members, and ascertain if Hameeda's accusations had any basis. The week passed. Then two weeks passed and then six.

Enough is enough, Samoli announced one day. It was time to confront the PO. The first step involved pinning her down. On an oppressively hot day in May, I accompanied Hameeda and Samoli to the PO's office in Kolkata's Alipore Court Complex. Samoli had got wind from her court contacts that the PO was coming to the office that morning. Everything and everybody in the court complex moved like molasses. People climbing the stairs rested at every landing, panting and sweating from the heat. The fans rotated once every few seconds, their blades weighed down by soot and a season's worth of cobwebs. The three of us leaned against the wall as time ticked by: fifteen minutes, then the half-hour gong, and then finally twelve noon, one full hour after we had arrived in the office. Even the stenographers who sat in the courtyard below us barely moved their fingers. A sizeable pause separated each click from each dull clack on their keyboards.

When the PO finally arrived, she did not seem to recognize Hameeda, feigning ignorance of the DIR Hameeda had already filed. She forced us to wait some more as she leisurely ate her lunch. Finally, she turned to us with a harassed expression. "Where is your DIR?" she abruptly demanded, shuffling papers around her desk as if to prove that she had never received the DIR in the first place. Samoli, having managed cases in the past, knew these tricks well and was ready. She swiftly whisked a copy of the necessary document out of her handbag and placed it on the PO's desk.

Samoli's preparation only irked the PO even more, who began complaining that she could not be expected to draw up a report so quickly. Hameeda lived where? Oh goodness, that village was more than two hours away. She had all these other cases that had been registered before Hameeda's. How could she travel to Hameeda's house on such short notice? At this, Hameeda timidly asked if the case would be processed in the promised sixty days allotted by the law. She had memorized everything Samoli had told her, and she remembered that this was one of the stipulations of the Protection of Women from Domestic Violence Act (PWDVA). The PO became incensed. She complained that the PWDVA had an unrealistic timetable. There was nobody to help her. She had to do everything herself.

It was at this point that Samoli made her interjection. "Madam, if you sign the form, we can fill it out." The PO ignored Samoli and continued to lament her workload until Samoli repeated the same statement. Samoli and Hameeda would collect the necessary witnesses, take statements, and complete an assessment of Hameeda's household goods. In essence, they themselves would write the PO's report for her. All the PO would do was add her signature.

Finally, the PO seemed to listen. She assumed a somewhat less hostile demeanor, admitting that Samoli and Hameeda were better positioned to collect the necessary information. Samoli used the opportunity to further cement the agreement. She highlighted both her own and Hameeda's abilities. She herself had "managed hundreds of such cases" in the past. Using the Bengali terms *khomota* and *yogota*, Samoli recounted how Hameeda worked hard and had many "capabilities." Taking her cue to speak up, Hameeda moved forward and recited all the ways she had supported herself and her unemployed, abusive husband. Hearing all of this, the PO nodded her head in agreement. She even became jovial. "Everyone says girls can't do anything, but you ladies are showing us [state officials] how to get things done!" Samoli and Hameeda giggled at the accolade.

Hameeda's and Samoli's interactions with the PO highlight how women asserted their capabilities in the process of being incorporated by law enforcement personnel. Both Hameeda and Samoli performed their own empowerment to offset and compensate for the real and supposed disempowerment of the state. But the interactions leave open the question of what kinds of aptitudes and orientations were needed for Hameeda and Samoli to pull off what they did. What exactly did women have to do to engage the law on the terms available to them? How did women move their complaints forward? What concrete capabilities did their engagements demand and engender?

The Practice of Law

By incentivizing the law and by incorporating women into the daily work of regulation, brokers and law enforcement personnel encouraged women to "run a case" (case *calano*). Women of diverse social backgrounds, women who had initially hoped to "run a family" (*sansar calano*), accidentally became enmeshed in this landscape in the process of seeking assistance. By contacting *atmiya sajana*, kin who possessed the prestige and connections to discipline their abusers, women opened their lives to interventions from a wider network of actors. These actors, who women referred to as *didi*s and *dada*s, had one foot in neighborhood and community life and one foot in political parties, nongovernmental organizations (NGOs), and women's committees (*mahila samiti*). Intervening in domestic disputes and encouraging women to engage with the criminal justice system, either illicitly or formally, provided a means for their own financial, social, and political enrichment. Brokers incentivized women's legal engagements, providing therapy, social networks, and material resources that made the law less costly and slightly more inviting.

Women experiencing violence thus found themselves propelled toward a set of state institutions that they had previously known little about, feared, and disdained. But law enforcement personnel made surprising concessions. If the woman was able to demonstrate her organizational connections, she received a modicum of cordiality and help. Law enforcement personnel bemoaned their own disempowerment and told women to use their organized helpers to carry out the law themselves. One could accomplish this by either doing the work necessary to move an official complaint through the criminal justice bureaucracy or jettisoning the formal process altogether and pursuing a parallel claim.

The "cases" that women ran were thus an amalgamation of various legal and extralegal ventures. Sometimes a formal complaint accompanied a parallel claim, enabling bargaining outside the law. In these instances, women registered an official case to negotiate extralegal settlements, using the threat of arrest and the promise of withdrawal as carrots and sticks to force their abuser's hand (Roychowdhury 2019). Women referred to these ventures, both official and parallel, through the language of the law. "I'm running a case." "The case is running." Similar to the way poor people in Brazil have been shown to "run after their rights," the women I met could not sit back and simply wait for legal procedure to take its course (Holston 2008). They had to actively strive, connive, and threaten people to acquire what the law promised.

This venture demanded and inculcated specific capabilities. Patience, tranquility, forgiveness, tolerance: this is what it took for women to keep their households intact in and "run a family." But "running a case" was a different ball game. First, one had to be able to risk estrangement, not only from husbands and in-laws but also from agnatic kin. Parents, siblings, uncles, and aunts, the very people who provided support when women remained in abusive marriages, frequently stopped supporting women who approached the criminal justice system. Second, one had to confront and manage state officials: courageously demonstrating organized connections, overcoming insults and neglect, and resolutely pursuing rights despite delays. Third, one had to be able to do what the state was supposed to do: figure out how to complete case-processing duties or find a way to acquire a semblance of rights outside a formal case.

Risking Estrangement

Ashu was in her late twenties and came from a middle-income Christian family. Born and brought up in Madhyamgram, a large town in North-24 Parganas, she epitomized the feminine virtues of patience and tolerance. Months before I arrived on the scene, she had approached Andolan hoping they would arrange a reconciliation. She, like the majority of the women I met, had been set on

Photo 1 Road to Burrabazar Police Station, Kolkata: Busy road in north Kolkata with a sign pointing to the local police station.

Photo 2 Bagdah Police Station, North-24 Parganas district: A rural police station in North-24 Parganas district.

Photo 3 Gender Workshop, Hooghly district: NGO workshop about gender inequality and legal reforms. In this exercise, participants were asked to draw institutions that govern women's lives.

Photo 4 Fortnight Campaign Against Violence, South-24 Parganas district: Members of a women's NGO gather on March 8, International Women's Day. At this moment, they wait the arrival of the Additional District Magistrate, who will give a speech on how women's groups can work with law enforcement personnel to counter domestic abuse.

Photo 5 Joint Workshop on Gendered Violence, South-24 Parganas district: Law enforcement, caseworkers, and women's rights activists discuss joint strategies against gendered violence.

"running a family." Andolan's caseworkers agreed to supervise a meeting with her husband, making no promises that the meeting would end in reconciliation. That meeting did not go as Ashu had hoped. Her husband neither admitted to the abuse he had inflicted nor apologized. Instead, he agreed to take her back on condition that her family make further cash payments on top of the hefty dowry he had already amassed through the marriage.

Despite their son-in-law's greed and violence, Ashu's parents scrambled to gather the money he requested. When they were unable to satisfy his demands, Andolan's caseworkers advised Ashu to conduct a *shalishi* to regain her possessions, specifically the gold jewelry she had received at her wedding. Ashu reluctantly agreed. She feared a *shalishi* would threaten her prospects of reconciliation. While less adversarial than a criminal or civil complaint, in the context of Andolan, *shalishi* enabled parallel claims, helping women access rights without a formal legal case. But for Ashu, the *shalishi* not only felt like the law; she feared it would lay the ground for future legal action. "If this doesn't work, they [Andolan] will tell me to do a case," she reasoned. And she wished to avoid a legal case at all costs.

Partly, she was convinced that "scheming" women registered domestic violence cases. She had no desire to become one of them. But her distaste for the law went beyond negative perceptions of legal claimants. It had to do with her family. "Mother and father have suffered so much during all of this, spending everything they had on the wedding. They had high hopes." She wanted her marriage to work out to honor their financial and emotional investments. And she was worried about the way her extended family interpreted the separation. "My uncles arranged the match. They think I did something wrong, that's why things didn't work out." Ashu's aversion to the law and her desire to reconcile at any cost had a great deal to do with the way a legal case might estrange her from those she loved best: members of her natal family.

While "running a family" appeared to simply be about maintaining affinal relationships, for women, it also entailed a deep commitment to staying on good terms with agnatic kin. Parents, siblings, aunts, and uncles: a woman's extended family members could be deeply invested in keeping abusive marriages intact. They invested money on weddings, frequently going into debt to entertain guests and provide dowry. And marriages cemented wider social networks, while divorce and separation brought social stigma not just for the woman getting married but also for her natal kin.

By "running a case," a woman threatened familial interests and, as a result, risked isolation. This was no small gamble. During interviews, women would routinely talk more about their own extended family rather than their abusers or the legally actionable abuse they had suffered. More than any other set of relationships, including marital relations and relations with children, the women

I met felt anxious and depressed about the effects legal actions had on the people they grew up with.

Agnatic relationships occupied a central place in women's lives for a number of reasons. First, they were socialized to expect a level of mistreatment and disregard from husbands and in-laws. But they had grown up experiencing love and affection, however gendered and partial, from their own families. Marital abuse did not violate their expectations. Estrangement from natal kin did.

Second, the fear of losing children was, of course, terrifying; but none of the women I talked to had been separated from their children for more than a few months. This may have been a random oddity of my research sample. But Indian courts follow a "tender years" principle with regard to child custody: divorced women are automatically granted custody of children under age six and most other children as well (Bose and South 2003). These legal mechanisms are buttressed by social norms that privilege maternal care and supervision of children. Thus, the women I met did not have to contend with separation from their children. Estrangement from natal families proved to be a greater risk.

Brinda, who lived some thirty kilometers to the south of Ashu, could attest to how difficult it was to challenge these relationships. It was her brother and parents who had taken her and her daughters in when she had nowhere to live. Natal families provided the support women needed when their husbands abused or abandoned them. Women who were estranged from natal kin confirmed exactly how difficult it was to survive without this support. Uma, living without electricity and unable to send her daughter to school, talked repeatedly about her regrets in this regard. "I have no one to rely on. That is a very hard place to land in this society."

What did it take to risk estrangement from one's parents, siblings, aunts, and uncles? Partha, the Andolan caseworker who supervised Ashu's case, had a fair amount to say on the matter. After advising hundreds of women over the years he had spent with the organization, he believed that women could only take this step when they were capable of having "self-esteem." "You have to respect yourself and realize that family should think of your well-being just as you think of theirs," he commented. To Partha, having self-esteem and being "selfish" were not the same thing. "This is the confusion our society makes. We tell girls they are being selfish when they express their own desires or wish to do something their parents disagree with. But we each have a right to dignity! That cannot come at the cost of pleasing everyone around us." Small of stature, with round glasses and a scratchy voice, Partha had a soothing presence. The fact that he was a man, advising women on family matters, lent him a certain authority not readily available to women caseworkers at the organization. He used this position to encourage women like Ashu to develop "self-esteem."

For Partha, who did not have to experience estrangement himself, distinguishing selfishness from self-esteem was relatively easy. For the women he counseled, this exercise was more difficult. Ashu wondered if the distinction was as real as Partha asserted and sought my advice on the matter. "If I decide to register a case knowing it pains my parents, is that self-esteem or selfishness? What do you think Poulami?" I was not sure how to answer her question.

That day, Ashu was back in Andolan's office. Her parents as well as one of the uncles who had arranged the marriage accompanied her. They sought Andolan's advice on how to proceed. Her husband had violated the *shalishi*: he had returned a small amount of jewelry and then falsely claimed to have nothing left. Partha was encouraging Ashu to register a 498A case, to "pressure" her husband into returning her gold.

The atmosphere inside the office was tense: hot and full of dust from the construction site next door. I recorded the session on my handheld recorder, which I was later thankful for, given the number of people arguing with each other in the room. Partha had called in Bani, who in turn was conversing with Neelu, Andolan's founder, on her cell phone. Everyone was talking at once. "*Didi* [Neelu] says enough is enough. Let's do a case," Bani announced to the room. A sturdy-looking woman in her early forties who was extremely near-sighted, Bani had a habit of pressing her thick glasses close to her face and leaning in when she talked to people. Hearing the advice, Ashu's mother started crying softly in the corner. Ashu looked distressed and mentioned that a legal case would place additional stress on her parents.

At this point, Ashu's uncle stepped in, arguing that a legal case would strain the family's social position. And after all, "misunderstandings happen. We acknowledge our own fault in this. We should have given our daughter [Ashu] a better education, then she would have managed the situation more skillfully." Hearing Ashu's uncle frame the abuse Ashu had suffered as a "misunderstanding" and cast blame on her for not "managing the situation," Bani erupted. "Sir, excuse me, but it is because of this kind of mentality that girls suffer in our society. How can you say it is her fault? We all know what kind of boy you married her to. You should have looked into the boy's background more carefully before landing her in that situation." Bani was visibly angry. And her words were biting, laying the blame squarely on the uncle for placing Ashu in a dangerous situation by fixing a bad match. As Bani paced the room breathing heavily, Ashu's uncle looked taken aback and became red in the face.

By this point, Ashu had begun to cry. It was unclear if she was crying because of the abuse she had suffered or because her mother was crying or because her uncle continued to blame her for the abuse she had suffered or because Bani had reprimanded her uncle. What was evident was the emotional pain she suffered, pain directly linked to the visible strain her natal kin felt and her fears of alienating them with a legal case. As a woman who had long been capable of the tolerance and self-sacrifice so integral to "running a family," Ashu struggled to adopt the quality of "selfishness" or "self-esteem" so necessary for "running a case."

Others argued that these capabilities were secondary. "You have to be able to withstand loneliness," Rupa, survivor-turned-caseworker stated succinctly. She had lived in her parents' house with her son since her separation, but the entire time she felt alone. "I live alone on one side. My parents and brother are on the other." Rupa used her living arrangements to describe an emotional barrier that existed between her and her natal kin. Her family never helped with her 498A case, refused to accompany her to court, and did not even want to hear she was pursuing a legal claim (even though it had been going on for ten years).

In a similar vein, Jhumpa mentioned that women who risked estrangement from their families had to be capable of living independently. "You have to have a place to live, some kind of work. Otherwise, it's not possible." Estrangement demanded not just self-esteem but self-sufficiency. One had to be able to feed and clothe oneself and pay for housing without relying on handouts.

Brokers both demanded estrangement and provided the means of making it possible. The services they provided—job training and loans, housing, medical care—proved invaluable in this regard. Rupa had become financially self-sufficient with Shadheen's help, first setting up a sewing business in her home and then conducting casework full time. Rupa used the money she earned to support her son and build a room and bathroom for herself in her parents' home. She also paid for her parents' living expenses, even though they refused to support her legal endeavors. "This is how I stay in their house," Rupa explained. When Rupa started having health complications, it was Shadheen's executive director, Dolly, who helped her attain medical care.

Meanwhile, Jhumpa had used seed funds from Andolan to set up a vending business. She used earnings from the business to pay her brother-in-law rent, maintaining a room in her marital home. And she reconnected with her brothers in her natal village, sending gifts to her nieces and nephews. While Ashu had no desire to live in Andolan's group home, the resource was available to her if she needed it, providing a safety net. The financial, residential, and health services their brokers provided allowed all three of these women to manage estrangement: to simultaneously gain independence from natal families so that they could "run a case" and to nurture some level of support and intimacy necessary for their emotional, social, and physical survival.

Confronting the State

Confronting one's family, contradicting their views, and disagreeing with their decisions was one thing. Confronting the state was another. Given the institutional setting within which law enforcement personnel operated, the main way women could make sure they were taken seriously was by demonstrating their organizational connections. They used brokers to gain credibility, hoping to be incorporated rather than suppressed by law enforcement personnel. Incorporation did not, however, guarantee respect, promptness, or good service. Madhura had to withstand disrespect as she sat in front of the officer in charge, who allowed her to register a case while refusing to meet her eye and calling her "kept." Hameeda had to withstand poor service and delays as the PO outsourced her job and refused to adhere to the PWDVA's time constraints. To "run a case," women had to learn how to manage law enforcement neglect and hostility. They had to talk to law enforcement, to put up with their insults and failures, all while putting on a brave and congenial face.

Law enforcement personnel were terrifying apparitions. The police were especially fearsome in this regard, with records of physical violence and sexual assault. But other members of the criminal justice system were not much better. POs, judges, court clerks: all took pot shots at women experiencing violence, treating them like second-class citizens. Women from marginalized backgrounds were more likely to be verbally abused and physically pushed around, but middle-income, upper-caste women were not immune to mistreatment. The abuser they faced was no longer someone they knew but rather a series of unknown officials with institutionalized powers of dismissal and dread. They had to become capable of contending with this new source of mistreatment. Those who grew a thick skin did well for themselves. They picked themselves up and kept moving forward.

But "running a case" entailed more than stomaching insults and encountering threats. Delays were commonplace. Law enforcement personnel sat in their chairs and refused to help, witnesses failed to show up to court, documents were routinely not processed or sent to the wrong department. Rupa, who had become a caseworker in the time it took her 498A case to keep puttering along in court, continued to spend a sizeable amount of time every month trying to get trial dates closer together, following up with the police regarding missing evidence. The delays she encountered had stretched her 498A case to ten years. She did what she had to do to keep her case going. She took time off from work, spent grueling hours on public transportation getting to and from various government offices, bribed the court clerk to move her next trial date closer, befriended a constable who could give her information on her ex-husband's dealings.

The evidence that went missing in Rupa's case (photographs depicting her husband's abusive behavior) pointed to another systemic issue: law enforcement negligence. Caseworkers and rights activists had the same complaint. "Things are not done in the proper way," Gouri, the AIN caseworker who looked for cases on TV and newspapers, summed up the problem. "You will take a girl to get a DIR registered, and then the document comes back with things missing." She went on to discuss the particulars of a case she was managing. "I'm helping a girl whose husband hit her on her head. She lost hearing temporarily in one ear. You know what the police didn't write in the report? That she lost her hearing! They don't think to mention that!" Gouri felt frustrated by these experiences not only because they hurt women's chances of redress but because she personally knew the law enforcement officer who had made the mistake. She tried to bring cases to officers with whom she had working relationships. Yet, their work remained thoroughly inadequate.

Working with the state thus required not only courage but also perseverance. Faced with delays and negligence, women had to be tenacious. As the PO of South-24 Parganas mentioned at the Nodakhali workshop, the "active" girls were the ones who got places. While women who "ran families" patiently waited for their abusers to reform, women who "ran cases" learned how to act strategically, overcoming the ills of the criminal justice system to resolutely move ahead. Observing women interact with caseworkers, listening to them learn how to run cases, was always instructive. The capabilities required to manage the state and its personnel became amply apparent at those moments.

Gouri had a number of open cases on her docket at AIN, including Koel's PWDVA case. This was the same Koel who had ended up at AIN after asking her *kaku* to arrange a reconciliation. Upper caste, with a graduate degree in accounting, with one of the highest incomes in my sample, Koel had originally found the criminal justice system to be an unpalatable place for women of her social class. She had registered a DIR but, according to Gouri, needed to learn how to "run a case." The DIR had been pending for some time, and Gouri wanted to know what Koel had done to follow up on the matter. While AIN's official discourse emphasized legal procedure and rules, in the intricacies of casework, the organization's employees instructed women on how to make the system work to their advantage.

"Did you go see her [the PO]," Gouri demanded? Koel shook her head sheepishly, indicating that the PO was hard to track down. "I don't know what to do with the case," Koel continued, her voice wavering as she explained that it might be best to drop the charges. Koel's husband, who had money and political connections, supposedly had the PO "in his pocket," meaning that he was either bribing her or threatening her job security. With brusque confidence, Gouri dismissed Koel's fears. "You can't just let the case go. You have to work hard if you want to keep it running." Suddenly, Gouri asked about Koel's brother's political connections. "Doesn't your brother have friends in the party?" In local parlance, "the party" is always the Communist Party of India (Marxist) (CPI[M]). If Koel's husband could get the PO in his pocket, so could Koel. Gouri urged Koel to get her brother to find out what the PO wanted.

Gouri's recommendations left much to the imagination. Finding out what the PO wanted meant that Koel had to figure out how to motivate her to do her job. The motivation would very likely take the form of an extralegal favor, be it cold hard cash or something that would make the PO's job easier. It was notably through political channels that Gouri encouraged Koel to take these actions. Her brother, who worked with the CPI(M), needed to figure out how he could influence this state official. Gouri, despite her belief in AIN's mission and faith in legal statutes, did not think Koel should rely on the law alone to provide succor. Koel had to develop the capabilities it required to run a case. She had to stick to it, not give up so easily, deploy the organizational and political resources she had at her disposal, identify cracks in the system and make them work to her advantage.

Most interactions with the state demanded both courage and tenacity. Women from marginalized backgrounds arguably had to muster up more courage because they had more to fear. And they had fewer resources at their disposal to help them remain tenacious. Twenty-five kilometers to the south of AIN's office, a woman facing multiple disadvantages struggled to develop the capabilities she needed to run a parallel claim. Najma, the landless Muslim sharecropper who was part of Shadheen's poultry production unit, had decided to register a General Diary Report (GD).

Najma was in her mid-twenties and thin as a wasp. The skin around her eyes and mouth had started to develop the fine lines that come with working in the sun. She was impoverished enough to qualify for a government-sponsored work program that provided one hundred days of guaranteed employment to the rural poor.[1] And the job she had gotten was road building, a backbreaking business that involved shouldering heavy bags of rocks and sand and mixing gravel. But her husband kept beating her and stealing her earnings, leaving nothing for her and her daughters to eat.

It wasn't the caseworkers at Shadheen who convinced Najma to register the GD. It was Sila, the one-time caseworker turned rogue broker who now headed her own informal *mahila samiti* while collaborating with Shadheen on specific cases. While Shadheen's caseworkers steered clear of informal arbitration, Sila had no such qualms. She promised Najma that a GD would help her avoid a formal case by forcing her husband to the negotiating table. "This way you can get him [Najma's husband] to compromise," Sila promised. "He will get scared." Najma was pleased with this middle ground.

The police station where Najma was scheduled to register her GD was well known to Sila. She was on a first-name basis with the sub-inspector and knew most of the officers from past cases she had brought to the station. Sila had the social clout necessary for mediating between Najma and the police. She was the daughter of a police officer, her husband had been well known in the area, her family had money, her mother-in-law was a schoolteacher, Sila herself had volunteered at the *panchayat*. Sila was also slightly scary: her latest feat included organizing nearly one hundred women in a nearby village and using them to surround a small police station that had refused to register a First Incident Report (FIR). She was also rumored to be friendly with Pora Kokhon, who had grown up in a village close to where Sila lived. Sila's dealings with the gangster were discreet and hard to pin down, but his shadowy presence was felt wherever she went, including at the police station that day.

Sila's organizational connections made Najma more threatening to the police than she would have been as a single, working-class, Muslim woman. But even with Sila on her side, Najma could not afford to take good behavior for granted. The day Najma was scheduled to register her GD, I arrived at the police station to find her waiting outside with her mother. Sila was on her way with members of the *mahila samiti*, but it was unclear how long we would have to stand there before their arrival. There was nowhere to sit outside the station, and the sun was merciless. I asked Najma and her mother if they wanted to wait inside. They reluctantly agreed.

We entered the station to find the lights of the front hall dimmed and a young constable wearing only a white undershirt above his regulation-length khakis. The lean muscles on his arm rippled as he flexed his fingers around his gun. He was tall and young. The hallway was long and dark. Other dark figures loomed further inside: more men. The police station sat among a sea of green paddy off the main road. I had the sense that whatever happened here could easily be forgotten.

If not exactly loquacious, Najma had talked easily enough when I met her at Shadheen. She colorfully described her husband's drinking habits and even had to be told to slow down on several occasions. But this police station was a different ball game. Having stepped inside, Najma shook her head and quickly retreated. I could understand why. Najma's mother stood mutely to one side. She was wearing a printed cotton sari, the kind that one buys from a cart at the edge of the bazaar, so cheap the dyes instantly run together into a see-through muddy brown once washed. Najma was wearing a newer version of the same. They were visibly poor. They were Muslim. They were women. And theirs was a woman-headed household. Najma's father had abandoned them for his second wife many years ago. They lacked male protection. Later, Najma would confess her fears: "the police sniff out weakness." She alluded to stories she had heard about custodial violence. Guided by this palpable fear, Najma preferred to wait outside in the scorching sun. She was brave enough to come to the station but wise enough to know her limits.

We exited the station, muttering excuses and took shelter in the meager shade of a tree outside the front gate. And there we waited. Najma and her mother did not have any water with them (a water bottle was an expense they could not afford). Neither did they have any food. I am not sure when they had last been able to use a bathroom. Men could simply urinate on the road. Women could not. At some point, Najma's mother smiled and told me her daughter was hardier than she looked. "So what if she is so thin?" Najma could do the "work of five boys on an empty stomach." It was her resolve and ability to overcome obstacles that gave her the strength to stand up to her husband, Najma's mother reasoned. "She's the one who convinced me we should come here," she explained while Najma quietly listened, eyes downcast.

Najma's resolve and tenacity would continue to be tested over the next few months as she moved forward with the informal arbitration Sila arranged. But that day, she still had to master the fear that gripped her. Thirsty, hungry, and covered in sweat from hours in the heat, she re-entered the station under Sila's protection. She opened her mouth and told a constable her name, address, and the name of her husband. She then proceeded, however haltingly, to narrate her experiences of abuse and express a desire to live separately from her husband. The police station was better lit now that Sila had demanded they turn on some lights. And the officers were polite because they knew who Sila was and did not want to ruffle her feathers. But for an illiterate Muslim woman who struggled to put food on the table and who had been trained all her life to avoid eye contact with the police, the experience demanded nerves of steel.

Doing the Work of the State

After risking estrangement from those they loved, confronting and forging working relationships with an abusive and negligent criminal justice system, women still had ground to cover if they hoped to "run a case." Incorporation came with certain conditions. Namely, women had to be able to do the work of the state, be it in the nitty-gritty details of an official case or a complete outsourcing of the legal process. Most women had never seen an FIR or DIR, far from knowing how to fill them out. Even if they knew what these forms were, they knew very little about what forms of evidence might help them prove abuse. They had never tried to convince people to serve as witnesses. Law enforcement personnel did not provide much by way of guidance.

Parallel claims were less inscrutable. They did not require literacy or arcane knowledge of what might prove convincing in a court of law. But they did require muscle and might to push the claim to completion and thus posed naked dangers for already vulnerable women. Doing the work of the state demanded a certain amount of rule breaking. One had to overlook and bend legal procedure, step outside the law, act as one of its executors, and carry out its coercive functions.

Koel, who was educated and from a privileged social background, quickly figured out what needed to get done with her PWDVA case. Following Gouri's instructions, Koel had mobilized her brother's CPI(M) connections to get her case moving. Feeling pressured, the PO agreed to forward the application for relief to the magistrate. But the PO refused to recommend maintenance on the report because Koel worked as an accountant and because the PO believed Koel's husband was unemployed. "He told her he doesn't have a job and she believed him. Can you imagine?" Koel was livid. The PO had refused to do her job and investigate her husband's claims. "He has money stashed everywhere but it's all in the black [black market]. I know he owns a building in Tollygunge that's not in his name." Koel was resolved to get the better of her scheming husband and bypass the PO. Koel's large dark eyes, accentuated by eyeliner, gleamed with anger.

We were sitting together at a chic coffee shop in South Kolkata. Koel had the money to pay several hundred rupees for a tea and muffin. And she had the social network she needed to gather information. A college friend of hers was related to a clerk at her husband's bank. This man had provided Koel printouts of her husband's transactions, including records of gold bullion he was storing in the bank vault in lieu of cash. In return for this help, Koel was helping the clerk's daughter register at a good private school in Kolkata. With bank records in hand, she had once again called on her brother's political contacts to intimidate the PO. Alongside the application for relief and the DIR, the magistrate would now see Koel's husband's bank records. The bank records only showed a fraction of her husband's assets, but according to Koel, they would at least raise doubts in the magistrate's head about her husband's financial status.

Koel could rely on private resources—money, a supportive family, and well-connected friends—to help her develop the capabilities she needed to do the work of the state. Women from marginal backgrounds had to rely on the skills and training their brokers provided. Hameeda learned what it meant to do the work of the state long before she found herself convincing the PO to let her and Samoli write the report for the magistrate's office. The work she did started with the DIR, which the PO was supposed to have guided her through but which she simply turned over to Hameeda and Samoli without any instructions. Much longer than FIRs, DIR forms have seven separate sections, each with multiple subsections that must be completed.[2] While the length of the form is a product of feminist efforts to provide greater information to courts, for women who are barely literate, the form poses significant challenges.

Hameeda and Samoli sat down together in Shadheen's offices with Mona, the external consultant, who led them through each section. Had Hameeda experienced sexual abuse? If so, what kinds? Each section had to be ticked off and details of every kind of abuse written out. Meanwhile, while the PO was supposed to have helped Hameeda secure a medical certificate and make a list of her *stridhan* (gifts given to a bride), she had done no such thing. Samoli arranged for the medical certificate, telling Hameeda which doctor to visit and how to have him fill out the form. Meanwhile, Hameeda was left on her own to remember the gifts she had received at her wedding, and she had to find someone to write down the list of items for her. She was lucky to have a sympathetic younger brother who was literate and willing to help.

Hameeda earned a modest income as a seamstress, working in a tailoring business run by her father and brothers. But beyond this financial stability, she had very few advantages. She had lived all her life in South-24 Parganas, had traveled to Kolkata once for a wedding, had never stepped foot in a courtroom before her case, and could barely read or write, having dropped out of school after sixth grade. Yet, to be capable of doing the work of the state, Hameeda had to regularly leave her village, weave in and out of the Alipore court complex, locate a particular doctor and ask him to fill out a certificate attesting to the abuse she had suffered, and struggle through and fill out a giant document she could not read. After the DIR, the application for relief to the magistrate seemed like a piece of cake. All it required was checking off boxes. She had to repeat her requests for particular orders and provide greater details of the expenses she had incurred and for which she was requesting compensation.

Doing the work of the state around PWDVA cases, while time-consuming and demanding a great deal of detailed information, did not require the same physical faculties as those called upon in a 498A case. Criminal investigations by their nature were more adversarial than civil suits. Section 498A housed the threat of arrest and as a result instigated greater backlash from friends and family members of those who were accused.

The suspicion that a 498A case had been registered against them led a number of alleged perpetrators to abscond in the hopes of avoiding arrest. Gathering evidence, recruiting witnesses, or documenting information of any kind under these conditions was not just difficult but also physically hazardous. It was because of the onerous and dangerous nature of the task that the police wished to avoid conducting investigations in the first place. By farming this process out to civilians, law enforcement personnel dumped a herculean task on to people who frequently lacked the means to carry out these operations.

Brinda realized she did not possess the capabilities necessary to do the work of the state once she decided to follow through with a 498A case. Not wanting to disclose her experiences as a sex worker, Brinda remained silent about her time in Kalighat when she approached the police. "498A is safest," Rupa had cautioned. Mona, Dolly, and the other caseworkers who knew the details of Brinda's history all thought she should avoid a trafficking case since these cases were known to turn against women and land them in prison on charges of prostitution. But a 498A case, because it dealt with a cognizable offense, demanded the police conduct an investigation and draw up a charge sheet that would be forwarded to the magistrate's office. The Bishnupur police agreed to register the FIR on condition that Brinda, Rupa, and other members of Shadheen help them with the task.

Later on, Rupa would lament that she had made some strategic mistakes in leading Brinda through the next steps. Namely, they had entered Brinda's husband's village late in the day without sufficient backup. The light had faded as they tried to locate neighbors who might be sympathetic to Brinda, those who were willing to give statements on her behalf. In the meantime, Brinda's husband had gotten wind that Brinda was back, looking to dig up dirt on him. He rounded up his cousins and found Brinda, Rupa, and Samoli inside a neighbor's house.

Rupa tried to reason with him and intimidate him, naming her credentials and warning him that Shadheen was not to be messed with. Brinda, panicking, tried to escape while Samoli and Rupa were engaged in argument. In the tussle that followed, Brinda's husband smacked Brinda over the face and then threw a hurricane lamp at her head. The lamp missed Brinda but hit Rupa instead, leaving a gash on her forehead where the glass broke and cut her skin open. Bloodied and in fear for their lives, the three women made a mad dash for the main road, where they hoped they would find an autorickshaw. They were not able to gather the statements they needed and remained shaken from their experiences a week later when I saw them again.

Doing the work of the state thus entailed taking on a set of physical risks that law enforcement personnel were unwilling to stomach. These dangers reached an acute level when women were tasked with parallel claims. The courage it took to confront the state had to be rechanneled to confront the very people who had abused them. It was impossible to be capable in this way without the support of brokers and the organizational resources they provided. Payel and Sobha, both of whom engaged in extralegal repossessions, relied heavily on Andolan and Shadheen to help them become capable of these exertions. But their capabilities also emerged through the state because it was law enforcement personnel who gave them license (going so far as to provide unofficial supervision) to behave in this way.

In Payel's case, it was the combined support of Andolan and the constable sent to "supervise from a distance" that enabled her to do what she did. The re-possession took place the day after Andolan met with the police and negotiated the arrangement. When Payel entered her husband's house, her husband stood mutely to one side as she screamed at him. She swept through the house, intentionally breaking clay pots and throwing clothes on the ground. At one point, she even slapped her husband, crying and loudly recalling everything he had done to her.

People who lived nearby watched the proceedings but did not interfere. Andolan's union exerted a soft form of coercion over their livelihoods. If they needed help negotiating collective contracts with landlords or accessing water and other resources in the future, it was to this union they would have to turn for help. Andolan also exuded more overt threats. The union members guarded the doors and physically crowded the inside of the house, creating a sense of physical peril. They looked on stone-faced while Payel screamed and threatened her husband. Meanwhile, the constable, visibly stationed at a nearby tree, tacitly supported whatever was happening in the house by not coming to Payel's husband's assistance. The constable was there to help Payel, and everyone knew it. His help, however distant and passive, transformed Payel from a woman victimized by violence into someone who deployed it.

Conclusion

"Running a case" was a specific mode of legal praxis, one that demanded special sacrifices—namely sacrificing existing emotional attachments to family and kin. It entailed a great deal of risk—approaching hostile officials and trying to get them to take one seriously. And it combined legal mechanisms with large doses of illegality—linking the ability to claim rights with the ability to violate legal procedure, ignore rules, and, when necessary, deploy violence. This way of relating to the law did not emerge from some inherent quality of the law or of rights. It was particular to the political and institutional environment that surrounded domestic violence.

Women had to risk estrangement because the people who offered help pushed them in opposite directions. Their families supported them as long as they did not pursue legal action, while brokers promised to help only if they engaged the law in some limited way. Meanwhile, they had to be courageous and determined because state officials were menacing and neglectful. And finally, to a certain degree, they had to be lawless because that is how the law could actually be utilized.

The way women "ran cases" extends ongoing debates in the social sciences about how Indian citizens make claims on the state. Partha Chatterjee's (2004) theorization of "political society" suggests that political parties and illegality are essential to underprivileged people's access to rights and state-based resources. For Chatterjee, it is the marginalized who approach the state through political society, leaving open the suggestion that those from more privileged backgrounds rely on more civil means.

Countering Chatterjee's insights, Gabrielle Kruks-Wisner's work in Tamil Nadu and Rajasthan demonstrates the opposite relationship between social background and claims-making strategies. She shows that women and caste minorities are much more likely to use formal government channels in seeking redress, while men and members of dominant castes have greater access to informal, nonstate mechanisms (Kruks-Wisner 2011).

My findings differ from both Chatterjee's theorizations and Kruks-Wisner's findings. I found very little distinction in tactics among the women I met. Women of all social backgrounds used a combination of civil and uncivil tactics, approaching the state through political intermediaries. The art of running cases comprised a whole set of practices whereby women engaged the law through organized groups and illegal acts. Bending legal procedure, doing the work of the state, convincing law enforcement to be helpful through threats and bribes: all of these practices were essential to the process of making rights claims. Women who were poor and not so poor, those who were upper-caste and lower-caste, Muslims and Hindus, city dwellers and those who lived in villages, all learned to engage the law through these subterfuges.

"Politics" was the reserve neither of the lower classes nor of dominant social groups. Incivility, or at least the threat of it, provided a pathway toward civil recognition for all. Middle-income, upper-caste women did not use bureaucratic channels or stand before the law as individual rights-bearing subjects. It was by communicating their ability to act outside the law, to violate it, to overpower it, to bend it to their whims, that women were able to carve out a space of legitimacy within it. Social background (caste, class, sexuality, religious ascriptions) did not guarantee recognition. Mobilization, threat, getting the job done: these were the only avenues for dealing with the criminal justice system without being silenced. Women of all social backgrounds either learned to play the game or fell behind.

9

Aspirational and Strategic

The Subjectivity of Law

"You wouldn't have recognized me fifteen years ago," Jhumpa laughed, her eyes gleaming as she threw back her head. Jhumpa liked repeating this particular phrase. In her early forties, Jhumpa looked much younger than her years. She was petite, with sharp, gleaming eyes and a mass of wavy, shoulder-length hair. Loud, confident, and upbeat, she spent several afternoons a week rehearsing skits with AIN's theater troupe. It was she who approached me wanting to tell her story, curious about my notebook, wanting to know about life in the United States.

Raised in a family of lower-caste, Hindu farmers in South-24 Parganas, Jhumpa described her upbringing as comfortable but sheltered. Against her rural background, her future husband cut a striking figure at the festival where they met. With a degree in accounting, born and brought up in Kolkata, he appeared suave and urbane. Jhumpa was flattered when he took a liking to her, even though, according to her own words, she was "dark and skinny," physical attributes not highly prized in Bengali women. Their wedding date was set, a dowry arranged by her parents, and the next thing Jhumpa knew she was living in a two-story house with her husband and in-laws in South Kolkata.

The marriage went well at first but soured over the course of multiple miscarriages. Jhumpa's husband blamed her infertility on what he perceived as her moral degeneracy, verbally and physically abusing her as punishment for her suspected sins. Her brother-in-law, who Jhumpa claimed was the truly wicked one in the family, egged her husband on, beating her himself when her husband did not seem to be in the mood. Eventually, Jhumpa's husband moved out of the house, taking a job in North Kolkata, where he began living with another woman. Abandoned to a violent brother-in-law who refused to feed her, Jhumpa took a job as a domestic worker to survive. Her employer, an elderly woman involved in various social welfare projects throughout the city, told her about AIN.

Hearing her say I would not have recognized her in the past, I imagined a bodily transformation. "Did you look different?" I naively asked. She assented

Capable Women, Incapable States. Poulami Roychowdhury, Oxford University Press 2021. © Oxford University Press
DOI: 10.1093/oso/9780190881894.001.0001

but mentioned there was more to it. "I was a village girl. You know, my hair was always in a braid. I didn't even wear *salwar kameez*, always *sari*." For Jhumpa, sartorial choices such as the *sari* and braided hair indexed a lack of cosmopolitanism. She went on to say, "I didn't know about any of this," gesturing at large at our surroundings. She had never heard of the laws that governed domestic violence. She was terrified of law enforcement personnel. Like so many women in her position, Jhumpa had initially asked AIN's caseworkers to discipline her husband and help her "run a family." But the caseworkers had refused to fulfill her wishes. Instead, they had proposed alternate solutions, solutions that involved legal claims.

By the time I met her, Jhumpa was running two separate cases, one under Section 498A of the Indian Penal Code and the other under the Protection of Women from Domestic Violence Act (PWDVA). A criminal suit does not logically accompany a civil case: criminal law promises arrest and incarceration for the perpetrator, while civil law promises protection and alimony from a free and gainfully employed perpetrator. Jhumpa was not overly concerned about these contradictions. If one case does not work out, the other one might, she offered by way of explanation. In her head, the two cases either provided ammunition for each other or helped her diversify her methods. At the very least, two cases were better than one because a second case provided an additional means to annoy and burden her abusive husband.

She scoffed at the idea of reconciling with him, eagerly hoping her legal campaign would mete out punishment, compensation, or at least headache. She felt righteous in her cause and rarely seemed afraid. Embracing her newfound independence, she had taken out a small loan to start her own vending business. And in whatever free time was left at her disposal, she taught other women how to follow her path, establishing and running her own *mahila samiti* in her neighborhood. It was Jhumpa who instructed me to pay close attention to AIN's screening of *Mann ke Manjeere* during the Fortnight Campaign. It was her favorite song, she announced. Shameem Pathan's daring style appealed to the identity she had embraced. Among the audience members, she whistled the loudest when the video ended.

The Subject of Rights

Jhumpa's narration of her life history mapped a subjective metamorphosis. She had once been a village girl who had neither known about the law nor realized the extent of her own deprivation. She worried about pursuing legal remedies, was concerned over how others would perceive her, and felt frightened of state officials. From there, she became a person who confidently and gleefully asserted her entitlements to housing, work, and food. She sought revenge for the injustices she had suffered. And she felt capable of pursuing her interests through the criminal justice system, going so far as to strategically pursue conflicting cases in the hope of pressuring and annoying her husband.

If the self is constituted through disciplinary regimes of truth, then what laws partly do is articulate normative conceptions of identity and desire (Foucault 1977). Key to the transformation Jhumpa described was the emergence of a new legal subjectivity. But the emergence of legal subjectivity cannot be taken for granted. For many people, especially those who have historically been marginalized or denied rights, turning to the law proves to be a difficult transition. In my research, the subjective gap women traversed involved moving from their initial desire to "run a family" toward "running a case."

Legal consciousness, how individuals perceive the law and respond to grievances, informs specific modes of legal mobilization. A relatively inclusive, multidimensional concept, legal consciousness connotes a broad set of thoughts, feelings, and behaviors related to the law (Bose and South 2003; Levine and Mellema 2001; McCann and March 1996). It includes how people understand legal rights, how and when they make use of laws, how they assemble legal concepts, and how they interact with legal institutions (Engel and Engel 2010; Ewick and Silbey 1998; Nielsen 2000).

Legal consciousness varies across demographic groups to be sure. Class, gender, race, age, and educational status are important determinants (Blackstone et al. 2009; Morrill et al. 2010). But how people think of the law is also shaped by legal praxis. Asking how people come to think about their actions in relation to the environment, Arun Agrawal found that rather than social identities based on gender and caste, it was the contingent practice of engaging in regulatory strategies that helped transform residents into environmental subjects (Agrawal 2005). Harsh Mander's work on communal violence in India traces a similar process from praxis to consciousness. In the process of claiming rights, Muslims who survived communal riots in Gujarat learned to think of themselves in new ways, and this transformation occurred even when they did not receive state-based compensation (Mander 2009).

The praxis of law is shaped by institutional context (Albiston 2005; Chua 2012; Hirsh and Lyons 2010; Reynolds 2019). Uneven institutional environments, such as the one we find in India today, engender multiple and sometimes conflicting orientations. Within these conditions, positive changes in feelings of individual efficacy and competency vis-à-vis the law can accompany negative evaluations of the legal system in terms of its fairness and effectiveness (Gallagher 2006; Holzer 2013).

The legal environment surrounding domestic violence claims provided fertile ground for a dual consciousness among the women I met. As they became embroiled in "running a case," their legal subjectivity became centered around what I call an "aspirational-strategic" consciousness. Women learned to think of the law in two seemingly contradictory ways. First, they started believing they deserved what the law promised, a life free of violence where they could exercise a modicum of control over their bodies and material possessions. In this vision, legal cases provided an avenue toward freedom, justice, and empowerment to which women could aspire.

Second, they learned to think of the law as a strategic field they could engage and manipulate. In this second vision, legal cases did not always follow set rules, nor did they necessarily guarantee official rights. Instead, the law was a site to be overpowered. Sometimes, one needed to overpower the law in order to access what the law promised but did not deliver. At other times, the law became a weapon to inflict retribution and settle scores through means the law did not promise, including annoying perpetrators, physically threatening them, and making them the topic of gossip and social disdain.

This "aspirational-strategic" subjectivity arose through routine encounters with brokers and with law enforcement personnel. And it differed significantly from subjectivities geared around "running a family." To aspire to rights, women had to recognize their violation and believe they merited compensation. There was no denying the abuse they had suffered, no sense that they should compromise for the benefit of the family, nor guilt that they had deserved what had happened to them. Meanwhile, to approach the law strategically, they could not simply think of themselves as helpless and incapacitated women who needed to avoid the state. Re-envisioning the law as a site that they could engage and manipulate meant they had to, at some level, take responsibility over their complaints, feel confident about engaging the state , and acknowledge that they had to do whatever it took to save themselves.

Learning to Aspire

It is through aspiration—the ability to envision a better future—that marginalized groups find the resources required to resist and change the conditions of their oppression. Aspiration expands people's "political horizons," creating a logic of patience that focuses on long-term asset building and cumulative victories (Appadurai 2004). The aspirational component of the legal subjectivities I encountered may surprise some readers. Here, the history of Indian democracy provides instructional material. Despite its limitations, the postcolonial Indian state has been relatively successful in producing citizens who feel both legally entitled and morally engaged with the state. A robust constitutional tradition, the judicialization of rights, and a strong culture of political participation and protest encourage citizen engagement (Mitra 2010). Laws and legal rights have played a central role in every single major social movement in India over the past five decades (Harriss 2013). This includes movements for women's rights against violence as well as mobilizations for food security, education, employment, and land rights (Khera 2013; Nilsen and Nilsen 2014; Roychowdhury 2016a; Ruparelia 2013b).

These political traditions create the foundations of legal aspiration. But envisioning the law as an aspirational site was no easy feat for individual women. Before one can aspire to rights, one must perceive one's experiences as injurious, naming concrete events as violations. Then, one has to formulate a grievance, blaming someone for the injurious act (Felstiner et al. 1980). Aspiration, after all, is itself a capability that is unevenly distributed throughout a society (Appadurai 2004). Those who are wealthy and socially dominant are taught to cultivate expansive aspirational horizons from a young age. Those who are marginalized do not necessarily receive the same training.

To a certain extent, the women who participated in this study were primed to overcome these barriers. They had come forward, acknowledged the harm they had suffered, and sought some kind of solution. But the solution they initially sought almost never involved the law. They hoped to reconcile and manage a household. They believed women who approached the state were malicious and "abusive." They had little desire to become one of those women. They also doubted that law enforcement personnel would help them. They feared state officials and worried that a legal case would be expensive and time-consuming. And many of them believed that disreputable women used the law to torture their husbands.

Given these institutional and normative barriers, the very act of running a case indexed a powerful kind of aspiration. By running cases, women announced to their families, abusers, and themselves that they were willing to take dramatic steps to end the abuse they suffered. In exchange for the possibility of a life without violence, they would allow caseworkers, political party cadres, the police, and the protection officer (PO) to root around their private affairs and possibly drag their family's good name through the mud.

Ashu, the middle-income, Christian survivor who sought help from Andolan, succinctly captured the importance of this transformation. When I first met her, she expressed a strong disdain for legal cases. The law was an "unrespectable" venture, and only "scheming" women used it. Even the *shalishi* that Andolan conducted worried her. She thought it might pave the path toward further legal action. By the end of my research, however, Ashu questioned her earlier stances. A friend of her father who was a retired lawyer had encouraged her to register a First Information Report (FIR) against her husband. Andolan's caseworkers ensured the FIR was registered by mobilizing their contacts at the Madhyamgram police. "What is respectability without a respectable life?" Ashu wondered. She no longer cared to earn the respect of people who did not care about her safety or well-being. This included neighbors who looked down on her as well as the uncle who had arranged her marriage and remained convinced that the breakup was her fault.

While states grant rights to individuals, the women I met came to realize they deserved rights after they saw other women requesting them. Women's organizations played an outsized role in producing aspirations. Women developed a sense of individual entitlement through communities of like-minded people they met in these spaces. Ashu's transformation was clearly enabled by the environment at Andolan, which promoted women's rights, and more particularly by her caseworker Partha's invocations for "self-esteem." While Ashu wondered if "self-esteem" and being "selfish" were as distinct as Partha believed, his repeated soliloquies potentially had a long-term effect.

Like Ashu, Sabiha, a low-income, Muslim woman from North-24 Parganas who was a member of Andolan's women's wing, was acutely aware that by registering a 498A case she was committing herself to an image of femininity she had previously denigrated. Similar to Ashu, Sabiha registered a case after her husband violated Andolan's *shalishi*. When Bani and Partha advised Sabiha to pursue 498A to "pressure" her husband, she agreed but only because she knew Andolan had helped other women in the peasants' union. In the past, Sabiha had looked down on women who left their husbands, judging them to be selfish. But getting to know women who had pursued cases, both legal and extralegal, made her reassess the ethics of legal claims. Mentioning these women's names, Sabiha reasoned that giving up her husband was a sacrifice she was willing to make to privilege other values she now held dear.

Sabiha blamed her conservative upbringing and illiteracy on her earlier lack of awareness. As a girl, she claimed she had been trained to be "subservient" to men. These days, she understood the "value" of an independent life, no longer fearing the "freedom" that legal cases promised. I did not interpret her comments as an affirmation of liberal values of individuality. Rather, by linking freedom and independence to Andolan's peasants' union, Sabiha intimated that she could only dream of a life free of violence because she was part of a new collective.

Women's organizations affirmed a new set of ethical commitments while making alternative forms of femininity visible. And they provided much needed expertise, without which women would not have known what to aspire to. In discussing AIN's role in her life, Jhumpa argued that she would never have registered a legal case without her caseworker's help. "I had never heard of 498A." It was her caseworker who told her about her legal options. By supervising the early steps of her legal claim, it was also her caseworker who made the promise of legal rights seem somewhat attainable. Meanwhile, it was through AIN's gender awareness programs that Jhumpa linked her own personal problems to a general predicament that other women faced. She learned that "girls also have rights."

Women's groups were not alone, however, in encouraging women to improve their situation. By incorporating organized women, law enforcement personnel also promoted women's aspirations. By acknowledging women's grievances and letting them move ahead with legal and extralegal ventures, law enforcement subtly informed women that they deserved more than they had. By encouraging women to get involved in legal administration and run parallel claims, they told women that they were capable of acquiring more than they had. The myriad exchanges and interactions that constituted incorporation created a landscape where the law functioned no longer simply as a threat or a form of denial but rather as a gendered promise of inclusion and empowerment for women who were oppressed.

Hema and Najma both internalized these cues while attending the Nodakhali workshop. Both of these women, once intent on avoiding the law because of their distrust of law enforcement personnel, glowed with a new sense of recognition. Before attending the workshop, Najma was convinced that law enforcement ignored poor, Muslim women like herself or did "worse" (violated them). After the workshop, she sought confirmation for her new perspective. "They were very respectful towards us, weren't they?" I sensed that she felt less afraid and more empowered by the interaction: people she had once feared were looking to her for assistance. These powerful men and women were not just acknowledging her existence by looking her in the eye; they were affirming her strength and ability as a woman and begging for assistance.

Hema similarly felt encouraged by her experiences that morning. This was the same Hema who had once told me she would "run towards her husband" if given the choice between him and the police. The police, who used to be "worse than the thugs they lock up," became respectable and approachable. "Not all of them are bad," she commented after the workshop was over. "Some of them see things from a girl's perspective." To Hema, the Nodakhali workshop made law enforcement personnel more sympathetic. But it also achieved something else. Their recognition of her as someone who was wronged and who deserved compensation validated that a harm had been done to her. Hema had always brushed off her husband's abuse as minor, saying that she could handle it for the sake of her children. The Nodakhali workshop marked a turning point in our conversations. Hema increasingly voiced critiques of her husband after the workshop. She seemed more resentful than she had been in the past, grumbling that violence should not be a woman's destiny.

I suspected that law enforcement affirmation was crucial for Hema and Najma in two ways. First, state officials' recognition of women as rights bearers transformed women's sense of their place within a broader polity.

As purveyors of the law, those who determined how the law was applied and adjudicated, law enforcement had the authority to mark what was and was not a violation. Their authority endured despite civilian skepticism and no matter how much law enforcement personnel themselves pleaded their own disempower-ment. The state yielded a "meta capital" that shaped women's desires, fears, and identities (Aretxaga 2003; Bourdieu 1994).

Second, law enforcement personnel influenced women's aspirations because they were disproportionately men. Hema's response to the officers at Nodakhali was gendered. She did not talk about the woman PO who opened the work-shop. She concentrated on the police officers who were both men. These men, the kind of men she had once feared as potential violators, were acknowledging her rights as a member of society and looking to her for help. The interaction validated her sense of what she did or did not deserve in a way the predomi-nantly woman-dominated world of Shadheen did not.

Daring to Be Strategic

As women came to believe they deserved the life the law promised, they simulta-neously asserted the need to strategically maneuver their claims. They envisioned the law as a tactical field they could and should manipulate. In their minds, extra-legal measures did not contradict a commitment to legal rights but rather helped ensure them. Politically pressuring law enforcement personnel, using criminal cases as bargaining chips against abusers, threatening abusers through criminal gangs, bribing witnesses and state officials: all of these actions were justifiable avenues to rights because the world was tilted in men's favor.

The strategic component of women's growing consciousness combined the language of law and legal rights with distrust of the state and tactical acceptance of illegality. It provided striking proof of what some have identified as a pop-ular understanding of the Indian state as simultaneously sublime and profane, a site that embodies an ideal of justice but which has become corrupted and is thus needful of extralegal action (Hansen 2001; Kaviraj 2005; Khilnani 1999). Nestled within women's evolving strategic visions was a scepticism of law en-forcement personnel and a suspicion that criminal justice institutions rewarded craftiness, rather than rule-abiding behavior. This part of their legal conscious-ness overlapped with commonplace understandings of law enforcement corrup-tion and malfeasance (Kapur and Vaishnav 2014; Vaishnav 2017).

But, on its own, legal cynicism can promote avoidance rather than engage-ment (Kirk and Matsuda 2011). It is important to remember that ordinary Indian women know very little about the state, about laws, or about the legal process (Corbridge et al. 2005). Thinking strategically about the law does not simply emanate from citizen distrust, nor in the case of middle- and low-income women is it all that commonplace. Strategic behavior was thus by no means a holdover of their prior lives but rather a direct artifact of their changing legal practices. "Running a case" provided new knowledge about the public sphere, training in the tactics and subterfuges of politics, and a level of confidence about how to mobilize against both law enforcement personnel and their abusers.

Women experiencing violence reimagined themselves as efficacious negotiators because they had a new set of resources with which to become familiar with the state. Brokers instructed them to use certain tactics and provided social networks and political power. These networks meant that women did not claim rights alone but through some kind of *dol* (gang), whose support made them feel that the law was something they could influence. Meanwhile, their routine encounters with law enforcement personnel created a sense that the law was something they could participate in. They learned about the inner workings of different government offices, who worked where, who could be influenced, and how.

Here, Jhumpa's recollections are again instructive. Thinking back to the time when she first decided to register a 498A case, Jhumpa remembered feeling acute fear of law enforcement personnel, wanting to avoid them at all costs. "The first day I went to court, I was trembling." But by talking to court personnel and entering a police station, all of these people and spaces that had been unfamiliar and intimidating became familiar and negotiable. "It's different now. Once you get accustomed, it's not so intimidating." Jhumpa had become accustomed to the actual spaces of the law, places like the Alipore court complex in South Kolkata, which had at one point intimidated her. Talking about specific law enforcement personnel, she mentioned that "Some people are helpful, others aren't." She had gotten to know who could be counted on and who could not. The state was no longer a monolith but rather a disaggregated set of offices and individuals.

None of this would have happened without AIN, without the knowledge and connections the organization provided. Still talking about law enforcement personnel, Jhumpa mentioned that she did not trust the police. But she had realized that most of them were lazy, rather than outright malicious. They needed motivation. "You have to force them to get to work," she chuckled. By force, she mentioned bribery and mobilizing connections through upper-level bureaucrats and political parties.

The idea that she could force law enforcement personnel to do anything at all was relatively novel for Jhumpa. At the beginning of her journey she had trembled in court, been afraid of the police. Now, she felt capable of partaking in the legal process and bending it to her will. This about-face was a product of Jhumpa's perception of AIN's institutional power. The elder sisters (caseworkers) knew important people in the criminal justice system, she mentioned. Their connections ensured that her PWDVA case moved forward. It was also a product of the new social network AIN gave Jhumpa. The women with whom she talked on the phone and who accompanied her to the movies also went with her to court and to meetings with her lawyer. This sense of support gave her the strength it took to keep going.

Of course, brokers provided more than moral support, knowledge, and political connections. Depending on who the broker was, they also provided credibility, muscle power, and the ability to do what the state was supposed to do. These provisions were amply evident to Uma, who received help from the police once she had organized support from Shadheen and Girish; to Najma, who found the courage to enter a police station with Sila's *mahila samiti* by her side; and to Hameeda, who learned how to fill out a PO's report through her caseworker Samoli. While these women remained suspicious of the law and its personnel, their access to organized groups allowed them to think of the law as a site that could be worked upon and worked to their advantage.

By creating these openings and allowing women to use them, law enforcement personnel promoted strategic behavior. Women would not have had to bribe, threaten, or illegally complete case-processing duties if law enforcement did their jobs and enforced legal procedure. Similarly, they could not have taken any of these steps if law enforcement were not receptive to such machinations. By incorporating women into the daily work of regulation, state officials reinforced a popular consciousness of law as a possible vehicle for social justice but a vehicle that required mobilization and manipulation to be realized in practice.

Women's disregard for rules and regulations was a direct response to a criminal justice system that rewarded political power and craft. It was the PO who demanded Hameeda illegally complete her report and then lauded her for her initiative when she agreed to do so. It was the police, at first hostile and physically threatening, who became friendly and pliable once Najma used a *mahila samiti* to mobilize shadowy threats. By creating these spaces and only responding to women who knew how to maneuver within them, state officials underscored both the necessity and the benefits of strategic action.

Law enforcement's role in encouraging strategic behavior became starkly visible when women ran parallel claims. Payel, who repossessed her property with help from Andolan, ended up taking items that may not have been hers. When I interviewed her after her repossession, she animatedly listed all the items she had grabbed from the house, including bed sheets, floor mats, and the memorable pack of ducks. But she avoided a direct answer when I asked her if the items she had taken were hers. Instead, she circuitously remarked, "We took what we could carry. The police officer was there." While conducting the interview, I was a bit confused about her response. What did "taking what one can carry" have to do with her claim to the property she took away? Why did she note the police officer's presence at the scene?

I later answered my own questions by thinking through her responses to other questions I asked her to answer. When I wondered why she had screamed at and hit her husband, she again noted the presence of the police officer at the scene. This portion of her statement is worth quoting at some length.

> I was just scaring him so he wouldn't be violent. The police, he was right there, next to us. You don't know these kinds of people [her husband]. You have to put the screws on them, otherwise they get the better of you. The officer [police] is a village boy. He knows how things work here.

Taken together, Payel's justifications for taking items that may not have been hers and for wielding physical force created a consistent picture. There was a reason she reminded me that the police officer was "right there" when she was hitting her husband. She intentionally discussed the police's upbringing and set him up as a foil to me, the non-resident Indian. For Payel, the police officer's presence meant something. It meant that whatever she was up to was necessary in order to achieve her desired outcomes.

Threats were how you got "these kinds of people" to behave, and the police officer knew it. Also, his presence confirmed that Payel's actions, including taking things that may not have been hers and hitting her husband, were within the boundaries of acceptable behavior, for if they had not been, the police officer, who was "there" and observing everything, would have stepped in and put a stop to it. For Payel, law enforcement supervision simultaneously emboldened her strategic use of illegality and violence while placing a stamp of approval on her actions. What she had done was necessary to achieving justice, and the police officer knew it.

If the state's supervision and encouragement emboldened women, its negligence and ill will were the main reasons they felt they had to be strategic in the first place. These strategic maneuvers spilled over, outside the realm of the criminal justice system, informing how women melded legal claims with extralegal negotiations in order to get a leg up on their abusers. After doing all the work required to move her PWDVA complaint out of the PO's office into the district magistrate's court, Hameeda ran out of steam. It was wedding season: she worked long hours to fulfill sewing orders and had no energy left to run a case. She asked Samoli to help arrange a settlement. "If I tell him I will withdraw the case, will he give me anything?" Hameeda asked Samoli's opinion. Samoli informed her there was no harm trying. She would run an arbitration behind Shadheen's back in her own home, using her independent *mahila samiti* to provide organizational legitimacy.

I arrived at Samoli's house to find everyone gathered in the new brick extension. Even the room seemed to be a strategic decision: Samoli wished to communicate her own social standing to give ammunition to the settlement. The mud portion of her house would not have served the same purpose. Samoli herself was a practicing Hindu, but the room was decorated with a multiplicity of religious paraphernalia. A plump baby Krishna eating butter stood next to Jesus and Mary on a nearby shelf. In a corner under the staircase, I spied a small shrine to Pir Baba, a Sufi saint.

Samoli's diversified religious practices provided a metaphor for her strategic approach to legal cases. Samoli felt little guilt about running an arbitration behind Shadheen's back. "How many cases are actually resolved in court?" Samoli demanded. I was unsure how to answer Samoli's challenge. Looking at Hameeda for confirmation, Samoli then asked if she was unhappy with the way things had turned out. Hameeda piped up at this point, addressing me. "This is what I asked for. The other *didi* [referring to Madhavi, the head of Shadheen's casework team] told me to keep running the case, but I can't anymore." Hameeda's parents also chimed in, corroborating their daughter's statements and claiming that the law was a waste of time.

Samoli interjected at this point. To my surprise, instead of confirming the law's uselessness, she argued *for* legal remedies. "If you need to, you will have to go back to the case," she scolded Hameeda. Later speaking to me one-on-one, she explained her logic. "I've been working with women for ten years now. The situation here was very bad when I began. Without the law, mediation has no force, you understand?" Samoli went on to explain that her association with Shadheen's casework team enhanced her ability to broker compromises. The fact that she understood the law and could help women like Hameeda pursue an official case were factors that functioned as a silent threat, providing credibility and force to the agreement.

"The boy [Hameeda's husband] is afraid now. He knows what she can do, so he is behaving himself. But don't count on it lasting." Samoli urged Hameeda to think of her domestic situation as a long-term negotiation. Just because things were working out now did not mean they would work out in the future. If the compromise fell apart, then the next step for Hameeda might have to be to return to the PWDVA case. "What do you say? To which, Hameeda hastened to shake her head. "Yes *didi*, I understand."

Samoli's strategic approach to the law combined legal measures with extralegal initiatives, and it was this amalgamation that she hoped to teach Hameeda to embrace. Samoli's opinions about the appropriate relationship between the law and extralegality rubbed off on Hameeda partly because Samoli provided care and help. But Samoli's teachings were also convincing because of the way state officials behaved. Hameeda, perhaps echoing something she had overheard Samoli say, argued that the law was best seen as a "weapon" that women had to know how to yield. One had to believe one deserved what the law promised but not be deluded into having too much faith in its institutions. It was only through this dual consciousness that one could hope to secure a semblance of what the law promised.

10

Justice by Another Name

What Women Gained from Running Cases

By "running a case," women experiencing violence developed an aspirational-strategic subjectivity. They acknowledged they had been abused. They also recognized that they were strong enough, smart enough, and courageous enough to compel abusers to the negotiating table and force law enforcement personnel to take them seriously. But what did they materially gain from their endeavors, if anything?

Among the seventy women who feature in this book, thirty-six registered an official complaint against domestic violence under either criminal or civil law over the time period covered by the study. This time period spanned two years of ethnography, plus interviews that traced women's legal engagements prior to and after ethnography was concluded, totaling a span of sixteen years. Over this period, thirty women registered First Information Reports (FIRs) under Section 498A. Meanwhile, six women registered Domestic Incident Reports (DIRs) under the Protection of Women from Domestic Violence Act (PWDVA), including one survivor who also registered a 498A case (Jhumpa).

Among those who registered a 498A case, three received verdicts in their favor (two convictions and one fine) and one received a verdict in her husband's favor (acquittal). The three women who received a favorable 498A judgment represented 8.3 percent of the women who registered a criminal case. This means that in my research sample, women who registered a 498A case had a low chance of success. Meanwhile, of the women who registered a PWDVA case, two received court orders guaranteeing protection, financial compensation, and rights to the joint household. These two women represented 33.3 percent of those who registered civil cases. This means that in my research sample, women who registered PWDVA cases had a higher chance of success than those who registered 498A cases. These numbers place my study's findings below the current countrywide conviction rates under both civil and criminal law. By 2018, the conviction rate for 498A was 15.9 percent, while 47.3 percent of PWDVA cases led to a court order (National Crime Records Bureau 2018).

Capable Women, Incapable States. Poulami Roychowdhury, Oxford University Press 2021. © Oxford University Press
DOI: 10.1093/oso/9780190881894.001.0001

In addition to the thirty-six criminal and civil cases women lodged, it is important for me to mention that another fourteen women pursued maintenance (alimony) claims under Section 125 of the Code of Criminal Procedure (CrPC), making the total number of "official" cases I encountered fifty. Section 125, which promises alimony to married women who are separated, divorced, or abandoned by their husbands, can provide a much needed lifeline to those who are unable to provide for themselves. The fact, however, that five women received official orders under CrPC 125 should be taken with a grain of salt. CrPC 125 is not a law against violence, and the fact that women use the law at all can be interpreted as evidence of the limitations of domestic violence legislation. As other scholars have already noted, women experiencing violence are forced to choose between punishment and financial survival (Basu 2006). Gains under Section 125 often come at the expense of convictions under Section 498A. And this is exactly what happened within my research sample.

So all in all, I can count the women who actually secured legal rights on the fingers of one hand. There were five of them. Even if I were to include maintenance orders under CrPC 125 in the bucket of successful legal claims, the fact remains that a small minority of the seventy women in this study received rights through the law. "Running a case" rarely led to convictions or court orders.

If the law rarely awarded rights, what did women get out of their legal engagements, if anything? What did "running cases" actually provide women in a context where legal rights were politicized but state capacity remained limited? While only a handful of women secured state-based redress, many women used the law to bolster extralegal bargaining. By "running cases," women were able to negotiate with abusers outside the criminal justice system. These negotiations allowed them to illicitly access money, possessions, housing, divorce or separation, and custody of their children.

Settlements

Both by registering official legal cases and by pursuing parallel claims, women negotiated five types of settlements outside the law: financial settlements, repossession of personal property, child custody, separation, and residential access. Some women received two or more of these settlements at once. Notably, while these outcomes are part of the orders the PWDVA promises, none of them are ensured by Section 498A, which only promises fines and imprisonment.

When discussing extralegal settlements, women used a particular vocabulary. They did not refer to gains outside the law as *bicar,* which connotes a juridical form of justice. Rather, they used words such as "atonement" and "justice for wrongdoing," terms that better captured extralegal, moral claims to justice.

The word *mimansa* ("compromise," "settlement," and "solution" in Bengali) provided a catch-all that described the process through which women attained illicit justice.

A financial settlement took one of two forms: a monthly allotment or a lump sum transfer of cash or other assets from the abuser to the survivor. Because monthly installments offered abusers multiple opportunities to default, women and the brokers who counseled them pushed for one-time lump sum transfers. Child custody settlements are relatively self-explanatory: women either regained access to their children or ensured that children continued to live with them. Repossession of personal property involved situations where women retrieved a host of personal items that their husbands initially refused to give back. Among these items, women sought gold jewelry, clothing, furniture, and kitchen utensils and appliances they had received as gifts during their marriage.

Meanwhile, residential access allowed women to live in their husband's or in-laws' house. While this was a less than ideal arrangement, for some women the option was either to remain in the same house or risk homelessness. Renting housing as a single woman is extremely difficult and nowhere more so than in West Bengal where property laws are weak and landlords are unwilling to rent to demographic groups they view as financially risky or troubled. These gendered hurdles in rental markets made housing an important resource for women, no matter how difficult the conditions that surrounded it. Finally, some women simply wanted to live separately from their abusers without facing harassment or being contacted. A separation allowed them to do that.

"Running a case" enabled illicit outcomes for a number of reasons. First, "running a case" did not necessarily entail a formal registered claim. In my sample, only 51.4 percent of women (thirty-six out of seventy women) registered either an FIR or DIR. Those who did not register an official complaint could still run a case through a parallel claim. Second, even when women did register a formal complaint, they tended to use legal cases to gain a better bargaining position outside the law. In other words, even those who registered an FIR or DIR tended to *also* run a parallel claim at some point, either right from the beginning or after facing delays and snags with their official cases.

The institutional landscape of domestic violence law encouraged extralegal gains. Both brokers and law enforcement personnel encouraged and enabled extralegality. Brokers taught women how to manipulate legal rules and procedures. It was through caseworkers, political party representatives, and members of women's committees, those who were experienced in the law, that women learned how to acquire a semblance of rights outside the criminal justice system.

Some brokers, like Bani and Partha at Andolan, or Girish, and Pora Khokhon, explicitly embraced illicit justice. They encouraged women to use legal claims to pressure abusers after community-based forms of discipline and surveillance reached their limits. Other brokers, like Gouri at AIN and the top management at Shadheen, remained ideologically committed to legal procedure and disavowed extralegality as undermining the legal process. But they were unintentionally dragged into facilitating illicit justice. At Shadheen, caseworkers as well as brokers who brought women to the organization, like Rupa, Samoli, and Sila, resisted the organization's official prescriptions and deployed extralegal tactics outside managerial supervision. At AIN, caseworkers were forced to choose between helping women in need and continuing to pursue a legal case. They sometimes chose to help women at the cost of their ideological principles.

Meanwhile, law enforcement personnel either looked the other way or provided institutional cover for informality. They actively rewarded extralegality, both because it was in their interest to reduce the number of open cases on their docket and because they did not wish to alienate women with organized support. As Hema noted, law enforcement personnel could be persuaded, through money or personal favors, to take a girl's side. Or, as in Jhumpa's words, they could be "forced" through organized pressure or the threat of physical violence. Encouraging extralegal settlements ensured that women either withdrew registered complaints or never registered a complaint in the first place.

Finally, extralegality prevailed because of the way this institutional landscape transformed women themselves. Simultaneously believing they deserved rights while recognizing that the criminal justice system was unlikely to award them, women who registered legal claims remained open to the possibility of using the case as a bargaining chip. They learned to use a number of illicit tactics to push their cases forward. They gathered their own evidence, illegally filled out and ferried government forms, cajoled and threatened witnesses to ensure they showed up to court, and bribed the court clerk to secure a speedy trial date. They also worked with multiple brokers at the same time, increasing their chances of receiving what they needed from one broker if the other refused or failed to deliver.

Jhumpa's settlement with her husband provided a case in point. She sought help from multiple brokers and used each broker to negotiate and enforce various dimensions of an out-of-court settlement. Through AIN, she registered a 498A case. Through the "boys at the local club," men who spent a lot of time lounging around the headquarters of the political party that dominated her neighborhood, she later registered a PWDVA case. The club boys helped Jhumpa because they were affiliated with the Trinamul Congress Party (TMC). Jhumpa herself was an ardent TMC supporter, while her husband and brother-in-law were affiliated with the rival Communist Party of India (Marxist) (CPI[M]). Party competition worked to Jhumpa's advantage. The TMC-affiliated club boys were happy to help their party sister. They also did not know about the 498A case Jhumpa had already registered through AIN. Neither did AIN know about Jhumpa's dealings with the club boys or her PWDVA case.

Alongside her two legal claims, Jhumpa asked AIN to help secure the deed to the apartment where she lived, an apartment owned by her absent husband. AIN agreed to help because they did not realize that Jhumpa had an outstanding PWDVA claim, through which she could eventually have been awarded residential rights. In the minds of AIN's caseworkers, Jhumpa simply had a 498A case and 498A did not provide access to housing. Interpreting Jhumpa's pursuit of a property title as a separate endeavor from her "case," AIN caseworkers got to work. They even called on the help of a local police officer who was on friendly terms with AIN's staff. This officer assisted Jhumpa in changing her locks and made sure her husband moved his possessions. All of this, needless to say, happened before a court could issue an official residential order for Jhumpa.

What AIN did not know was how Jhumpa perceived the title. To her, the title was not separate from her PWDVA case or her 498A case. It was a settlement, part of a bargain she had cooked up with her husband in exchange for letting the official cases go. The extralegal negotiation had begun long ago, when Jhumpa's husband got fed up with receiving court summonses. He informed Jhumpa that if she stopped showing up to court and granted him a divorce, he would give up his claim on their apartment. She agreed, using AIN to square the deal without informing them it was a deal. Jhumpa also elicited the support of her local club boys to ensure that the settlement continued to hold water. They promised to watch over the area and make sure her husband did not try to muscle his way back into the apartment. Once again, Jhumpa did not inform AIN of this other dimension to the title or how she planned to enforce it.

With the apartment deed in her hands, a divorce in the works, the locks changed, and the local club boys looking out for her, Jhumpa felt completely disinterested in doing any of the work necessary to drive either her PWDVA or 498A case forward. I had the sense that the main reason Jhumpa registered a PWDVA case behind AIN's back had to do with further shoring up her side of the bargaining table. Referring to her husband, she discussed their mutual interests in negotiating outside the law. "He wanted the divorce anyway, so he could marry [again]. But it doesn't matter. He's out of my life and I get to stay in our house."

A title to an apartment in South Kolkata was an incredible resource for Jhumpa. While Jhumpa was not low-income in the way I have classified that category, she teetered near the edge. Her income varied greatly from month to month depending on the earnings she made from her vending business. She was by no means financially secure. The only security she had was the apartment in which she lived. It would have been impossible for her to rent a room in her neighborhood on her finances. The promise of free housing was thus incredibly important to Jhumpa, as was a life free of her husband's control. These outcomes trumped Jhumpa's desire for a conviction or a court order. They were concrete gains she could count on in the here and now, unlike the uncertain outcomes of criminal justice bureaucracies known for their delays and mistakes.

The Class Dynamics of Extra-legal Gains

While women of all social backgrounds ended up settling, social background influenced what kinds of legal cases women registered, how long they held on to an official case before negotiating, and how likely they were to register an official case in the first place. Low-income women comprised 52.8 percent of women in my research sample (thirty-seven of seventy) but only 30.5 percent of women who registered cases (eleven low-income women registered a domestic violence complaint out of a total of thirty-six claimants). They also disproportionately registered criminal, rather than civil, cases. Of the six women who registered DIRs in my sample, only one (Hameeda) was low-income. Meanwhile, nine out of thirty registered FIRs involved low-income women.

Low-income women were more likely to pursue 498A cases than PWDVA cases partly because 498A guaranteed the services of a public prosecutor, lowering the financial burden of a legal claim. Section 498A also had the added benefit of having mandatory arrest procedures. For low-income women and the brokers who represented them, the threat of arrest was a key disciplinary mechanism through which they could force abusers to the bargaining table. The threatening features of 498A mattered because low-income women had to settle official cases quickly, while women with greater financial resources could afford to wait longer to negotiate extralegal compromises. For low-income women, formal remedies exacted a heavy toll because legal cases had long timelines. They could not afford to take time off from work, had a harder time finding childcare, and could not afford to pay bribes or even the money it took to get to and from various government offices. As a result, they were relatively more eager to pursue extralegal solutions.

Some low-income women explicitly used case registration as a bargaining agent for out-of-court negotiations. Najma, the landless Muslim survivor from South-24 Parganas who lamented that the police did not respect poor women, registered a General Diary Report (GD) because it would help her negotiate a private deal. When the GD failed to have the intended consequences, Sila brought Najma back to Shadheen to discuss the possibility of registering a 498A. To the organization, Najma was merely registering a legal case, but behind the scenes Sila assured Najma that the threat of arrest would bring her husband to the negotiating table.

When I questioned Sila about her logic, she explained her rationale. "Who has the ability to run a case? The girls I work with, they have to earn money." Sila believed settlements were essential for women without financial resources because they needed money quickly and could not afford to wait around for a court order. Remarking on Najma's situation, Sila continued to justify her tactics. "This girl [Najma], she's doing the one hundred-day work program [National Rural Employment Guarantee Act]. Her husband sells the rice she buys for her children to buy alcohol for himself. They are starving." Sila paused, motioning with her hands that the rest was self-explanatory. A woman in such dire financial conditions could not see a 498A case to completion, she intimated. And there was the matter of the costs entailed in "running a case."

When I looked unconvinced by her rationale, Sila pointedly asked, "You tell me, how can she take time off work, pay bus fare [to get to court], going up and down to Kolkata for who knows how long?" Highlighting Najma's financial needs and the lengthy nature of criminal trials, Sila felt justified in advising her to use the law for illicit purposes. Najma was poor enough to qualify for government-guaranteed work and financially desperate because her good-for-nothing husband stole what little she earned. The most pressing concern was to get Najma's husband out of her life, not to wait around for the state to deliver on its promises.

Najma agreed. This was why she had approached Sila in the first place. Mentioning the names of other women who had registered cases, she acknowledged that they had not received an official verdict. But according to her, an official verdict was never something they sought. Nor for that matter did she. "Their husbands gave them back their clothes and jewelry." In Najma's view, this was the outcome they had intended from the very beginning, and it was the ideal outcome.

Najma did not feel guilty about employing Shadheen's and Sila's services simultaneously. Like Jhumpa, she felt that two brokers were better than one. If Shadheen could help her with a legal case, she was happy to see where that might lead. If Sila could use that case to contract a quick settlement with good terms, so much the better. Najma's and Jhumpa's simultaneous use of multiple brokers indexed a wider practice whereby women strategically engaged with not just their abusers and law enforcement personnel but also with brokers who provided mediation services.

Brokers who catered to low-income women's concerns knew how to arrange settlements with great speed and, like Sila, actively embraced these outcomes. Sabiha, the low-income Muslim woman from North-24 Parganas who was a member of Andolan's women's wing, received advice from Bani on how to get something concrete outside the law by registering a legal case. Sabiha's husband initially refused to financially provide for her and their daughter, claiming that she had "abandoned" the marriage even though it was he who had beaten her and then moved in with his mistress. Bani advised her to first see if he would budge by sending the union's members to harass him. When Sabiha's husband moved to his new girlfriend's village to avoid the union, Bani gave the go-ahead for 498A. "Hit him with a case." Bani and Sabiha believed that a criminal case would "burn" him out of hiding, driving him to the negotiating table.

Over time, Sabiha's 498A case did in fact have the desired effect. Weary of dodging an arrest order, Sabiha's husband agreed to give her a sum of $15,000 RS (roughly $250 at the time) if she agreed to a divorce and withdrew the case. The disbursement process took another few months to be completed and was policed by the union. Reflecting on the compromise, Sabiha concluded that the monetary settlement provided the best outcome for her. She had no desire to send her husband to jail, where he would lose his job and thus the ability to financially provide for her. Nor did she have the time or money to fight a trial. When she was not out in the fields, she cleaned people's homes for a living. Taking time off from these jobs meant losing valuable wages. And the bus fare to and from the district court house was itself a financial burden.

While low-income women like Sabiha and Najma entered 498A cases with the express purpose of attaining an out-of-court settlement, those who could afford to keep a case going held on as long as possible. The ability to wait allowed them to negotiate better terms for their agreements. Women who had a range of social and financial connections thus had a leg up in the illicit negotiating process over those who could only count on civil society intervention.

Sharmila's trajectory from legal suit to settlement provides a case in point. A much loved only child born and brought up in a middle-class, upper-caste Hindu family in South Kolkata, Sharmila was shocked by the treatment her husband and his family meted out after her marriage. Tall, broad-shouldered, and outspoken, Sharmila had been raised to expect affection and consideration from those around her, affection she could still count on from her natal family. Her parents supported her decision to leave her abusive husband, telling her to return home, paying for the consultation fees of a private lawyer, and encouraging her to seek help from AIN.

With the help of her AIN caseworker, Sharmila eventually registered a 498A case. But in the process, she also deployed family connections. "My family has always been with the CPI(M)," she explained. Her grandfather had "built" the neighborhood where they lived, arriving as a refugee from what is now Bangladesh to a swampland in the southernmost part of a smaller, less densely packed Kolkata. Her grandfather's early connections to the CPI(M) had established her family as a central figure in the political and social life of her neighborhood. As a member of that family, Sharmila enjoyed a range of privileges, including public support for her return home. She also happened to be childhood friends with her local *dada*, the political fixer who mediated between neighbor-hood residents and the CPI(M).

Learning of her family history, AIN's lawyer advised her to work closely with her *dada* on her 498A case. I could not precisely tell what the lawyer had in-tended when giving this advice because the accounts of the lawyer's advice came to me secondhand through Sharmila. But Sharmila's *dada*'s political connections did come in handy when she approached the police. He accompanied her to the station and on another occasion called ahead of her arrival, easing the reg-istration and investigation process. Sharmila also admitted to using her *dada* to send "sweets" to the inspector in charge of the police station. Feeding a govern-ment official "sweets" is a euphemistic way of talking about giving bribes in West Bengal. Neither AIN's lawyer nor Sharmila's caseworker were informed of these behind-the-scenes arrangements.

Sharmila's familial relationship with her *dada*, while initially good for moving the case ahead, eventually ran into its limits once the case entered the court. Her *dada* and his party affiliates had contacts among the court clerks and even with the district magistrate, but the court was a juggernaut that ran at its own pace. When I met Sharmila, it had been four years since she registered her case. Having once been bent on sending her husband to jail, she now felt less motivated by that goal. Her husband had willingly granted her a divorce and returned large chunks of her dowry once he became aware of her political connections. With a shrug of her shoulders, she announced that she was relieved to have her jewelry back. She was also glad that the case had "made [her husband] suffer for a bit." By using a range of illicit means, from political pressure to bribery, to move her of-ficial case forward Sharmila ended up convincing her husband that she was not to be ignored. Once he scrambled to appease her, she herself felt less motivated to keep fighting a legal battle.

A situation akin to this transpired for Riya, an upper-caste Hindu woman born and brought up in North Kolkata. The only daughter of an upper middle-class family, she had received a hefty dowry that included gold jewelry passed down through several generations of women. For a year after their separation, her husband kept making excuses about returning her dowry, claiming that he still hoped for reconciliation. After Riya registered a 498A case, all conversation stopped between them and Riya fretted over her family heirlooms, worried her husband had sold everything for profit.

Similar to Koel's wealthy husband, Riya's husband had extensive holdings. He owned several houses he had bought with "black" money. Riya adopted a similar extralegal strategy as Koel, even though they were officially pursuing very dif-ferent legal cases (Koel had registered a PWDVA case, while Riya was pursuing 498A). Riya also went to the bank and got her hold on a teller who could send her documents. By unearthing her husband's property deeds, Riya hoped to give her lawyer evidence of her husband's poor character to use in court. Yet, in the end, her husband was far more afraid of losing his property than hoarding her gold. Upon hearing that she had these documents in her possession, he suggested a compromise: if she dropped the 498A case, he would return not just her jewelry but also the furniture her parents had given her and a chunk of the money she had been gifted upon their marriage. Satisfied with this bargain and tired of fighting a case, Riya admitted that she no longer cared if her husband went to jail. "I have what I went in with. He doesn't get to keep anything of me," she explained with a sense of satisfaction.

Conclusion

What did women materially gain from "running a case?" A handful of them received legal rights. Others made illicit gains. This research affirms the broader picture coming from India's National Crime Records Bureau: most women do not register formal legal cases, and when they do, they rarely secure state-based rights. Beyond this official story, I also found a hidden world of illicit settlements, separations, property repossessions, residential agreements, and child custody arrangements.

Illicit gains should not be dismissed as unimportant. For individual women, they spelled the difference between financial survival and destitution, between having housing and being homeless, between acquiring a sense of justice and finding none. The stories underlying extralegal settlements also indicate that legal reforms have helped expand normative commitments to women's rights— among law enforcement, brokers, and women themselves. By engaging the law in this way, women imagined an expanded realm of possibilities for their lives and sometimes succeeded in attaining otherwise unattainable material and social resources.

Finally, the very process whereby women attain the illicit speaks to the way laws do matter and have created positive social change. Without laws on the books, it is unclear if women would have been able to negotiate at all. By providing women with "weapons" against their abusers, Section 498A and the PWDVA have created a space within which extralegal negotiations can take place and, to some degree, gendered wrongs can be made right.

Meanwhile, the classed basis of who is better able to extract concessions raises troubling questions about the social biases baked into a system where rights are not guaranteed by the state but rather set up to be rewards for those who are most capable of acquiring them. If Sila is correct in her assessment, the ability to negotiate extralegal settlements is an important asset for poor women. But it is important precisely because the criminal justice system performs so abysmally.

If the state provided speedy justice, women like Sabiha and Najma would not have to rush into compromises just to feed themselves. Extralegal settlements are only an asset when legal settlements are compromised or nonexistent.

Here, it is important to pause and recognize the full implications of what kind of woman has to rush into a settlement. Sabiha and Najma were poor to be sure. But they were also marginalized in a number of other ways. They were both Muslim and barely literate and had lived all their lives in villages outside Kolkata. Meanwhile, Sharmila and Riya could both afford to hold out for a better settlement. They had the financial resources to do so. But they also had significant social resources: family support, friends in political parties, influential contacts at banks. Their access to such resources may have been connected to their social background. They were not just middle-class; they belonged to dominant social groups: they were Hindu and upper-caste. They both lived in Kolkata and were well educated.

These facts, when grouped together, create the following contradictory picture. Marginalized women needed illicit gains more pressingly than their more privileged counterparts. But they also had fewer resources with which to secure a beneficial settlement. At the margins, the extralegal outcomes of "running a case" were thus more important for those facing the greatest disadvantages. But when thought about in terms of total assets, it was the women who already enjoyed substantial financial and social advantages who made the greatest gains.

The Allure and Costs of Capability

I was about to head to Shadheen when I saw an incoming call from Rupa on my phone. We were supposed to meet at the office, but she was sick. Could I come to her house instead? she wondered. She was making lunch. We could eat together, she cajoled. From my apartment in Kolkata, getting to Rupa's house in South-24 Parganas required several modes of transportation. I had to walk, take two different buses, then an autorickshaw, and then walk again. Mulling the distance, I reluctantly agreed. If we did not meet that day, I would not see her before I left Kolkata. I was scheduled to return to New York later that week. Research, at least the concentrated time of immersive ethnography, was coming to an end.

Rupa lived in a village shaded by large trees. Her house was made of brick, the rooms situated around a courtyard with a hand-operated water pump in one corner. The first time I had visited Rupa's house, she had dutifully introduced me to her parents. Short and curt, introductions over, she quickly steered me away without allowing me to meet her brother or his wife. Rupa's portion of the house consisted of one large room that she shared with her son and an adjoining bathroom she had built with her own income. The room was outfitted with a large wooden bed, a small black and white television, and an aluminum armoire that contained all of her and her son's earthly possessions. She was especially proud of the bathroom, which had previously been an open-air shower with a tiny walled latrine. The new bathroom was covered with a tile roof, housed a small fan for the hotter months, a mirror, bottles of shampoo, and two bars of soap, one for the sink and one for the toilet. I noticed she kept the bathroom locked to keep the rest of her family out.

On that first visit, Rupa had been in good spirits and clearly in the mood to capitalize on my presence. She had invited several women to come and meet her "friend" from America. And she had paraded me around the village, drawing me into neighbors' homes and encouraging me to consume numerous syrupy sweets at every pit stop. I was a special part of the institutional landscape that helped Rupa build a career and gain social credibility. Thanks to Shadheen and her personal contacts with local law enforcement, Rupa had become someone

Capable Women, Incapable States. Poulami Roychowdhury, Oxford University Press 2021. © Oxford University Press
DOI: 10.1093/oso/9780190881894.001.0001

other women in the village turned to for help, both with domestic disputes and with any other issue defined as women's business. I was thoroughly aware of the fact that Rupa was using me to further bolster her image as a woman of some means, someone who knew "an American," someone who was capable of getting the American to visit her home. Given the time and effort Rupa had spent helping me, I found her attempts to use me to amass social capital small compensation for everything she had contributed to my research.

Rupa's ascent within her natal village was no small feat, and she knew it. She had worked hard to achieve her current status and talked about herself through the language of capability she heard reverberating through the halls and corridors she inhabited. "Earlier, I didn't dare do anything by myself. Now, I have capabilities in the palm of my hand," she explained in an extended interview. Rupa measured her achievements in relation to where she had been ten years back: an abandoned and abused wife who had returned to her parents without money or friends. She had felt ill-treated by both her family and others in her village, cast at the bottom of the social ladder.

Through her engagement with the law and its institutions, she had not only gained self-confidence, she had built herself a *pakka* bathroom, one made of concrete and cement, not cheap mud.[1] She introduced other women to Shadheen, where she had assumed the status of a legal expert and professional working woman. She accompanied women to that ultimate site of fear and hope: the criminal justice system. She conversed with the people who occupied these unknown and intimidating spaces with relative ease. And she provided a kind of protection for the women under her wing from the violence and neglect these very same people could inflict on those they regarded as unworthy of their attention.

On my first visit to her house, Rupa embodied the model of a capable woman, the kind of woman who could access rights if she put her mind to it. Rupa, of course, had not accessed rights. Not legal rights provided by the state at any rate. Her 498A case remained pending. But she seemed to have acquired something else, something that was neither the same as official rights nor akin to an illicit settlement. Rupa saw herself in the image of capability she encouraged other women to adopt. She identified as someone who could take care of herself and get things done. "I'm not afraid of anyone. I have friends everywhere. I even have the DM's personal number on my cell phone," she boasted, mentioning the name of the District Magistrate, who epitomized the heights of judicial power that a woman of her social background could only have hoped to hear about on television.

Around the time I first visited her house, Rupa was invited to join a panel on women's rights at Jadavpur University. She was the sole caseworker to have been invited and the only woman at the event without a high school degree. She was asked to provide a ground-level picture of legal cases, and she relished her position. This panel invitation turned into a foray into the world of popular media.

A journalist who attended the panel later contacted Rupa, asking if she would be willing to speak on the radio about her work.

Rupa could not have been prouder of these invitations. Speaking to college students at an elite university, sitting on a podium with upper-class, upper-caste women in expensive *saris* who had fancy degrees and fancy job titles, Rupa felt recognized and validated. This was where she belonged, among these kinds of people, looked to as an authority on the topic under discussion. "The radio didn't invite anyone else," she mentioned excitedly. The journalist had picked *her*, deeming her words worthy of mass distribution.

In comparison to the first time I visited Rupa, my second visit revealed a darker side to her life. She had been sick on and off for the past month, taking time off from work to get some rest. She was having complications with her menstrual cycle, bleeding heavily week after week, and people at Shadheen suspected she had fibroids. What was certain was that she was in severe pain and could not afford to see a specialist. Thankfully, Shadheen was raising money on her behalf, and Dolly was looking for a doctor who could provide treatment. But until that happened, Rupa could not perform the capability she had been so proud of on my previous visit. She was literally incapacitated. After lunch, she lay prostrate on her bed in a loose nightgown. Her stomach was swollen, and she was having a hard time walking.

Despite being prostrate, she kept her phone by her side and answered numerous calls related to cases she was supervising. She wished me to know that she was doing her best to stay abreast of developments: checking in on law enforcement personnel who were managing open cases, conversing with alleged perpetrators, giving abused women directions to Shadheen, and walking through existing cases and next steps with other caseworkers. She admitted that her job wore her out: all the travel, waiting around in heat and sun without access to bathrooms or food, the emotional energy needed to convince women to engage the law and then confront law enforcement personnel. She complained that Shadheen did not pay her enough for her efforts and that she felt underappreciated by those she attempted to help.

Further weighing her down, her own 498A case had hit another snag. Her husband had filed a countersuit alleging Rupa had been unfaithful to him. He was claiming that it was adultery that had led to the dissolution of their marriage, not domestic abuse. Rupa was anxious about the countersuit not because it had any basis but because it would further demand her time and attention. She recognized that the countersuit was, at best, a diversionary tactic and, at worst, a threat to her 498A case. With more than a tinge of sadness in her voice, she sighed that perhaps her life's achievement would be to help other women win their cases. "After trying for so long, I haven't been able to do anything for myself."

Rupa wanted me to spend the afternoon at her place. I had the sense she was lonely with only her son to keep her company during her convalescence. She mentioned the names of people who had visited while she was ill, including Samoli and Sila. Mona had called to check how she was doing. Rupa clearly felt hurt by those who had failed to check in, noting that after so many years of work, you would think people would care that she was ill. As she spoke, I realized that my visit meant more to her than I had realized. This time, I was not there to help boost her social position within the village. She wished to relate to me as a friend, someone who cared about her well-being and was willing to spend time at her side.

When I finally left, she had her son escort me back to the main road. As we walked, the boy chatted about his desire to enroll in a computer course. I encouraged his aspirations, while a small voice in the back of my head wondered if Rupa could afford to send her son to private training programs. My autorickshaw arrived, and I jumped in, waving goodbye to the person who was Rupa's responsibility and her main source of affection. It was a clear day, but I sensed the dark clouds hovering over Rupa's head. Ill, unable to work, cooped up in a house with people who provided little by way of care or attention, with a young son to feed and raise, she worried about the future. It was a future that was uncertain. She might be fine, chalking out a living, acquiring notoriety. Or she might be proven an adulteress rather than a victim of violence, no longer physically capable of helping either herself or other women.

It may seem strange to begin and end this book, a book about women experiencing violence, with Rupa. She appears throughout the chapters in her role as a caseworker at Shadheen. But she was not just a caseworker. She herself had been abused and she was a legal claimant. While her 498A case remained pending, she became proficient enough in the law to secure full-time paid employment at a large and well-respected women's NGO, built a *pakka* bathroom, fought to gain social standing within her village, became friendly with law enforcement personnel, spoke at a prestigious university in Kolkata, appeared on a radio program, and expressed a great deal of pride in her abilities to accomplish so much with limited education. She also struggled with depression and loneliness, encountered violence from men she was helping prosecute, felt exhausted by the hours and physical strain demanded by her job, could not afford treatment for ongoing physical ailments, and worried about what would happen to her and her son when her parents died and her brother kicked her out of their family home.

There was a certain irony as well as a cruelty to Rupa's life. The law had given her nothing it promised. But it had given her a livelihood, social recognition, and self-confidence, all while leaving her physically enfeebled and lonely. This contradiction is not coincidental to the topic of the book: it is its central finding.

"Running a case" forged real capabilities among women who became familiar with and embedded in the institutional landscape surrounding domestic violence claims. These women were able to translate their new knowledge and connections with brokers and law enforcement personnel into meaningful forms of empowerment: jobs, education, social networks, and a sense of self-worth. These are important achievements. For women struggling on the margins of social recognition and poverty, for those who had experienced the long-term psychological effects of intimate abuse, they spelt the difference between an impoverished life (both materially and emotionally) and one that was sustainable and evoked pride.

Empowerment came, however, at a price. First, and perhaps most obviously, if the only way one could get anything out of the law was by wheeling and dealing outside of it, rights were by no means a guarantee but rather a privilege afforded to those with the ability to acquire justice outside the state. Second, wheeling and dealing was exhausting and dangerous. "Running cases" entailed a number of risks that led some women to feel overwhelmed, withdraw, or, similarly to what happened to Brinda and Rupa, get physically attacked in the process of doing the work of the state. Finally, the discourse and practice of capability produced the illusion that those who could not run cases were somehow defective or not up to the task, not fit to survive. Capability, in other words, also created its alter ego, the woman who was "incapable" and undeserving.

Empowerment

In addition to receiving possessions, housing, and money through illicit settlements, women secured jobs, expanded their social networks, went back to school, and developed a sense of self-confidence. Unlike illicit justice, these achievements did not result from negotiations with their abusers. They emerged through sustained engagement with the institutions that surrounded domestic violence allegations, namely brokers and the criminal justice system.

The most perceptible manifestation of this kind of empowerment was to be found in the lives of women like Rupa, Samoli, and Bani. These women experienced intimate violence, contacted various women's organizations looking for help, became familiar with local police and courts, and, in the process of making the rounds of these various institutions, entered training programs that helped them become caseworkers. By becoming embedded in organizations like Shadheen and Andolan, they gained proficiency in the law and women's rights. By getting to know the ins and outs of the criminal justice system, by forging close contacts with police and court clerks, they were able to steer other women's allegations through an overwhelmingly inhospitable bureaucratic environment.

None of these women, need it be reiterated, received rights through the state. But by running their own cases, they did forge a livelihood for themselves where they helped other women run cases.

Illicit justice and empowerment were not mutually exclusive processes: they worked together. Women who negotiated extralegal settlements achieved various forms of empowerment through their illicit endeavors. Najma received a settlement with Samoli's help, while continuing to work with Shadheen on various livelihood development initiatives. Ashu registered a 498A in the hope of negotiating a settlement through Andolan and simultaneously used the organization to convince her family she needed to return to school. Sharmila negotiated a divorce and retrieved pieces of her dowry through a settlement with her ex-husband, while also using her affiliation with AIN to establish a *mahila samiti* in her own neighborhood, an organization she headed and took great pride in. Meanwhile, through her interactions with law enforcement personnel around her 498A case, she met and began an intimate relationship with a police officer. Over time, this relationship evolved to include certain professional dimensions. The police officer introduced women in Sharmila's *mahila samiti* to the police station where he worked.

Empowerment had concrete dimensions, such as jobs, education, and social networks; but it also involved a range of more nebulous, yet life-changing, elements. For Jhumpa, these elements included new emotional attachments, a sense of self-confidence, and what can only be described as a right to the city and its public spaces. In the process of "running a case" (or, in her situation, two formal cases and one parallel), Jhumpa learned to address the police. She forged alliances with the Trinamul Congress Party (TMC) boys at the local club. She navigated public transport so that she could ferry herself to and from AIN, her home, and various government offices. And she arranged a settlement with her husband.

Meanwhile, by becoming affiliated with AIN, she became part of a world where separating from an abusive husband seemed both reasonable and commonplace. AIN's theater troupe and women's network provided a community of other women in her predicament. These women reaffirmed that Jhumpa was not alone in her endeavors. She used her training and connections to AIN to forge her own *mahila samiti* in her neighborhood in south Kolkata. Because she had these broader connections and experiences, she was able to convince other women that she was someone who was "capable" of helping them solve problems.

When I attended one of Jhumpa's *samiti* meetings, I found a group of twenty or so women of low- and lower middle-class backgrounds, settled on the pavement facing the Durga *dalan* of the neighborhood. For readers unfamiliar with the setting, a Durga *dalan* is a permanent stage that is frequently located in the center of Hindu neighborhoods and villages, a place where the statue of the Hindu mother goddess, Durga, resides and where the Durga Pujo is celebrated.[2] It is simultaneously a place of immense social significance as well as a space that offers a legitimate site for a women's gatherings, situated as it is under the watchful eyes of the mother goddess.

Members of the *samiti* came from the brick houses surrounding us as well as the *basti* (a slum) that ringed the borders of the neighborhood. Sitting on jute mats they had spread on the pavement, talking loudly about various issues impacting their domestic lives, they formed a voluble entity in the center of the neighborhood. That day, Jhumpa had brought a young wife who was being beaten by her in-laws to the group to seek advice. She had plans to introduce the woman to the TMC club boys and bring her to meet a caseworker at AIN.

As members in the *mahila samiti* questioned the young woman about her experiences, residents of the area walked by, some saying a polite hello, others looking irritated that the group had gathered in such a prominent place. Dismissing negative reactions, Jhumpa focused on the progress she had made. She remarked how a few years back, none of this would have been possible. People in the neighborhood refused to acknowledge her presence. "Now, you see what I have built?" Other women in the area wanted to join the meetings.

Pointing to a tall, thin man standing against a nearby tree, she smirked. It was her brother-in-law, the man who used to drag Jhumpa through the street by her hair. At that moment, he cut a pathetic figure, stooped and cowering in the distance. "His wife joined my group." Jhumpa gestured again, pointing to a woman with a prominent limp who stood at the edge of the *samiti* gathering. The limp, according to Jhumpa, was her brother-in-law's doing. Nowadays, she would complain about him, and he would stand looking ashamed, cackled Jhumpa with a sense of vindication.

Through the course of the *samiti* meeting, Jhumpa moved with energy and spoke with confidence. Some of this may, of course, have been staged for my benefit. But I noticed that none of the other women looked askance or viewed Jhumpa's behavior as out of the ordinary. The symbolic significance of the events I observed cannot be overstated. A few years back, Jhumpa had been a publicly humiliated and abused woman viewed by others in the neighborhood as an embarrassment best avoided. She was thoroughly disempowered. Others refused to even acknowledge her existence, far from coming to her assistance when she was abused in public. From that position, she had become someone others wanted to know. She had the ability to organize a women's group and attract members. She also had the authority to convene that group not only in public space but at the religious and social center of the neighborhood: in front of the goddess Durga herself. Jhumpa was empowered enough to go so far as to publicly laugh at one of her past abusers and co-opt his wife into her organizational project.

Jhumpa not only felt empowered, she was empowered. Her experiences of
empowerment were significantly gendered. She had become a woman of some
worth. Her ability to do so emanated directly from her own battle against domestic violence and the status it gave her as a woman who could engage the
law, negotiate an extralegal settlement, and boast connections to AIN and the
TMC. Most palpably, she became empowered relative to a man who had violently humiliated her in the past. She turned the tables on him, forcing him to
stand mutely in a corner while she led public discussions of his ill behavior. Also,
she became a woman who others turned to for help, while in the past she had
been a woman in need of help that everyone denied. Finally, and perhaps most
subtly, she became a woman entitled to occupy and inhabit public space, a space
coded as masculine in South Asia.

Some weeks later, I met Jhumpa on one of the side streets of Gariahat in the
late afternoon, once the midday sun had subsided. By the time I arrived, the
street's shop owners were stirring from their post-lunch naps, laying out their
mats, waiting for their afternoon tea to arrive. I eventually spied Jhumpa making
her way down the street. She had brought a friend with her, someone she thought
I should talk to about my research. On the phone, Jhumpa had described her as
someone who had really suffered in her marriage.

Jhumpa looked energetic, wide-eyed, and slightly festive. She had carefully
applied lipstick and eyeliner and donned a bright pink *salwaar kameez* for the
occasion. She seemed comfortable and confident, striding ahead of her friend,
holding her by the hand to guide her over the uneven sidewalk. Her friend, a
short, fair-skinned woman with a heart-shaped face and black-rimmed glasses,
looked slightly overwhelmed by Jhumpa's rapid pace. She was clad in a well-
starched *sari* and took small, dainty steps.

Once we had been introduced and Jhumpa and I had a moment to catch up,
I motioned toward the tea stall at the corner of the street, one adorned with
a canopy and locally known for its brew. I offered to buy the women tea and
biscuits. Jhumpa excitedly agreed. Her friend, however, looked discomfited. "She
is shy about these things," Jhumpa remarked, alluding to the fact that drinking
chai on the street was considered indecent by many women. Jhumpa went on
to explain how they had both been raised in a particular way: straight to school,
straight back home, and then off to a husband's house. After marriage, neither
woman had been allowed out of their marital homes unescorted. "They locked
us in the house. But we ran away!" Jhumpa laughed gleefully. But her expression
soon turned somber. With a distant look in her eyes, she explained how back
in the days when her husband and brother-in-law still beat her, she had never
thought she would be having *chai* on the street.

Something that to me was a simple act, lacking little thought or preparation,
was something entirely less routine and more meaningful for Jhumpa. Drinking

chai at a street stall unaccompanied by male relatives, this act indexed how far she had come. It marked the passage of time and her distance from her friend, a woman who had not yet run a case or forged the comfort with the public sphere legal engagements inculcated. Jhumpa's eager embrace of the *chai* signaled her own capabilities. The dust of the street, its association with men, meant that only an empowered woman could do what she was doing.

Survival of the Fittest

Capability had a way of getting into women's heads. They had their own ways of measuring it, some that were immediately discernible to me as an outside viewer and some that required greater sensitivity: drinking *chai* on the street, organizing a *mahila samiti*, occupying prime realty in the center of the neighborhood, humiliating their abusers in public, displaying social connections to political party cadre and women's rights activists, having an "American" visit their home, building a bathroom, addressing elite students, speaking on the radio, helping other women run cases. While these various forms of empowerment were real, in the sense that they improved women's lives, they were also dangerous. The small, incremental advantages women accrued by "running cases" helped stabilize daily life, while leaving them vulnerable to major shocks.

The discourse and practice of women's capability that arose within the legal institutional landscape surrounding domestic violence was perilous because it *did* have the power to convince and transform. It made new kinds of feminine subjects: women who saw themselves in its image. It created a common sense whereby brokers, law enforcement, and women themselves agreed that it was women's responsibility to move their claims forward. It provided an excuse for the criminal justice system's poor performance, shifting the focus from law enforcement to individual women. And by doing so, it reinforced the false notion that women who fell behind did so because they were simply unfit. Capability helped secure a system that was overwhelmingly stacked against women, setting the terms of legal engagement at an impossibly high level.

The danger of capability, its ability to transform how women thought about their lives and the lives of other women, was evident in Jhumpa's case. By embracing the idea that she was indeed empowered and had come a long way from her past, Jhumpa forgot to criticize the situation in which she found herself. Instead of getting upset and recognizing that she may have been forced to negotiate because her legal cases were taking too long, Jhumpa felt proud that she had arranged a settlement on the side. Instead of wondering why her brother-in-law was still roaming around after beating her and crippling his own wife, she took solace in her ability to laugh at him in public. And by noting her distance from her relatively timid friend, Jhumpa confirmed the notion that it was her friend who needed to overcome her fears and get used to hustling around and confronting various dangers.

Unlike Jhumpa, who remained upbeat about her prospects, Rupa identified the contradictions in her situation. Rupa went so far as to broach a critique, not just of the criminal justice system that refused to recognize her victimhood but also of the nongovernmental organization that paid her a meager salary. But these critiques surfaced only after she became too physically ill to embody the capability she had once cherished. Walking in great duress and unable to bend over, she blamed her present incapacity on her prior attempts to be capable. "You think this job is easy?" she wondered aloud as if answering a question she had posed to herself. It was the strain of running cases, both her own and other women's, that had aggravated her illness, she argued. Lying alone on her bed day after day, Rupa's was forced to confront the holes in the ideology of capability she so cherished.

Rupa's interpretation of her decline was impossible to confirm but plausible given the physical and emotional challenges casework entailed. In the months before she became bedridden, Rupa had finished a blockbuster year, managing the largest number of cases among Shadheen's casework team. She had also been attacked by Brinda's husband. The peak of her illness coincided with the hottest months of the year, when average temperatures hovered around 110 degrees Celsius in West Bengal and rainfall was at a minimum. Working within such conditions was difficult, occasionally life-threatening, for even the healthiest of people.[3] And given the usual routines of casework, which included traveling long distances on crowded, open-air public transport and then waiting around in equally crowded and hot police stations and courts, it was not entirely surprising that Rupa felt that she would be healthier if she had a different lifestyle.

The fact that it took Rupa so long to critique the environment that surrounded her, and within which she had been enmeshed for upward of ten years, shows the power and cunning of capability as a model for women's citizenship. Capability felt empowering and thrilling. In the process of trying to be capable, women lost sight of the dangers their actions posed and the risks to which they were exposed. Critique was muted by the pleasures of being recognized by the state and by brokers, of negotiating illicit settlements, of acting strategically and demonstrating an occasional show of force against people who had previously denigrated them.

Sobha, the low-income Hindu woman who ran a parallel claim with Rupa's help, was seduced by her own capability in the process of doing the work of the state. Sobha, if one needs a reminder, had received the blessings of the police to go retrieve her possessions from her husband's house. Rupa brokered the arrangement months before she fell ill. No official case was registered, but in the absence of formal oversight, the police station sent a constable to supervise the repossession from a distance. Much like the proceedings around Payel's extra-legal repossession in North-24 Parganas, where Bani and members of Andolan's union had provided muscle power and threat, Sobha's repossession went forward under the auspices of Shadheen's caseworkers and self-help group members.

When we arrived at the house, Sobha's husband was away. Sobha's mother-in-law, a woman who had previously hit Sobha and encouraged her son to be abusive, was reduced to meek protests in the face of a sizeable group of aggres-sive women. "These are mine," Sobha shouted, grabbing a metal spatula and shaking it threateningly in her mother-in-law's face. Rupa, who was still healthy and energetic at the time of the events, ordered people around, standing with her hands on her waist in the middle of the house. In the end, Sobha succeeded in repossessing not just her clothing and personal effects but also a sizeable number of household items and several ducks from the backyard. Once loose from their pen, the ducks flew into a nearby pond. The constable overseeing the process ended up chasing after the ducks and getting himself completely wet.

According to Sobha and Rupa, the operation was a smashing success. Sobha had her possessions, and Rupa had pulled off yet another intervention. While narrating the events to an audience at Shadheen, the two women could not stop laughing at the constable's antics. Knee-deep in water, trying to grab a slippery duck, the constable's visible ineptitude made the women feel adept in compar-ison. Both Sobha and Rupa were exhilarated by their accomplishments.

"It was very quick," Sobha noted, comparing the extralegal repossession to the possibility of a long withdrawn legal case. While Rupa did not say it out loud, she also found the parallel claim to be fortuitous: it proved with great force that she as an individual, powerful caseworker could do whatever she wanted. The repossession helped spread not just Shadheen's name but her own. This is why she had readily volunteered her services for the undertaking without informing Dolly or Madhavi, her supervisors, of what was about to happen.

Sobha's and Rupa's sense of empowerment emerged within an institutional landscape that encouraged women to be assertive, "active," and to get what they could by whatever means were at their disposal. This landscape made capa-bility not just tolerable but in the seeming interest of individual women who were able to embody it. Sobha and Rupa readily, and rather eagerly, accepted their responsibilities as administrators of the justice the state promised but refused to guarantee. These responsibilities could have gone seriously wrong, exposing both women to danger. But because everything went in their favor, the experience produced a surge of endorphins, filling them with a sense of their own power and competence. Neither women acknowledged that perhaps they should not be having to take such risks while a police officer stood safely at a dis-tance. They sensed the danger involved and reveled in their ability to overcome it. Instead of feeling resentful at the police, they identified the constable as a vulnerable and slightly inept ally who needed *their* help.

Rupa would later wonder about these ventures but only after she was attacked by Brinda's husband. It was when they were harmed by their attempts to be capable that women questioned the terms on which they could chalk out a life for themselves outside of a violent relationship. To my knowledge, Sobha never reached that place. Like Jhumpa, who felt her life was on track, for the time being, everything seemed to have worked in Sobha's favor.

Women like Jhumpa and Sobha, those who did not experience any major failures, tended to explain other women's setbacks as being a result of personal deficiencies. Sobha summed it up neatly when I asked why she was always so optimistic. "I've always been this way. A lot of girls, they like to complain. But they are weak. They aren't able to do anything themselves." Sobha clearly believed that she had gotten where she had not because she was lucky but because she possessed innate qualities other women lacked. Other women got discouraged and complained because they were unfit. She was brave enough and hardy enough to do what was necessary to have a better life.

Explanations of women's incapacities abounded when someone returned to an abusive relationship. Madhura, who had been so violently attacked by the thugs Ashok hired, dropped her case weeks after Shadheen's caseworkers worked so hard to get the case registered. She stopped picking up phone calls and simply vanished. Jhinuk called her incessantly but Madhura's phone remained switched off. Namita, Rupa, and Samoli began a concerted search for her, drawing on all their contacts in the villages that surrounded Shadheen's office. Everyone at the organization was terrified that Ashok had killed Madhura or that he had kidnapped her, taken her phone, and was holding her hostage.

Sila finally heard rumors through her contacts. It appeared that Madhura had left the district, traveled to an aunt's house in another part of the state to get away from Ashok. Everyone sighed in collective relief and interpreted Madhura's disappearance as an attempt to protect herself from retaliation. Assured of Madhura's physical safety, caseworkers continued to wonder how to reach her and what to do about the police report she had filed. They could not move forward without her. Ashok might use Madhura's absence as a way to discredit the allegations. This stalemate continued for another couple of weeks, with Dolly, Mona, and the casework team still hopeful that Madhura would return once she felt safe again. But Sila's intelligence provided a different story. After weeks of absence, Madhura had resurfaced in Ashok's company. They were in a relationship again.

Nobody knew what to make of the situation, grasping at various explanations. Mona's anxiety that Madhura had been forced under threat of further violence to return to Ashok was quickly dismissed. According to Sila's informants, Madhura looked happy and well fed and had taken to giving herself airs, talking disparagingly to her neighbors again. In light of this information, Madhavi intimated that she had known from the very beginning that Madhura did not have what it takes to run a case. "Didn't I say it then? Will this girl really be able to run a case?" Madhura was incapable of driving a case forward, and her return to Ashok proved it.

Rupa agreed with Madhavi's assessment, mentioning that Madhura was weak-willed. "At every step, the girl was of two minds." Sila snorted when I asked her opinion, explaining that it was all about money. Her contacts had told her that Madhura was walking arm in arm with Ashok wearing an expensive *sari*. Sila raised her eyebrows in distaste to let me know what she thought of Madhura's character. Jhinuk and Namita sided with Sila, calling Madhura "naughty." She had "used" the NGO's services just like she "used" Ashok for money.

Aside from Mona, who continued to worry about the constraints that might have forced Madhura to return to a violent man, everyone else at the NGO was angry at Madhura for wasting their time. They reasoned that she had withdrawn the charges because she was innately deficient: either because she lacked the ability to work hard and drive a case forward or because she was indecisive and greedy. The failure of the case was Madhura's fault. It was not the fault of a state which failed to protect her from retaliation. Nor was it the fault of Shadheen for pushing her into an adversarial legal case without providing her with a place to stay or any form of supervision. Nor was it the fault of the society that surrounded Madhura, one which provided young, poor women with very few financial or social options and which castigated them no matter what kinds of decisions they made. The discourse and practice of capability gave birth to the false idea that it was women's individual inabilities that caused problems, not the institutional and structural forces that made women's lives so difficult.

The fact was that "running a case" was hard. It was not easy to be "capable" in the way brokers and criminal justice institutions demanded, especially for low-income women with little education, limited social networks, and few financial options outside marriage. Running hither and thither trying to pressure law enforcement personnel, gather evidence, and negotiate extralegal deals: all of this was completely exhausting and overwhelming. Mona, who was older and had seen many women come and go from Shadheen, understood the challenges. Rupa, after falling ill, finally admitted it. Capability drove some women to give up. If this is what it took to get ahead, better to withdraw. Survival itself became a burden given the conditions under which it had to be eked out.

Brinda, the low-income, lower-caste, nearly illiterate woman who approached Shadheen for help after being abused and trafficked by her husband, gave up on running a case. She decided to withdraw the First Information Report registered under 498A after that fateful evening when she was attacked by her husband and his relatives. To Shadheen's credit, everyone respected her decision and left her alone, perhaps because Rupa herself had been injured in the confrontation. For a few weeks, Brinda continued working quietly in Shadheen's sewing unit but no longer wished to discuss her case or talk about her husband. "What option does a girl like that have," Mona sadly remarked. "There is a limit to what we can do [to help women access the law]. She has to first stay alive." But survival, it would seem, was not something Brinda necessarily wanted. Shortly before I left West Bengal, Brinda was admitted to the hospital after a suicide attempt. She was badly burnt. She had lost the use of one her hands, and her once beautiful face was covered in pink scabs. When I asked what had happened, she simply remarked that "staying alive is difficult."

12

Conclusion

Capability Without Rights

Six years before I started my research in West Bengal and some 1,240 km to the southwest, the central Indian city of Nagpur erupted in protest. Two hundred poor, Dalit women from a slum entered an open courtroom. Once inside, they confronted a mob boss by the name of Akku Yadav (Nandgaonkar 2004). Yadav had allegedly raped and tortured many of the women in the room, using sexual violence to extort money from slum residents for over ten years. But he was never charged for any of his offenses, having bribed and threatened local police to do his bidding. That day, he was on trial for other crimes. His victims seized the opportunity to dole out the punishment they believed he deserved. Grabbing him from police custody, they collectively stabbed him, rubbed chili powder into his wounds, and castrated him. Yadav later died from his injuries (Ramesh 2004).

The police did nothing to stop the violence in the courtroom that day. Later, they made a feeble attempt to arrest five of the so-called ringleaders. But their plans quickly backfired. Central parts of the city came to a standstill. Women's organizations, civil society groups, and a number of political parties clogged the streets and engaged in a *dharna* (civil disobedience involving fasting and sitting until one's demands are met). They were not protesting on Yadav's behalf. They supported the women who had killed him. After unsuccessfully battling popular unrest, the police released the five women and dropped all charges.

Some of the women involved in the killing went on to receive funding from the Indian government as well as the Clinton Global Initiative. They used the money to establish a women's organization, the Kasturba Nagar Community Project, in their slum. One of their leaders, Usha Narayan, became a transnational women's rights icon. She gained support from several nonprofit groups, including the M. Night Shyamalan Foundation. And she was featured in Nikolas Kristof and Sheryl WuDunn's emancipatory narrative about women's empowerment in the global south (Kristof and WuDunn 2009).

Capable Women, Incapable States. Poulami Roychowdhury, Oxford University Press 2021. © Oxford University Press
DOI: 10.1093/oso/9780190881894.001.0001

Why end with this story? What does this event have to do with this book? Like the cities and villages of West Bengal, Nagpur had the same dangerous cocktail of gender-based violence and state neglect. An incapacitated, sexist, and corrupt criminal justice system did very little to enforce women's rights, refusing for ten years to help lower-caste, poor women experiencing horrific levels of abuse. But law enforcement personnel also did little to prevent those very same women from taking over sovereign functions. The police claimed they were afraid to intervene in the courtroom in case the women turned around and attacked them.

Furthermore, the political dynamics of gendered violence in Nagpur brought together a cast of characters and juxtapositions similar to those present in West Bengal. Nongovernmental organizations (NGOs), political parties, and neighborhood associations in Nagpur provided associational strength to women who, after years of withstanding abuse and state neglect, collectively organized and took the law into their own hands. And their violent usurpation of the law provided a pathway toward social recognition, financial resources, and a modicum of physical and personal safety in their daily lives.

What happened in Nagpur in 2004 thus represents an extreme example of phenomena I have traced throughout these pages. It highlights how women claim rights against gendered abuses in India and showcases the pervasive and intimate linkages between illegality, violence, and the law. Meanwhile, my work in West Bengal allows us to conceptualize events like Nagpur not as exceptional affairs but as part of a broader pattern of governance. By encouraging women to administer the law, the Indian criminal justice system provides an avenue toward diverse capabilities rather than rights per se. And this situation is visible both in the routine, unpublicized regulation of domestic violence in West Bengal and in the spectacular, transnationally visible execution of a rapist in Nagpur.

Incorporation and Capability

How do women negotiate rights against violence in India and with what consequences? How do law enforcement personnel respond to their claims? The central finding of this book is that women negotiate rights in India not by performing victimhood but by becoming "capable": deploying collective threats and doing the work of the state themselves. They do so because law enforcement personnel do not protect the virtuous but *do* feel threatened by organized women. As a result, rights negotiations do not necessarily lead to better enforcement or more woman-friendly legal outcomes. Instead, they allow some women to make gains outside the law: repossess property and children, negotiate cash settlements, join women's groups, access paid employment, develop a sense of self-assurance, and become more active members of the public sphere.

Indian law enforcement personnel govern gendered violence by "incorporating" organized women into regulatory functions. They encourage these women to be assertive and do their work for them: gather evidence, fill out paperwork, round up witnesses, deliver subpoenas. When that fails or seems beyond reach, they tell women to run parallel claims outside the law, providing supervision from a distance and allowing women to acquire housing, property, and children outside formal legal channels. Incorporation, a tactic of governance, is distinct from state protection, the concept that dominates existing theorizations of law and gender violence. When law enforcement personnel incorporate women, they are not using legal measures to impose social control. Neither are they basing their responses to women's claims on the degree to which they think the woman in question fits hegemonic definitions of appropriate femininity. They are doing something quite different.

Law enforcement "incorporated" women because they felt disempowered by the conditions that surrounded them. They reasoned they could neither enforce the law nor afford to alienate women with organizational resources. They were highly attentive to women's organizational connections, rather than their gendered performances per se. Even when they felt sympathetic toward docile, passive women, they told them to remain silent and return home. To women who effectively disrupted and threatened their livelihood, personal safety, and daily routines, they turned over the reins of justice. This governmental regime was not organized around saving virtuous women, reordering private relationships, or managing problem populations. It was marked by a concerted lack of control, an unwillingness to regulate interpersonal violence, and an outsourcing of state functions to politically mobilized civilians.

By incorporating organized women, law enforcement personnel demanded and engendered "capability" among women. To move forward within this landscape, women learned to be assertive, to get things done, and, at times, to be downright violent themselves. They mobilized support, expanded their political and social networks, learned about the public sphere, figured out the inner workings of criminal and civil law, confronted their abusers. If they hoped to survive, they learned not to be meek but to be "active." Sitting back and waiting for the state to rescue them was not an option because the rescue team never came. The only pathway toward some form of safety involved capability: taking the law into their own hands and completing the hard work that incapable and unwilling state officials refused to complete.

Registering cases; showing up to court; talking to the police; spending time with caseworkers, women's right activists, and political party cadre; negotiating extralegal settlements; threatening abusers and in-laws: all of these discrete acts made up "running a case." And each act required a set of aptitudes that forced women to orient away from the subjectivity required to "run a family." The women who managed to complete these tasks came to think of themselves differently. Through a new set of reiterative practices in and around the law, they re-envisioned who they were as women. And this re-envisioning highlighted courage, resourcefulness, financial and emotional independence.

Capability's Advantages and Perils

As numerous scholars have pointed out, state protection for "good victims" casts women in a subservient role, not as agents capable of changing their circumstances but as docile creatures needful of state largesse (Young 2003). In order to be protected by the state, you have to live up to heteronormative notions of femininity: act chaste, meek, virtuous (Bumiller 1987; Kapur 2002; Minow 1992). Aggressive behavior, anger, and self-defense are not allowed. The victim identity is not just restrictive and difficult to emulate; it systematically discriminates against minorities and marginalized women. No matter what really happened or how they actually behaved, women who are poor, undocumented, racial minorities, trans, or queer are rarely deemed "good victims" (Crenshaw 1991; Freedman 2013; Incite! 2007; Razack 2004; Seal 2010).

For women negotiating rights, relating to the criminal justice system as a "capable" woman was preferable to performing victimhood in three important ways. First, to be a good victim, one has to look helpless, frail, and passive. But it is difficult to be all of those things and put up an effective legal battle. Women are punished for being too assertive, even though defending oneself from violence and pursuing legal rights require a great deal of assertiveness (Maguigan 1991; Shepard and Pence 1999). By becoming capable, the women I met eluded this trap. Their performances emphasized aggression, perseverance, and resourcefulness as meaningful forms of feminine conduct. These are the very qualities one needs to leave a violent situation and to "run a case." And in this way, women who learned to be "capable" experienced less of a gap between the discursive demands of the law and its actual operative practices.

Second, to a certain degree, marginalized women could hope to be convincingly capable in a way they could not necessarily pretend to be helpless or meek. Unlike the good victim, a subject position that demands the gentility and innocence of privilege, capability calls for the kind of resourcefulness that women of disadvantaged backgrounds may be better socialized to inhabit. This shift in focus created openings for low-income, lower-caste, Muslim women: women who might have had little access to state recognition under a model of virtuous victimhood.

Marginalized women also had a shot at becoming capable because, unlike victimhood, capability was *not* an individual status. Working with survivors of violence in a very different time and place, Sally Merry noted how making a legal claim is a difficult decision for women because it forces them to choose between two very different gendered subjectivities: a socially embedded subjectivity, where their relation to the outside world is mediated by kinship, and an individual legal subjectivity, where they stand alone in relation to the state (Merry 2003). Capable women did not stand alone before the state. They were only able to stand and be acknowledged because of their organizational references. Women became capable by demonstrating their social and political connections, becoming embedded in various organizations, and engaging in disruptive behavior. Organizations gave underprivileged women a leg to stand on. Without organized support, they were invisible to the state. But with it, they were granted a modicum of consideration.

Finally, in the process of becoming capable, women accessed real skills and resources. They joined women's organizations, formed friendships, gained a working knowledge of the public sphere and the criminal justice system, and confronted and worked with law enforcement personnel. Some women used these opportunities to secure paid jobs, expand their social networks, and negotiate illicit settlements. Even the ability to pursue extralegal concessions can be interpreted as a positive achievement. Sobha and Payel, both low-income, lower-caste women with limited education, pursued parallel claims that provided access to valuable material goods. And they did so under the unofficial aegis of the police. The importance of these gains cannot be overstated, especially for women who exist at the margins of subsistence.

Despite its advantages, becoming "capable" proved to be a double-edged sword for women. Women who tried to be capable had to work hard and take significant social and physical risks. These acts were seductive, generating an ephemeral sense of empowerment that at times was disconnected from the reality and harshness of their lives. The notion that they were "capable" encouraged women to think that doing the work of the state was a reasonable way to escape violence. After all, they had fought to attain this position. Not every woman was met with such regard. The other option was being silenced and told to go away. Incorporation was an achievement and capability its reward. Or, at least, that was the idea even when being capable entailed danger and uncertainty.

Simply becoming capable by no means assured a woman full and equal citizenship based on substantive rights under the law. Rather, capability was all women got out of waging legal battles. They rarely received rights. And not all of them were equally positioned to acquire even that. Gathering evidence, rounding up witnesses, threatening people who abused you, having the courage to disagree with law enforcement personnel, grabbing your possessions without explicit help from the criminal justice system: exceptionally lucky women carried off such initiatives. Others could not.

When placed alongside the disadvantages women already faced, the need to be capable was at times counterproductive and cruel. To be "capable," women had to shoulder a new burden of responsibility, work, and physical hazard on top of all the vulnerability they already experienced. Becoming capable did not guarantee that any given individual would lead a safer life. Nor did capability as a framework for women's identities necessarily enhance gender equality. The social world that made women disproportionately vulnerable to violence, unable to exit violent situations, unable to attain jobs, and unable to live outside heterosexual, heteronormative families remained relatively unchanged.

When state officials assess worthiness through the trope of victimhood, women are forced to perform docility and incapacity in exchange for entitlements. Meanwhile, when state officials recognize and valorize capability, women are forced to fall back on their own organizational, social, and financial resources— no matter how meager those resources may be. In this sense, marginalized women had a tough time becoming capable. While they may have been socialized to act assertive and able to join the kinds of associations that could provide a modicum of legibility, by dint of their social status, marginalized women had fewer of the other kinds of resources needed to act capable. It is telling that among my research sample women who were educated, middle-class, and from Hindu, upper-caste backgrounds tended to make the most of "running cases." They also disproportionately lived in urban areas. This included Koel, Sharmila, Ashu, Uma, and Riya. Meanwhile, those who suffered the most from running cases or had to settle a case quickly were poor, uneducated, lower-caste, Muslim, and lived in villages. This included Madhura, Brinda, Sabiha, and Najma.

Finally, the discourse of women's capability provided an excuse for the criminal justice system's continued poor performance. Discussing alternative forms of marriage regulation, Gopika Solanki (2011) has argued that the Indian state's shared adjudication model with religious and other societal groups can help balance cultural rights with gender equality. But this is not the story I have documented here. Here, law enforcement personnel actively delegated authority to women to escape their own obligations. The discourse of women's capability allowed a defensive and weak state to preserve itself against disgruntled and organized civilians while maintaining a semblance of order and political legitimacy.

Neither does the story of women's capability in this book mirror Amartya Sen's theorizations. For Sen, capabilities are what people come to have when their rights are recognized and assured by democratically accountable states (Sen 1999). But in the halls and offices of the Indian criminal justice system, "capability" was not the product of rights. It was an alternative to rights. The discourse of women's capability provided a convenient way for law enforcement personnel to contain and manage rights assertions. By allowing women to register cases, by encouraging them to illegally regain possessions, state officials appeared more responsive and supportive than they had in the past. But they allowed women to engage the law only if they did not have to lift more than the proverbial finger. Women were welcome to lead lives free of violence if they themselves were able to regulate and control the violence that victimized them.

Theoretical Extensions

What can the Indian case tell us about how and why law enforcement personnel govern gendered violence in the way they do? Developing, postcolonial democracies, where social movements confront weakly institutionalized states, are where we are most likely to find incorporation and capability. In these contexts, rule of law is contested, and state officials are forced to compromise with civilians in ways that redistribute authority and undermine their own monopoly over violence (Chavez 2003; Cheesman 2015).

Similar to my findings, studies of Latin America and South Africa show how law enforcement personnel manage everything from interpersonal violence to powerful drug cartels through processes that closely resemble incorporation. Faced with crime, they do not intervene or impose social control. Rather, they form contingent alliances with local actors and allow civilians to duke it out themselves (Gordon 2019; Steinberg 2008; Tuckman 2019).

Meanwhile, civilians who live in these areas become similarly capable as the women in my field site: working strategically with law enforcement to find localized solutions to security and rights (Goldstein 2012). They negotiate rights by approaching the state through organizations with established records for disruption and violence. They do this because collective strength is the only way to be taken seriously by the state (Holston 2008; Houtzager et al. 2002; Paret 2015; Super 2016; Willis 2015). And the end result is not necessarily rights per se but a range of aptitudes and a modicum of safety that demands their own labor and creativity (Auyero and Berti 2016).

While developing postcolonial democracies are most likely to house the institutional and political conditions conducive to incorporation and capability, post-welfare countries may not be immune to these governmental strategies or citizenship practices. Post-welfare states also suffer from capacity constraints. And they house marginalized social groups who are politically active and fed up with state negligence.

Incorporation shares boundaries with documented processes of devolution where state officials govern at a distance and "empower" lower-level authorities, nonstate actors, and citizens with decision-making responsibilities and resources (Barry et al. 1996; Burchell 1996; Cooke and Kothari 2001; Leve and Karim

2001). Meanwhile, capabilities mirror broader discourses of "participation" and "responsibilization" where civilians are told to be responsible for their own personal safety and manage social conflict (Cruikshank 1999; Ferguson and Gupta 2002; Hindess 2010; O'Malley 2004). Private prisons, citizens' watches, and state support for local militias in the United States and Canada provide concrete examples of these broader governmental initiatives (Garland 2012; Hannah-Moffat 2010; Rose 2000; Simon and Feeley 2003).

As a result, the landscape for incorporation and capability may traverse academic classifications of post-welfare/postcolonial, developing/developed. A more accurate read of the possibilities could take governance voids into account as well as the existence of organized groups that yield a certain authority over violence. In poor, urban areas of the United States, for example, we find extensive "legal cynicism": a historically and socially constructed distrust of legal authority that emerges from generations of neglect and violation at the hands of law enforcement personnel (Kirk and Matsuda 2011). This distrust motivates practices of self-help where residents simultaneously contain and deploy interpersonal violence to settle disputes and terrorize opponents (Anderson 2000; Contreras 2013; Vargas 2016).

These spaces, while enclosed by states with relatively higher capacities, are ripe for the kinds of practices I found. Law enforcement personnel who work under such conditions may come to behave similarly to those who feature on these pages, throwing up their hands and claiming they are disempowered and unable to enforce the law and then reassigning governmental duties to civilians. Similarly, marginalized people who seek redress against violence may, in the process of interacting with the institutions around them, come to re-envision themselves as "capable" of managing social conflict and interpersonal violence themselves.

The Possibility of Rights

The stories in this book highlight three points about the relationship between rights and enforcement capacity. First, strong states are not uniquely able to abuse and violate civilians. Weak state capacity can also lead to dramatic instances of governmental abuse and rightlessness. The Indian criminal justice system's neglect, its inability and unwillingness to enforce rights, creates serious challenges for social justice. Second, where rights are not enforced, civilians behave in ways that further undermine enforcement. Many of the women in this book actively and, at times, quite eagerly tried to be "capable." They found capability to be the only sensible way forward given the context in which they found themselves. Finally, state officials' coping strategies further limit their abilities to administer rights. On a case-by-case basis, incorporation provided a solution for managing and containing legal claims. But when aggregated, the various acts of incorporation taking place in different corners of the criminal justice system undermined women's access to state-based compensation and restitution by further dispersing sovereignty and authority outside the state.

What should be done about these entanglements? What needs to happen in order for women to actually secure rights against violence in contexts where criminal justice institutions remain sexist and incapacitated? One possible "solution" to the issues I have traced on these pages is to make the Indian criminal justice system more capable. This is the direction scholars focused on access to justice often recommend (Rhode 2004; Risse et al. 2013). And there is something important here that cannot be dismissed. If part of the problem with the Indian criminal justice system is that there are not enough police or judges or protection officers and they are not well compensated or well trained, women could have a better chance at securing rights if the Indian government took crime prevention more seriously and budgeted for crime control.

Another way forward is to go in the opposite direction. Here, the problem that needs solving is not state capacity but rights as a framework for women's emancipation. This is the direction many postcolonial scholars take. Since rights are not a forum for legal neutrality, formal equality, or objectivity, let us get rid of them. Narrow legal definitions exclude the complexity of human experience (Smart 2002). And the exclusions become more pronounced in postcolonial spaces where the public/private distinction does not govern social life, and as a result, state regulation of ostensibly "private" affairs often leads to greater rigidity and inflexibility than when these practices are governed by nonstate legal institutions (Menon 2004).

A variation of the postcolonial critique of rights is visible in Gayatri Spivak's (2004) notion that "responsibilities" are a more salient category than rights in the South Asian context. It is also evident in Ratna Kapur's (2005) claim that legal statutes against sexual violence fail to gain traction in India because they frame notions of consent and violation in terms of a liberal discourse that contradicts popular understandings.

I am not a fan of either of these solutions. The alternative to the situation in India today is neither a state with a complete and total monopoly over violence nor a state where there are no rights to fight over. Let me be clear about what I mean. Those who argue for enhanced state capacity seem to forget that very capable criminal justice systems evidence their own distortions. In fact, the comparative case that motivated this book—the United States—provides a model of a frighteningly "capable" criminal justice system. And as we know from extensive documentation, the capability of that institution has by no means been a friend to women facing violence.

American law enforcement personnel systematically use their capabilities to terrorize sex workers and low-income women of color, arresting them instead of the men who abuse them. They violently impose social control and engineer a gendered, racialized, and classed order where select women are awarded rights while others are not, all depending on the whims and ideologies of the police officer or judge who happens to preside over their complaint.

The one advantage women in India have over their American counterparts is that they can, from time to time and with the right organizational resources, overpower and frighten law enforcement into taking them seriously. The events at Nagpur, terrifying and symptomatic as they are of the gross violation poor, lower-caste women face, are also electrifying because of the violence and retribution those same women eventually unleashed. An event of that nature is unimaginable in the United States, partly because two hundred women armed with kitchen knives would have a very difficult time confronting the armed authority of American police. A capable state forcing women to be good victims and disentitling them at will is not preferable to an incapable state forcing women to be capable and abandoning them to deprivation and retaliation.

Meanwhile, the postcolonial critique of rights places too much faith on local, community-level solutions to women's issues at the behest of state-based remedies. Given the history of women's oppression at the hands of their own communities, this alternative appears to be one of taking women out of the frying pan and dumping them straight into the fire. The postcolonial critique of rights also leaves one wondering why the law matters at all to so many people. How do we understand the appeal and charisma of the law in a context of citizen distrust and delivery failures? What explains the resilience of rights in these conditions?

Within India, it is not just women facing violence but a range of social groups who appeal to the state using a language of rights. This includes informal workers seeking protections as citizens and Dalits and Adivasis making claims on land and natural resources (Agarwala 2008; Kumar and Kerr 2012; Nilsen 2013; Subramanian 2009). Outside India, we find a similar coalescence around the law and rights as markers of meaningful political exchange between states and citizens. An ever-expanding list of governments ascribe to and adopt human rights standards (Ackerman 1997; Klug 2011). The law pervades politics and popular culture not just in India but in a growing number of countries that suffer from similar, if not more extreme, forms of lawlessness.

One way of explaining the appeal of rights in these contexts is to note, as Jean and John Comaroff do, that the law mediates ever-growing inequalities spawned by neoliberalism. Citizens seek an impartial arbiter to make sense of the confusion and difficulty of everyday life, and the law promises to be such an arbiter (Comaroff and Comaroff 2008). An alternate explanation of the law's uses foregrounds dark political forces. Rights may be a tool in the rise of what Achille Mbembe (2001) refers to as the third, and most nefarious, political configuration in postcolonial societies: necropolitics. The appeal of rights, in this vision, has to do with their instrumentality in advancing various forms of oppressive and exclusionary majoritarian politics (Vishnupad 2017).

Recent events in India, namely the rise of Hindutva and its elected representation in the unprecedented two-term parliamentary majority of the Bharatiya Janata Party (BJP)–led government of Narendra Modi, make this last possibility worthy of careful consideration. Modi's government is aggressively pursuing a project of "legal" warfare against protestors and minorities, especially Muslims. In August 2019, Modi revoked the special status of Jammu and Kashmir. Then in December 2019, his government passed the Citizenship Amendment Act (CAA), which excludes Muslims from becoming naturalized citizens of India, and the National Register of Citizens (NRC), which disproportionately targets Muslims for disenfranchisement (Kesavan 2019). Meanwhile, BJP-led state governments have cracked down on peaceful protestors by appealing to "due process" and "rule of law" (Mathur 2020). These various policy changes highlight how legal mechanisms are used to exclude and repress.

The appeal that rights held in my field site was partly, but not fully, explicable through these theories. Women did pursue rights because their lives were shaped by vast inequalities, though to what degree those inequalities can be blamed on neoliberalism is hard to say. Simultaneously, domestic violence law also proved to be a mechanism of nefarious political agendas. Brokers used women's rights as a platform to advance their own political interests, while law enforcement personnel encouraged women's legal engagements to strengthen their shaky position. But the law's appeal did not just have to do with these forces. The women in this study as well as the brokers who supported their claims found rights appealing because rights provided one of the only available avenues toward some form of political power and social justice.

First, people pursued rights because it made them proximate to the state. Showing up with a police officer, even without an official case and even when that officer stood at a distance, was better than showing up without an officer. The officer's presence changed the meaning and validity of extrajudicial seizures, providing social credibility to those carrying out the act. If you could get the state on your side, however reluctantly and however minimally, you had a compelling ally. The presence of the state helped frighten foes and elicit consent among possible sympathizers.

Rights are appealing because *even* in weak institutional environments the state yields what Pierre Bourdieu (1994) identified as a "meta" power. Despite massive delivery failures, ordinary Indians continue to see the state as the ultimate guarantor of positive freedoms and welfare (Sundar 2011). A weak state is better than no state. And a weak state still provides a kind of protection and legitimacy that other institutions in the territory (be it an NGO or a thug) have difficulty supplying.

Second, rights are appealing because they can, under certain circumstances, serve as a tool of justice. As Thomas Blom Hansen (2017) has already noted, the people in India who *consistently* appeal to constitutional principles and the rule of law are left-leaning activists and minorities who have been historically oppressed: Dalits, tribals, Muslims, and women. The social basis of who is consistently demanding legal rights indicates that rights may, optimistically enough, provide oppressed people an opportunity to improve their conditions.

Here, it is important to remember that against the tide of xenophobic, discriminatory mobilization of the Hindu Right, countervailing forces continue to use the language of rights as bases of inclusion. Repeated protests on college campuses against the CAA and NRC have accompanied a continuous 24/7 sit-in protest against Modi's government organized by women who live in Shaheen Bagh, New Delhi (Gauri 2020). On January 8, 2020, an estimated quarter-billion Indians went on strike. In what may be the largest strike in world history, workers protested Modhi's "anti-worker," "anti-people" policies, calling for equality and rights under the law (MacLeod 2020).

For women facing violence, legal rights were at times useful in imperfect and unexpected ways. Turning to the law, feeling entitled to make a legal claim, these acts formed the basis of women's recognition of themselves as people who deserved something better than they had. This self-recognition was individually oriented. But it was also a collective achievement, forged in dialogue with rights activists and brokers, through emerging relationships with other women with similar experiences, and through direct confrontations with law enforcement personnel. Rights were not guaranteed. One had to work hard and take risks to try and attain them. Sometimes this struggle paid off, though not necessarily in the ways one expected, and sometimes it left women exhausted and despondent.

By foregrounding the limited, yet important possibilities of rights, this book conceptualizes the domain of the legal in a way that pushes against popular views of rights put forward by both legal formalism and legal realism (Unger 1982). In my field site, the law neither reflected objective rules and procedures nor did it simply disguise domination. Rather, it provided a site where unequal social actors with competing interests confronted each other and forged compromises. The law was a strategic network-based enterprise that involved ceaseless negotiation. Negotiation was necessary because the law *was* porous to politics, including the politics of the underprivileged. Politics was at the center of how laws worked, what governance looked like on the ground, and how gendered identities and practices evolved in relation to the state.

If enhancing state capacity on its own cannot improve this current stalemate and if getting rid of the rights framework altogether undercuts women's ability to negotiate in the first place, then how do we move forward? Here it seems to me that the simple answer is also the most difficult to attain: a concerted effort to attack the social inequality that gives rise to violence against women. It is this inequality that makes criminal justice solutions necessary in the first place, while rendering the very administrators of the law biased and hostile toward women's claims.

Attacking social inequality obviously means dismantling patriarchal domination: certain men's ability to terrorize women. But in India, it also requires a lot of other steps. It demands a dissolution not just of patrilocal marriage but of the compulsory nature of heterosexual marriage. Women should be allowed to live alone or love other women. It also entails getting rid of son preference and the social devaluation of girl children. It requires women's access to employment and equal pay, education, and access to secure housing and natural resources, such as clean water. It demands solutions to landlessness, poverty, and increasing income inequality. It means getting rid of the caste system, Brahmanical hegemony, and pervasive and institutionalized discrimination against Muslims and Adivasi populations. Without sustained social transformation, pumping more resources into law enforcement personnel or replacing rights with alternate frameworks may prove quite disastrous.

SECTION IV

APPENDICES

Appendix A

METHODOLOGICAL DISCUSSION

The data presented in this book comes from two sources: participant observation and in-depth interviews. Three sets of actors served as research participants: women experiencing violence, individuals and organizations that helped them (caseworkers from nongovernmental organizations [NGO], women's rights activists, members of *mahila samiti*, labor unions, private individuals, politicians, criminals), and law enforcement personnel (police, protection officers, court clerks, judges).

A qualitative analysis was indispensable to my research goals. Law and society scholars have shown that the gap between "law in books" and "law in action" is relatively axiomatic. This gap is large indeed in India. Data available through the National Crime Records Bureau and the National Judicial Data Grid lacks key pieces of information (such as how many allegations of violence do not become registered complaints). Basic features of crime statistics, such as the recorded number of First Information Reports, rely on self-reporting from police stations, many of which simply fail to report (Puri 2016). Data quality is compromised by the very institutional conditions that shape rights administration: the limited capacities of the criminal justice system. Law enforcement personnel routinely ignore procedural scripts, and civilians pursue illicit tactics.

If both law enforcement personnel and the people they govern are doing things that are not recorded, it was only by observing everyone that I could hope to learn what they were actually up to. Ethnography allowed me to understand *how* law enforcement personnel administer women's rights, including all of the processes they have a vested interest in keeping off the record, and *how* women claim rights, including via illicit means. While interview data helped me understand research subjects' discursive framings, ethnography allowed me to observe how they actually behaved (Jerolmack and Khan 2014; Khan and Jerolmack 2013).

West Bengal as a Case

I based my study in the state of West Bengal. To what degree does this state tell us about what may or may not be going on in other parts of the country? West Bengal, after all, is one state in a relatively diverse country. It is a fiercely politicized place, with a long history of mass mobilization and political party formation that began with the troublesome movements the British tried to escape by relocating their imperial capital to Delhi. More recently, this political culture has encompassed strong women's movements which focus on gendered violence. West Bengal is also notoriously weakly institutionalized. Criminal justice institutions suffer a range of infrastructural constraints. District courts and local police stations are in poor shape, and the state government has refused to appoint the appropriate number of protection officers.

Yet, despite West Bengal's distinct character and unique history, it is comparable to other parts of India. First, political mobilization against gendered violence actually has a longer history in other states (John 2019). Women's rights in West Bengal were historically subsumed under the Communist Party of India (Marxist)'s broader economic agendas. Until recently, violence was sidelined by a class-centered vision of social justice. In Mumbai and Delhi, by contrast, women's organizing was from its inception freer of communist control and more able to focus on violence (Ray and Katzenstein 2005). And Mumbai and Delhi are by no means the only places where we find active women's networks and organizations that focus on violence. Some of the largest groups exist in rural north India, including the Gulabi Gang, whose estimated 400,000 members spans Uttar Pradesh (Biswas 2007).

Just as we find similar political formations around women's rights in other parts of the country, West Bengal's institutional landscape proves to be comparable to other states. Along a number of measures of criminal justice capacity, from personnel to salaries, West Bengal emerges close to or slightly below all-India averages. Certain parts of India, of course, fare significantly worse than West Bengal, including the aforementioned state of Uttar Pradesh (National Crime Records Bureau 2018). Meanwhile, the southern state of Andhra Pradesh has made relatively greater progress in carrying out policing and court reforms and resolving staffing issues with protection officers. Existing studies of the Protection of Women from Domestic Violence Act (PWDVA) show improvement in case registration and court orders in exactly this state (Bhatia 2012; Ghosh and Choudhuri 2011). If there is a place where we could find a different governmental strategy and citizenship model, it would be in Andhra.

The Actors and Approach

The first set of actors in this book are women experiencing domestic violence (seventy total). Table A.1 provides details on their social backgrounds and the kinds of organizations from which they received help. These organizations included women's organizations (women's NGOs and women's associations), political parties (TMC or CPIM), and other organizations (labor unions, neighborhood associations, criminal networks, and for Muslim women mosques and religious organizations). To understand how these women claimed rights, I followed them through the various stages of their allegations, beginning with their attempts to seek help from various brokers, their first interactions with law enforcement, arbitrations, the registration of a First Information Report or Domestic Incident Report, trial, sentencing, and court orders (in the rare case where a woman received an official verdict).

Table A.1 includes two pieces of key information. First, it shows that the women I tracked were a diverse group who varied by: residential location (city

Table A.1 **Sample of Women Experiencing Violence**

Residential Location	Religion	Caste	Income	No Help	Help from Women's Org	Help from Political Party	Help from Other Group
45 rural (villages outside Kolkata)	30 Hindu	6 Upper Caste	5 Middle	2	3	2	1
			1 Low	0	0	1	0
		24 Lower and Scheduled Caste	7 Middle	2	5	2	3
			17 Low	3	12	7	4
	10 Muslim	N/A	1 Middle	0	0	0	1
		N/A	9 Low	2	6	4	6
	5 Christian	N/A	4 Middle	1	3	1	1
		N/A	1 Low	0	1	0	0
25 urban (Kolkata)	20 Hindu	14 Upper Caste	11 Middle	3	8	6	3
			3 Low	1	2	1	0
		6 Lower Caste (no Scheduled)	2 Middle	0	2	1	1
			4 Low	1	3	2	1
	5 Muslim	N/A	3 Middle	1	1	1	2
		N/A	2 Low	1	1	0	1

or village), religion (Hindu, Muslim, Christian), caste (applicable for Hindus), and income (low income defined as a woman living on less than $1 per day). I purposefully sought out a diverse sample because I wished to understand if and how a woman's social background impacted law enforcement responses to allegations of violence. Existing research indicates the ascriptive categories I sampled on are particularly salient for women's abilities to claim rights (Panda and Agarwal 2005; International Institute for Population Sciences 2017).

A larger proportion of the sample came from rural areas (villages outside Kolkata) because approximately 71 percent of India's population lived in villages when the study was conducted. For further information, refer to the World Bank website: http://data.worldbank.org/country/india. Similarly, a larger proportion of the sample were Hindus because at the time of the study 80.5 percent of India's population was Hindu, Muslims accounted for 13.4 percent, and Christians accounted for 2.3 percent. See www.census.com/india.gov.in for more information.

"Caste" refers to a complicated system of social stratification among Hindus, rooted in occupational segregation and cultural notions of ritual purity and pollution. Religion and caste affiliation are ascriptive, inherited, and maintained through endogamy; they are also *legal* categories in India. The Indian government classifies citizens according to religion and caste for the purposes of welfare services as well as family law (which defines rights to marriage, divorce, alimony, inheritance, and child custody). It is important to note that both Section 498A and PWDVA apply to all women irrespective of religious affiliation.

I assigned caste and religious categories according to research subjects' self-identifications. "Upper" caste includes Brahmins (priestly caste) and Baidyas (merchants). "Lower" caste includes Sudras (laborers) and scheduled caste (untouchables). "Upper" and "lower" are legally recognized classifications within India. Classifying women's income level proved to be a tricky business, partly because I was conducting research with women who did not always earn their own money and because financial deprivation is often a feature of domestic violence. Because of these constraints, I classified women's income by personal consumption: the amount of money they consumed on a daily basis. If someone reported living on $1/day or less (at the time the study was conducted, $1 was roughly equivalent to 50Rs), I classified her as low-income. If she was living on anything between $1 and $3 (50–150Rs) per day, I classified her as middle-income.

Table A.1 provides another set of key information: women's organizational resources. It shows that women of diverse social backgrounds received organized help. This is interesting because one might expect relatively privileged women to have greater access to institutional support. I do not think this feature of my sample is accidental or unrepresentative of the general population. Rather, it speaks to the broader literature that shows how organizations of various kinds have taken up the project of women's rights, speaking to different demographic groups and operating in both urban and rural areas.

The table also shows that women sought help from multiple organizations at the same time. The same woman was likely to approach a women's NGO, a neighborhood association, and a representative of her ruling political party either concurrently or sequentially. Women consciously diversified their help seeking behavior. They approached different organizations for different kinds of resources (for example, women's organizations provided counseling and job training, political parties helped them access electricity and food). They also believed having a combination of actors behind them would provide greater leverage over the criminal justice system.

The second group of actors that feature in this book are thus the organized actors women turned to for help: those who mediated between women and the state. These intermediaries formed a complex and contradictory layer of society, most accurately characterized as members of Partha Chatterjee's "political society." They consisted of organizations and individuals who at times shared little in common other than their interest in mediating domestic conflicts. I call this diverse crew "brokers" because they brokered between women, abusers, families, and the state. In studying brokers, I hoped to understand four things. Who were they? Why did they help women? How did they help women? What effects did their mediations have on women's access to justice?

I conducted twenty-six in-depth interviews with brokers in West Bengal. This included seven NGO caseworkers, three *mahila samiti* organizers, four women's rights activists, three people in management positions in women's NGOs, two lawyers, two private brokers, one well-known criminal, two elected officials, and two men who conducted "party work" (were affiliated with and campaigned professionally for political parties).

Within this broader set, three organizations became key ethnographic sites because they were well known for helping women facing violence. I have called them AIN, Andolan, and Shadheen. I divided my time by organization, dedicating one or two days per week to each site depending on the week and the pace of case-related activities at each place. Within each venue, I observed a range of organizational initiatives: staff and board meetings where organizational members discussed internal challenges, intake sessions where caseworkers met women experiencing violence, case-processing activities where caseworkers accompanied women to criminal justice institutions (Shadheen and AIN), arbitration sessions (Andolan), training workshops for members and caseworkers (Shadheen), and women's support group meetings (AIN). In addition, I reviewed financial reports (Shadheen and AIN), memos, publicity documents, and self-assessment studies (AIN and Andolan).

Alongside the time I spent within these organizational settings, I dedicated approximately ten hours every week within the halls of the criminal justice system: observing how police stations, protection officers, and court personnel interacted with women experiencing violence. In total, I conducted around 880 hours of participant observation with law enforcement personnel.

I supplemented this participant observation with seventeen in-depth interviews: ten police officers (two inspectors in charge, one officer in charge, two sub-inspectors, five constables), four judges (two high court judges, two district magistrates), and three protection officers. Interview questions focused on three sets of issues: how law enforcement personnel perceived women who asked for help (gendered, classed, and caste-based ideologies), the key challenges they faced while going about their work (political and structural constraints), and their decision-making strategies around concrete cases (managerial tactics).

I conducted interviews during three separate time periods: during the ethnography which spanned 2009–2011 and then again in follow-up visits in 2015 and 2016. Interviewing people over the course of six years helped me gain a longer perspective on the trajectory of people's lives beyond the ethnography I conducted. All interviews were conducted in Bengali, my native language and the language of my informants. Interviews lasted anywhere from one to four hours and were loosely structured and conversational in nature.

I avoided conducting interviews in women's homes if they were still living with their abuser. With women brokers, once I got to know them quite well, I did visit their homes. With law enforcement personnel and *dadas* I made sure to only meet them in their offices or in a public place like a cafe. I used interviews to understand how respondents thought of the law, what kinds of strategies they believed were effective forms of engagement, their gendered ideologies, and how they conceptualized their surroundings and their own actions.

Sampling, Recruitment, Researcher Position

I used a snowball sampling technique to recruit all research participants (Duvvury et al. 2002; Panda and Agarwal 2005). Meeting women and members of women's organizations proved to be relatively easy. I first scheduled meetings with well-known women's rights activists in West Bengal. Through them, I gained introductions to women's organizations that provided legal aide to women in three different parts of the state: the capital city of Kolkata and two adjoining districts, North-24 and South-24 Parganas. The people I met within these venues in turn introduced me to other women, caseworkers, *mahila samiti* members, and rights activists in their personal networks. Given the issue I was studying and the people I hoped to meet, snowball sampling was not just convenient but necessary for accessing people who may otherwise have refused to meet me (Atkinson & Flint 2001). Because I was already "vouched for," I was able to establish trust with research participants.

Snowball sampling is critiqued for producing representational bias (Kapur 2013; Pound 1910). Given that it was indispensable to access and to ensure my personal safety, I mitigated the method's shortcomings in two ways. First, I enhanced the diversity of my observational sites (Griffiths et al. 1993; Van Meter 1990). I conducted ethnography in five courts and six police stations in four different districts, and I sought out law enforcement personnel through a number of reference points. Second, I sought the replication of results across observational sites and during interviews in order to strengthen theoretical generalizations (Kirchherr and Charles 2018).

My gender and social background enabled rapid access and relatively quick integration into sites that were women dominated. Caseworkers at women's NGOs, members of women's committees, and women experiencing violence: all of these people were relatively comfortable and willing to speak to me and have me trail them around. As a woman, I could easily enter these women's homes and personal lives. Speaking Bengali fluently helped ease entry, especially with women from relatively disadvantaged backgrounds where English would have interrupted our abilities to mutually coexist. Coming from the United States and having an elite American university attached to my name also helped. NGOs and rights activists who might otherwise have ignored me saw me as a potential future resource, someone their organization could get to know and who might help expand their social networks.

Over time, I gained what some sociologists have termed an insider/outsider status (Weiss 1995). I became part of the local work cultures of several women's organizations, was allowed to sit in on high-level managerial meetings, and was included in sensitive intake sessions. I also became a recognized figure in police stations and courtrooms, accompanying caseworkers and women experiencing violence. This position came with certain advantages as well as drawbacks. Access was its main advantage. Meanwhile, my ability to ethically, emotionally, and analytically separate myself from research participants turned out to be the main drawback of being an insider/outsider. People often mistook me for a caseworker or a lawyer or a women's rights activist, expecting that I would provide advice and legal help. I had to work hard to disappoint them. Some of the caseworkers and rights activists I shadowed became friends, people I confided in and whose company I enjoyed. Thinking and writing critically about their actions became intellectually difficult and emotionally fraught, and I could only do it with some amount of time and distance.

These intimacies also underscored my own privilege relative to those I studied. Despite our presence together in the same spaces for the length of two years, I eventually left, while they stayed behind. The very time and distance that made the intellectual act of interpretation and analysis possible were resources that I had at my disposal, resources that eventually led to a well-paid job, the ability to travel, and a well-appointed apartment. The trajectory for women experiencing violence was far less secure, with relatively little scope for mobility, both physical and financial. The trajectory for caseworkers and rights activists, meanwhile, depended on the financial viability of the organizations within which they existed.

While my gender and social background created intimacy, and all the hazards that came with it, with the women I met, it proved to be a hindrance as well as a useful tool in completely different ways with the men who feature on these pages: *dadas* (political party cadre, male politicians, private brokers, and criminals) and law enforcement personnel. While I managed to interview some of these people, I think I would have made quicker headway if I had been a man.

Because public and private spaces are so heavily gendered in India, I could enter women's homes but I could not easily inhabit the public spaces where *dadas* spend their time. Sitting around in a political party's club house, lounging at an outside *chai* stall, or smoking cigarettes and drinking in the evenings with a bunch of men: I could not reasonably do these things without raising eyebrows and giving off the impression that I was a "loose" woman who was sexually accessible. Similarly, the patriarchal and largely male world of Indian law enforcement personnel is not always the most hospitable place for a young woman. With the police, it is not just a matter of giving off the wrong impression; it is also a safety issue. Given their record of abusiveness toward women, I had to be careful as a woman researcher.

To access *dadas* and law enforcement personnel, I relied on referrals from relatively powerful people: family friends who were politicians or part of the law enforcement world and well-known lawyers. Once I had established rapport with a particular law enforcement official or a *dada*, I asked him to refer me to other people in the same position in different districts within West Bengal. This strategy afforded me the opportunity to interview and observe people working in a range of settings across the state, both rural and urban, while ensuring my physical safety and the integrity of my research methods.

My sampling tactics with law enforcement personnel are, I believe, quite revealing of the role social networks play in guiding law enforcement responses to women. Like the women who approached the criminal justice system through organized groups, I too thought it best to always have my organizational, professional, and personal contacts on display. "She comes from such and such organization" or "she knows so and so senior bureaucrat" provided the armament I needed to deal with law enforcement personnel on what I hoped would be my terms, rather than theirs.

There was no individual, unmediated access (Naples 1996) and no abstract bearer of rights who could walk through the door and register a report or demand an interview. Neither was access guaranteed by social background. Despite my upper-caste Hindu last name and my upper-class paraphernalia (my clothes, my phone), I could not count on being classified as a "virtuous" woman worthy of respect. My ability to be recognized as someone meriting time and consideration depended on my demonstrated linkages to politically influential people and organizations. Thus, in the end, while my gender was something I had to think about and manage, and which potentially restricted my access, it also revealed, at a very embodied level, the social and political processes that structured women's relationship to the criminal justice system.

Analytic Strategy

If all of this information gives you the idea that I conducted a carefully planned study, you are misled. West Bengal's status as an "ideal case" was thoroughly fortuitous because I initially intended to study something else. The place itself accidentally generated a completely new set of research questions.

I first went to West Bengal in the hope of understanding the gendered effects of microfinance. Needless to say, that is not what I ended up studying. But it was through microfinance banks, a host of NGOs, women's organizations, and microfinance self-help groups that I ended up meeting the people who became my "target" population: women who were dealing with intimate abuse. Domestic violence was where the action was, so to speak. The truth of the matter was that everyone, from the self-help group members to the street vendor who sold me *chai* in the morning to newspaper editors to my relatives, was talking about violence against women. And they all had strong opinions about "the issue" that such violence indexed, with some people lamenting that women were oppressed and needed help, others arguing exactly the opposite, and still more projecting apocalyptic fears of family disintegration and societal decline.

By listening to the buzz around me, I felt my way toward a powder keg. In 2012 the keg exploded: the gang rape of Jyoti Singh Pandey in Delhi provided the match that ignited the flames (Roychowdhury 2013). The massive protests that seized the country after Delhi confirmed what I had started intuiting within the villages and cities of West Bengal. Gender-based violence was a political issue for diverse organized interests, including feminists, political parties, student groups, and neighborhood associations. After years of grassroots organizing and high-level negotiations between legislators and prominent women's rights activists, gendered violence was no longer a private affair discussed in hushed tones. Average people were concerned, openly debating and, under certain circumstances, willing to mobilize around particular incidents. And this politi-cization bore down on law enforcement personnel, demanding new managerial solutions.

My observations and interviews generated data that was most amenable to sociological traditions of abductive analysis. Abduction uses surprising and anomalous empirical data to construct theoretical insights (Timmermans and Tavory 2012). The anomaly at the heart of my findings is the process I describe as "incorporation." I did not expect law enforcement personnel to narrate their powerlessness either to me or to women who approached them for legal assis-tance. Neither did I expect them to reassign administrative duties or tell women to run parallel claims. In fact, what surprised me most was their attempt to "in-clude" women and appease them in some limited fashion. Incorporation is not the same thing as case suppression, which is what I had expected. Neither is incorporation like protection, which is what most academics who study gender and law theorize. Over the course of my research, it was the difference between suppression, protection, and incorporation that provided the key empirical comparisons motivating my theoretical analysis.

Appendix B

KEY LEGAL REFORMS

	Section 498A, 1983	**PWDVA, 2005**
Type of law:	Criminal	Quasi-civil, quasi-criminal
Covers:	Married men and women	Married women, women in live-in relationships, daughters, sisters, mothers
Prosecutes:	Husband or wife	Husband, live-in male partner, father, brother, other male relatives, in-laws
Definition of violence:	Physical and mental cruelty	Physical, sexual, financial, verbal, and emotional abuse
Available remedies:	Imprisonment and fine for convicted person	Orders of protection, temporary child custody, financial compensation, alimony, residential rights
Legal proceedings initiated by:	First Information Report	Domestic Incident Report
Legal representation:	Public prosecutor	Private lawyer appointed by aggrieved woman
Standard of proof:	Beyond reasonable doubt	Preponderance of probabilities

Prior to 1983, married women could seek limited remedies against domestic violence under religiously defined matrimonial law. This included the Hindu Marriage Act 1955, the Parsi Marriage and Divorce Act 1936, the Dissolution of

Muslim Marriages Act 1938, the Indian Divorce Act 1869, or, in the case of an interfaith union, the Special Marriage Act 1954. Matrimonial law recognizes physical and emotional "cruelty" as grounds for divorce, maintenance (alimony), and residential rights. Apart from matrimonial law, married women could also claim maintenance through Section 125 of the Code of Criminal Procedure, 1973.

Another route available to married women was criminal law, which was universal. Married women could use general provisions, including: Sections 319–326 against hurt and grievous hurt; Sections 336 and 340 against wrongful restraint and wrongful confinement; Section 376A against sexual intercourse after separation; Section 503 against criminal intimidation; Sections 312–315 against offences related to causing miscarriage; Sections 299, 300, 304, and 307 against culpable homicide, murder, culpable homicide not amounting to murder, and attempt to murder. Finally, if they were Hindu, they could use the Dowry Prohibition Act, 1961 if they experienced dowry-related harassment, abuse, and murder.

Addressing violence in the home through general criminal provisions proved, however, to be a difficult task. These provisions suffered from a misplaced burden of proof. Given patrilocal kinship arrangements, married women had a difficult time proving violence in intimate settings "beyond a reasonable doubt" because of the paucity of corroborating witnesses, most of whom were likely her abuser's kin (Agnes 1992). The domestic space also arguably called for different criteria to measure injury and hurt. Even when women do not suffer "grievous hurt," routine violence can cause physical and emotional trauma (Shepard and Pence 1999). Conventional criminal procedure left victims vulnerable to further violence. Criminal complaints are usually registered after an offense has been created, but someone who lives with her assaulter may need protection before she is attacked, at the moment she apprehends danger.

Similarly, the Dowry Prohibition Act and religiously defined matrimonial laws had their own limitations. First, these laws did not pertain to all women. Matrimonial law created a patchwork of different provisions available to women depending on their religious affiliation (Subramanian 2014). It was based on the false presumption that marital practices are distinct and separate across religions. The Dowry Prohibition Act also made the same erroneous assumption, extending rights exclusively to Hindu women even though the practice of dowry is prevalent among Muslims, Christians, and other religious groups across India (Caplan 1984; Chacko 2003; Waheed 2009). Even for Hindu women, the Dowry Prohibition Act did little to challenge the structural conditions of dowry, which involved patriarchal and compulsory marriage. Nor did it recognize the role natal families play in enabling dowry violence by exerting tremendous pressure on women to have arranged marriages, to have lavish weddings, and to tolerate violence in the marital home (Agnes 1999).

Finally, CrPC 125 provided maintenance but only if women satisfied a set of problematic stipulations. A woman could claim maintenance only if she could prove her husband had abandoned her, not if she herself had left the relationship. CrPC 125 is thus not only *not* set up to protect women from violence, one could argue it creates the conditions for the opposite situation: forcing women to stay in abusive situations in the hopes of future financial support.

Section 498A of the Indian Penal Code was introduced in 1983 to rectify some of these limitations. Section 498A criminalizes "physical and mental cruelty" within marriage. It pertains to all married women, irrespective of their religious background. It is a cognizable, non-compoundable, non-bailable offense. In other words, the police have the authority to arrest accused parties and conduct investigations without a warrant (cognizable). Cases cannot be withdrawn or compromised once they have been registered (non-compoundable). Finally, accused parties cannot negotiate bail terms directly with the police without a court hearing (non-bailable).

A 498A case carries a maximum sentence of three years and a monetary fine if violence is proven in court. Plaintiffs are guaranteed access to free legal representation through the office of the public prosecutor. Both men and women can register cases under the law. Section 498A does not recognize sexual or financial violence. It restricts entitlements to legally recognized husbands and wives and does not offer civil remedies.

Cases registered under Section 498A are processed by the police and district courts. A 498A case begins with the registration of a First Incident Report (FIR) with the police, who are then legally mandated to complete several tasks: locate and bring the accused into custody, conduct an official criminal investigation, draw up a charge sheet detailing the results of their investigation, and forward the charge sheet along with a copy of the FIR to the district magistrate's office for trial. The magistrate's office oversees bail hearings and works with the public prosecutor and the police to locate witnesses and gather evidence for trial. Since India officially abolished its jury system in 1973, it is the magistrate who delivers an official verdict at the end of a trial.

Section 498A has been dogged by criticism from all sides. Pro-family organizations and men's rights activists believe 498A gives unscrupulous women a weapon with which to "abuse" their husbands (Kishwar 2003). Meanwhile, those who represent and work with women facing violence note that many women express dismay at the possibility of imprisoning their husbands and, as a result, shy away from registering cases (Mehra 1998). Feminist activists and scholars furthermore argue that 498A places women in a double bind. Since the law strictly provides criminal remedies, it does not give women much needed civil protections to housing, divorce, or protection (Basu 2015). And Section 498A does not include provisions for maintenance, creating potential conflicts with remedies available through CrPc 125. By incarcerating the offender and removing him from his place of employment, Section 498A forces married women to choose between punishment and financial survival.

The limitations of criminal law led to another round of legal reforms in 2005. The Protection of Women from Domestic Violence Act (PWDVA) is a quasi-civil, quasi-criminal law. PWDVA proceedings follow civil law until and unless a court order is violated, at which point future action falls under criminal law. Unlike 498A, PWDVA is gender-specific, granting relief only to women and girls. PWDVA is not restricted to married women; it also covers women in "live-in" relationships and unmarried women facing abuse in their natal families. Aggrieved women can lodge complaints against spouses, in-laws, and their own fathers and brothers (the only exception being that PWDVA cases cannot be registered against a birth mother). PWDVA recognizes a range of abuses, including physical, sexual, financial, verbal, and emotional abuse. It also provides a range of civil remedies: orders of protection, temporary child custody, residential rights within the marital home, alimony, and financial compensation.

PWDVA is a quasi-civil, quasi-criminal law. It follows civil proceedings unless a court order is violated, at which point future action falls under criminal law. While 498A cases largely involve the police and courts, PWDVA cases rely extensively on a third unit of the criminal justice system, protection officers (POs). POs coordinate between various parties and supervise each stage of the case. A PWDVA case officially begins with the registration of a Domestic Incident Report (DIR). An aggrieved woman can register a DIR with any of the following people: the police, a local service provider (an officially recognized women's organization or nongovernmental organization), a medical examiner, a magistrate's court, or directly with her district's protection officer (PO).

After a DIR is registered, the PO must conduct an independent investigation, draft an application for relief, and forward the application along with a copy of the DIR to the district magistrate's office. The PO is also responsible for serving court notices and ensuring that the aggrieved woman has access to a shelter, medical facilities, legal aide, counseling, and, if need be, a women's organization. Meanwhile, the district magistrate oversees trial proceedings, including the granting of interim orders and has the power to ask service providers to supervise and support individual women. The police are called in the event a court order is violated, at which time criminal proceedings are initiated. According to PWDVA bylaws, each step of this process must adhere to strict timelines, with notices served within two days of an application being filed and the final order passed within sixty days.

Appendix C

FIRST INFORMATION REPORT

District:

Police Station:

F.I.R. Number:

Date:

Act: _____ Sections: _____

Other Acts & Sections: _____

Occurrence of Offence: Date from _____ Date to _____

Information received at Police Station: Date _____ Time _____

General Diary Reference: Entry No. _____ Time _____

Type of Information: Written/Oral

Place of Occurrence: Direction and distance from Police Station _____
_____

Address: _____
_____

In case outside the limit of this Police Station:

Name of Police Station _____ District _____
_____

Complainant Information:

Name _____

Father's/Husband's Name _____

Date/Year of Birth _____ Nationality _____

Identity Document _____

Date of Issue _____ Place of Issue _____

Occupation _____ Address _____

Details of known/suspected/unknown accused with full particulars (attach separate sheet if necessary)

Accused 1: _____
_____

Accused 2: _____
_____

Accused 3: _____
_____

Details of Incident:

Appendix D

DOMESTIC INCIDENT REPORT

UNDER SECTIONS 9 (B) AND 37 (2) (C) OF THE PROTECTION OF
WOMEN FROM DOMESTIC VIOLENCE ACT, 2005 (43 OF 2005)

1. Details of the complainant/aggrieved person
    a. Name of the complainant/aggrieved person:
    b. Age:
    c. Address of the shared household:
    d. Present address:
    e. Phone number, if any:
2. Details of respondents:

Sl. No.	Name	Relationship with aggrieved person	Address	Telephone No.

3. Details of children, if any, of the aggrieved person:
    a. Number of children:
    b. Details of children:

Name	Age	Sex	With whom at present residing

4. Incidents of domestic violence:

Sl. No.	Date, place and time of violence	Person who caused domestic violence	Types of violence	Remarks
Causing hurt of any kind, please specify.				
I. SEXUAL VIOLENCE (Please tick mark [√] the column applicable)				
			• Forced sexual intercourse • Forced to watch pornography or other obscene material • Forcibly using you to entertain others • Any other act of sexual nature, abusing, humiliating, degrading, or otherwise violative of your dignity (please specify details in the space provided below)	
II. VERBAL AND EMOTIONAL ABUSE				
			• Accusation/aspersion on your character or conduct, etc. • Insult for not bringing dowry, etc. • Insult for not having a male child • Insult for not having any child • Demeaning, humiliating or undermining remarks	

			• Ridicule • Name calling • Forcing you to not attend school, college, or any other educational institution • Preventing you from taking up a job • Preventing you from leaving the house • Preventing you from meeting any particular person • Forcing you to get married against your will • Preventing you from marrying a person of your choice • Forcing you to marry a person of his/their own choice • Any other verbal or emotional abuse (please specify in the space provided below)	
III. ECONOMIC VIOLENCE				
			• Not providing money for maintaining you or your children • Not providing food, clothes, medicine, etc., for you or your children	

		• Forcing you out of the house you live in • Preventing you from accessing or using any part of the house • Preventing or obstructing you from carrying on your employment • Not allowing you to take up an employment • Non-payment of rent in case of a rented accommodation • Not allowing you to use clothes or articles of general household use • Selling or pawing your *stridhan* or any other valuables without informing you and without your consent • Forcibly taking away your salary, income or wages etc. • Disposing your *stridhan* • Non-payment of other bills such as electricity, etc. • Any other economic violence (please specify in the space provided below)	

IV. DOWRY RELATED HARASSMENT				
			• Demands for dowry made (please specify) • Any other detail with regard to dowry (please specify) • Whether details of dowry items, *stridhan*, etc. attached with the form. Yes/No	
V. Any other information regarding acts of domestic violence against you or your children				

(Signature or thumb impression of the complainant/aggrieved person)

5. List of documents attached:

Name of document	Date	Any other detail
Medico legal certificate		
Doctor's certificate or any other prescription		
List of *stridhan*		
Any other document		

6. Order that you need under the Protection of Women from Domestic Violence Act, 2005:

Sl. No.	Orders	Yes/No	Any other
(1)	Protection order under section 18		
(2)	Residence order under section 19		
(3)	Maintenance order under section 20		
(4)	Custody order under section 21		
(5)	Compensation order under section 22		
(6)	Any other order (specify)		

7. Assistance that you need:

Sl. No.	Assistance available	Yes/No	Nature of assistance
(1)	(2)	(3)	(4)
(1)	Counsellor		
(2)	Police assistance		
(3)	Assistance for initiating criminal proceedings		
(4)	Shelter home		
(5)	Medical facilities		
(6)	Legal aid		

8. Instruction for the Police Officer assisting in registration of a Domestic Incident Report:

Wherever the Information provided in this Form discloses an offence under the Indian Penal Code or any other law, the police officer shall—

(a) inform the aggrieved person that she can also initiate criminal proceedings by lodging a First Information Report under the Code of Criminal Procedure, 1973 (2 of 1973)

(b) if the aggrieved person does not want to initiate criminal proceedings, then make daily diary entry as per the information contained in the domestic incident report with a remark that the aggrieved person due to the intimate nature of the relationship with the accused wants to pursue the civil remedies for protection against domestic violence and has requested that on the basis of the information received by her, the matter has been kept pending for appropriate enquiry before registration of an FIR.

(c) if any physical injury or pain being reported by the aggrieved person, offer immediate medical assistance and get the aggrieved person medically examined.

Place:

Date:

Name: (Countersignature of Protection Officer/Service Provider)

Address:

(Seal)

Copy forwarded to:
1. Local Police Station
2. Service Provider/Protection Officer
3. Aggrieved person
4. Magistrate

NOTES

Section I
Chapter 1

1. Collaboration between local social movements and transnational institutions animated a legal sea change. Before any laws existed, women began organizing at the local level to provide support services to themselves and other survivors of violence: Shepard, Melanie, and Ellen Pence. 1999. *Coordinating community responses to domestic violence: Lessons from Duluth and beyond.* Thousand Oaks, CA: Sage. Meanwhile, the ratification of the United Nations Convention on the Elimination of all Forms of Discrimination Against Women (CEDAW) in 1981 focused global attention on the issue of violence. Signed by 188 member states, including India, CEDAW marked the first international effort to address abuse within the home. Violence against women was no longer something people talked about in hushed tones; it had attained the status of a global human rights issue: Schneider, Elizabeth. 2000. *Battered women and feminist lawmaking.* New Haven, CT: Yale University Press. Social movement organizing ushered in new policies across the developed and developing world: Htun, Mala, and Laurel Weldon. 2012. The civic origins of progressive policy change: Combating violence against women in global perspective, 1975–2005. *American Political Science Review* 106(3):548–569; Naples, Nancy A., and Manisha Desai. 2002. *Women's activism and globalization: Linking local struggles and global politics.* New York and London: Routledge. This reversal housed a promise: the birth of a new era of gender equality, one where states would ensure women's full and equal participation in the polity by regulating their disproportionate vulnerability to physical, sexual, and emotional harm at the hands of men.

2. Prior to the passage of Indian Penal Code Section 498A in 1983, married women could seek limited remedies against domestic violence under personal laws. In addition to 498A and the Protection of Women from Domestic Violence Act (PWDVA), women have rights to alimony upon divorce and are protected from dowry-related abuse. Section 498A offers the promise of a fine and imprisonment if the perpetrator is convicted in court. PWDVA provides civil remedies including orders of protection, maintenance (alimony), child custody, financial compensation, and residential rights. For a detailed discussion of existing legal provisions, please refer to Appendix B: Key Legal Reforms.

3. Legal reforms have had one discernible positive effect: they have allowed women to make legal claims. Far greater numbers of women report domestic abuse in India today than they did in the past. Between 2007 and 2018, cases registered under criminal law increased by 138 percent, rising from 75,930 to 104,551. Women registered cases even as actual rates of violence decreased. In 2006, some 37.2 percent of surveyed women had experienced some form of domestic violence in their lifetime. By 2016 that average had fallen to 31 percent. For more, please refer to the following: International Institute for Population Sciences. 2017. *National Family Health Survey 2015–2016: India.* Mumbai: Government of India, Ministry of Health

and Family Welfare; National Crime Records Bureau. 2018. *Crime in India 2017 full report.*
New Delhi: Government of India, Ministry of Home Affairs.

Chapter 2

1. Married Hindu women could also use the Dowry Prohibition Act of 1961 in cases of dowry-related harassment, abuse, and murder. Dowry involves the transference of money, jewelry, property and other assets from the bride's family to the groom's as a condition of marriage. Under the Dowry Prohibition Act of 1961, the giving and taking of dowry is illegal in India. But the practice continues to be popular among Hindus, Muslims, and Christians. Dowry-related abuse involves the use of violence to extract ongoing payments from a woman's natal family. For more, refer to Banerjee, Priya. 2014. Dowry in 21st-century India: The sociocultural face of exploitation. *Trauma, Violence, & Abuse* 15(1):34–40.
2. A series of social and economic transformations triggered the fall in women's employment. First, increased educational enrollment of young women keeps them out of the workforce: Rustagi, Preet. 2013. Changing patterns of labour force participation and employment of women in India. *Indian Journal of Labour Economics* 56(2):215–241. Second, rising middle-class household incomes allow women to opt out: Neff, Daniel F., Kunal Sen, and Veronika Kling. 2012. The puzzling decline in rural women's labor force participation in India: A reexamination. GIGA Working Paper 196. German Institute of Global and Area Studies, Hamburg, Germany. Finally, economic restructuring has depressed employment opportunities for women while expanding formal sector employment for men: Neetha, N. 2014. Crisis in female employment. *Economic and Political Weekly*, November 22, 2014.
3. Refer to Appendix B: Key Legal Reforms for detailed information on procedural requirements.
4. IPS officers fill the top positions within the police bureaucracy, including the chief ranking officer of each state (the director general of police) and each district (superintendent of police). Members of the IPS have almost no contact with civilians. The PPS falls under state police and includes the heads of individual stations (officers and inspectors in charge) as well as investigators (sub-inspectors and assistant sub-inspectors).
5. In West Bengal, at the time of this study, a newly recruited constable on average earned a monthly salary of RS 20,000 (approximately $300 USD) with the possibility of promotion after a full twenty years of service (Times News Network 2012)!
6. The Bureau of Police Research and Development report results were based on extensive surveys conducted with 12,156 police station staff, 1,003 station house officers (officers in charge of a station), and 962 supervisory police officers. The survey was implemented in 319 police districts across the country, spanning twenty-three states and two union territories.
7. Mathura was raped by two police officers after being arrested for eloping with her boyfriend. The Sessions Court acquitted the two police officers charged with rape. The court reasoned that Mathura could not be raped because she was already sexually active. On appeal, the Supreme Court also acquitted the defendants because of "insufficient" physical evidence, citing that Mathura had not actively resisted the officers.
8. The NNPM combined five separate organizations: Mahila Sachetana Gabeshana (a resource center), Mahila Pathagarh (a library), Mahila Pathachakra (a study circle), *Ahala* (a newspaper), and Prabati Mahila Samiti (the Progressive Women's Union). Prabati Mahila Samiti later became affiliated with the CPI(M).

Section II

Chapter 3

1. In the Hindu epic *The Ramayana*, Sita is married to the god-king Rama. When Rama is banished from his kingdom, Sita follows him into exile. Before departing on a hunt, Rama encloses Sita in a sacred *gondi*, cautioning her not to step outside. Sita does step outside and is quickly abducted by the demon king Ravana.
2. Married Hindu women in West Bengal mark the center fold of their hair with vermillion.

3. Hindu wives do not have legal rights over marital property in India. Muslim women are entitled to one-eighth of their husband's property if they have children and one-fourth if they are childless, but as discussed in Chapter 2, Muslims in West Bengal have increasingly adopted Hindu succession practices that disinherit married women.

4. Hindu daughters enjoy equal rights as sons to parental property under the 2005 Amendment to the Hindu Succession Act, 1956.

Chapter 6

1. By 2009, the average income in the area hovered around $1 per day, and over 30% of the population was illiterate (Government of West Bengal 2009).

2. A direct translation of the term for "middle class" in Bengali is tellingly "civil people" or "civilized people" (*bhadralok*).

3. Madhura could not register a 498A case because the criminal law is only available to legally married women.

4. A lady constable is an official rank designation for women constables within the Provincial Police Service.

Chapter 7

1. Section 406 refers to "criminal breach of trust." It is routinely used to repossess personal property such as jewelry, furniture, cars, and even housing that was gifted to the wife during the time of her marriage by either her own family or her husband's.

2. Anganwadi centers were founded in 1985 by the Indian government to counter child hunger and malnutrition. These days they are the mainstay of public healthcare and education in rural areas. They provide contraception, family planning, nutritional education and supplements, and preschool activities. Many anganwadi workers are also now trained to identify and intervene in cases of domestic violence.

Chapter 8

1. The Mahatma Gandhi National Rural Employment Guarantee Act (NRGA) provides one hundred days of paid work to the rural poor. The NRGA was passed in 2005, the same year as the PWDVA.

2. Please refer to Appendices C and D for a detailed look at a First Information Report and a Domestic Incident Report.

Chapter 11

1. *Pakka* refers to dwellings that are designed to be solid and permanent. This term is applied to housing in South Asia made of stone, brick, cement, or concrete that takes substantial resources to build. *Pakka* is opposed to *kaccha* (raw), connoting a temporary, cheaper dwelling made of mud and straw.

2. Durga Pujo is one of the largest public festivals in the world, occupying a central place in Bengali Hindu religious and social life. The goddess Durga (otherwise known as Parvati) sits at the apex of celebrated deities in the state, and the Durga Pujo lasts ten days.

3. Due to climate change, India has been plagued by a rising tide of heat-related deaths and illnesses. An estimated 2,422 people died in 2015, with low-income people and those who worked outside disproportionately affected. Since 2015, the Indian government has introduced several low-cost measures, including free water and reflective roof paint, that have helped save lives.

REFERENCES

Ackerman, Bruce. 1997. The rise of world constitutionalism. *Virginia Law Review* 83(4):771–797.

Agamben, Giorgio. 1998. *Homo sacer: Sovereign power and bare life*. Stanford, CA: Stanford University Press.

Agarwal, Bina. 1994. *A field of one's own: Gender and land rights in South Asia*. Cambridge: Cambridge University Press.

Agarwala, Rina. 2008. Reshaping the social contract: Emerging relations between the state and informal labor in India. *Theory and Society* 37(4):375–408.

Agnes, Flavia. 1992. Protecting women against violence? Review of a decade of legislation, 1980–89. *Economic and Political Weekly* 27(17):WS19–WS21, WS24–WS33.

Agnes, Flavia. 1999. *Law and gender inequality*. Delhi: Oxford University Press.

Agnes, Flavia. 2005. The violence against women campaign: Where have we failed? InfoChange India. http://infochangeindia.org/women/192-women/analysis/159-the-violence-against-women-campaign-where-have-we-failed.html.

Agrawal, Arun. 2005. Environmentality: Community, intimate government, and the making of environmental subjects in Kumaon, India. *Current Anthropology* 46(2):161–190.

Albiston, Catherine. 2005. Bargaining in the shadow of social institutions: Competing discourses and social change in workplace mobilization of civil rights. *Law & Society Review* 39(1):11–50.

Alvarez, Sonia. 1999. Advocating feminism: The Latin American feminist NGO boom. *International Feminist Journal of Politics* 1(2):181–209.

Amsden, Alice H. 2001. *The rise of "the rest": Challenges to the West from late-industrializing economies*. New York: Oxford University Press.

Anderson, Elijah. 2000. *Code of the street: Decency, violence, and the moral life of the inner city*. New York: W. W. Norton & Company.

Andres, Luis, Basab Dasgupta, George Joseph, Vinoj Abraham, and Maria Correia. 2017. Precarious drop: Reassessing patterns of female labor force participation in India. Policy Research working paper WPS 8024. World Bank Group, Washington, DC.

Appadurai, Arjun. 2004. The capacity to aspire: Culture and the terms of recognition. In *Culture and public action*, edited by Vijayendra Rao and Michael Walton, 59–84. Stanford, CA: Stanford Social Sciences.

Arendt, Hannah. 1976. *The origins of totalitarianism*. San Diego: Harcourt.

Aretxaga, Begoña. 2003. Maddening states. *Annual Review of Anthropology* 32(1):393–410.

Arnold, David. 1986. *Police power and colonial rule, Madras 1859–1947*. Delhi: Oxford University Press.

Atkinson, Rowland, and John Flint. 2001. Accessing hidden and hard-to-reach populations: Snowball research strategies. *Social Research Update* 33(1):1–4.

Auerbach, Adam, and Tariq Thachil. 2018. How clients select brokers: Competition and choice in India's slums. *American Political Science Review* 112(4):775–791.

Auyero, Javier. 2001. *Poor people's politics*. Durham, NC: Duke University Press.

Auyero, Javier, and María Fernanda Berti. 2016. *In harm's way: The dynamics of urban violence*. Princeton, NJ: Princeton University Press.

Banerjee, Priya. 2014. Dowry in 21st-century India: The sociocultural face of exploitation. *Trauma, Violence, & Abuse* 15(1):34–40.

Banerjee, Sumanta. 1999. Marginalization of women's popular culture in nineteenth century Bengal. In *Recasting women*, edited by Kumkum Sangari and Sudesh Vaid, 127–179. New Brunswick, NJ: Rutgers University Press.

Bardhan, Pranab. 2001. Sharing the spoils: Group equity, development, democracy. In *The success of India's democracy*, edited by Atul Kohli, 226–241. Cambridge: Cambridge University Press.

Barry, Andrew, Thomas Osborne, and Nikolas Rose. 1996. *Foucault and political reason*. Chicago: University of Chicago Press.

Basu, Amrita. 1994. *Two faces of protest: Contrasting modes of women's activism in India*. Berkeley: University of California Press.

Basu, Srimati. 2006. Playing off courts: The negotiation of divorce and violence in Kolkata. *Journal of Legal Pluralism and Unofficial Law* 38(52):41–75.

Basu, Srimati. 2012. Judges of normality: Mediating marriage in the family courts of Kolkata. *Signs* 37(2):469–492.

Basu, Srimati. 2015. *The trouble with marriage: Feminists confront law and violence in India*. Berkeley: University of California Press.

Baxi, Pratiksha. 2005. The medicalisation of consent and falsity: The figure of the habitué in Indian rape law. In *The violence of normal times*, edited by Kalpana Kannabiran, 266–311. New Delhi: Women Unlimited.

Baxi, Pratiksha. 2010. Justice is a secret compromise in rape trials. *Contributions to Indian Sociology* 44(3):207–233.

Bayat, Asef. 2013. *Life as politics: How ordinary people change the Middle East*. Stanford, CA: Stanford University Press.

Bayley, David. 1983. The police and political order in India. *Asian Survey* 23(4):484–496.

Bayley, David, and Philip Stenning. 2016. *Governing the police: Experience in six democracies*. Piscataway, NJ: Transaction Publishers.

Bedi, Tarini. 2007. The dashing ladies of the Shiv Sena. *Economic and Political Weekly* 42(17):1534–1541.

Benford, Robert, and David Snow. 2000. Framing processes and social movements: An overview and assessment. *Annual Review of Sociology* 26(1):611–639.

Bernstein, Elizabeth. 2012. Carceral politics as gender justice? *Theory and Society* 41(3):233–259.

Bhatia, Manjeet. 2012. Domestic violence in India: Cases under PWDVA. *South Asia Research* 32(2):103–122.

Bhattacharya, Chandrima. 2015, November 26. Domestic violence topper for seven years. *The Telegraph*.

Biswas, Soutik. 2007, November 26. India's "pink" vigilante women. BBC News. http://news.bbc. co.uk/2/hi/7068875.stm.

Blackstone, Amy, Christopher Uggen, and Heather McLaughlin. 2009. Legal consciousness and responses to sexual harassment. *Law & Society Review* 43(3):631–668.

Bloemraad, Irene, Anna Korteweg, and Gokce Yurdakul. 2008. Citizenship and immigration: Multiculturalism, assimilation, and challenges to the nation-state. *Annual Review of Sociology* 34:153–179.

Bose, Sunita, and Scott J. South. 2003. Sex composition of children and marital disruption in India. *Journal of Marriage and Family* 65(4):996–1006.

Bourdieu, Pierre. 2011. The forms of capital (1986). In *Cultural theory: An anthology*, edited by Imre Szeman and Timothy Kaposy, 81–93. Chichester, UK: John Wiley & Sons.

Bourdieu, Pierre. 1994. Rethinking the state: Genesis and structure of the bureaucratic field. Loic Wacquant and Samar Farage translation. *Sociological Theory* 12(1):1–18.

Brass, Paul. 1997. *Theft of an idol: Text and context in the representation of collective violence.* Princeton, NJ: Princeton University Press.

Brass, Paul. 2005. *The production of Hindu–Muslim violence in contemporary India.* Seattle: University of Washington Press.

Bumiller, Kristin. 1987. Victims in the shadow of the law. *Signs* 12(3):421–439.

Bumiller, Kristin. 2008. *In an abusive state: How neoliberalism appropriated feminist movements against sexual violence.* Durham, NC: Duke University Press.

Burchell, Graham. 1996. Liberal government and techniques of the self. In *Foucault and political reason,* edited by Andrew Barry, Thomas Osborne, and Nikolas Rose, 19–36. Chicago: University of Chicago Press.

Bureau of Police Research and Development. 2015. *Data on police organizations as of January 1, 2015.* New Delhi: Government of India.

Burt, Ronald. 2005. *Brokerage and closure: An introduction to social capital.* New York: Oxford University Press.

Burton, Barbara, Nata Duvvury, Anuradha Rajan, and Nisha Varia. 2000. *Domestic violence in India, part 2: A summary report of four records studies.* New Delhi: International Center for Research on Women.

Burton, Barbara, Anuradha Rajan, and Nandita Bhatla. 2002. *Domestic violence in India, part 5: Women-initiated community level responses to domestic violence.* New Delhi: International Center for Research on Women.

Buzawa, Eva, and Carl Buzawa. 2003. *Domestic violence: The criminal justice response.* Thousand Oaks, CA: Sage.

Caldiera, Teresa. 2000. *City of walls: Crime, segregation, and citizenship in Sao Paolo.* Berkeley: University of California Press.

Campbell, Jacquelyn. 2002. Health consequences of intimate partner violence. *Lancet* 359(9314):1331–1336.

Caplan, Lionel. 1984. Bridegroom price in Urban India: Class, Caste and "Dowry Evil" among Christians in Madras. *Man* 19(2):216–233.

Centeno, Miguel. 2002. *Blood and debt: War and the nation-state in Latin America.* University Park: Pennsylvania State University.

Chacko, Elizabeth. 2003. Marriage, development, and the status of women in Kerala, India. *Gender & Development* 11(2):52–59.

Chatterjee, Partha. 2004. *The politics of the governed: Reflections on popular politics in most of the world.* New York: Columbia University Press.

Chatterjee, Partha. 2013. *Lineages of political society: Studies in postcolonial democracy.* New York: Columbia University Press.

Chavez, Rebecca Bill. 2003. The construction of the rule of law in Argentina: A tale of two provinces. *Comparative Politics* 35(4):417–437.

Cheesman, Nick. 2015. *Opposing the rule of law: How Myanmar's courts make law and order.* Cambridge: Cambridge University Press.

Choo, Hae Yeon. 2013. The cost of rights: Migrant women, feminist advocacy, gendered morality in South Korea. *Gender & Society* 27(4):445–468.

Chowdhry, Prem. 2004. Caste panchayats and the policing of marriage in Haryana. *Contributions to Indian Sociology* 38(1):1–42.

Chua, Lynette. 2012. Pragmatic resistance, law, and social movements in authoritarian states: The case of gay collective action in Singapore. *Law & Society Review* 46(4):713–748.

Coker, Donna. 2001. Crime control and feminist law reform in domestic violence law. *Buffalo Criminal Law Review* 4(2):801–860.

Collins, Patricia Hill. 1998. The tie that Binds: Race, Gender, and US violence. *Ethnic and Racial Studies* 21(5):917–938.

Comaroff, Jean, and John L. Comaroff. 2008. *Law and disorder in the postcolony.* Chicago: University of Chicago Press.

Commonwealth Human Rights Initiative. 2007. *Police reform debates in India: Selected recommendations from the National Police Commission.* New Delhi: Commonwealth Human Rights Initiative.

Connelly, Clare, and Kate Cavanagh. 2007. Domestic abuse, civil protection orders and the "new criminologies": Is there any value in engaging with the law? *Feminist Legal Studies* 15(3):259–287.

Contreras, Randol. 2013. *The stickup kids: Race, drugs, violence, and the American dream.* Berkeley: University of California Press.

Cooke, Bill, and Uma Kothari. 2001. *Participation: The new tyranny?* New York: Zed Books.

Corbridge, Stuart, Glyn Williams, Manoj Srivastava, and Rene Veron. 2005. *Seeing the state: Governance and governmentality in India.* New York: Cambridge University Press.

Corsilles, Angela. 1994. No-drop policies in the prosecution of domestic violence cases: Guarantee to action or dangerous solution. *Fordham Law Review* 63(3):853–881.

Crenshaw, Kimberle. 1991. Mapping the margins: Intersectionality, identity politics, violence against women of color. *Stanford Law Review* 43(6):1241–1299.

Cruikshank, Barbara. 1999. *The will to empower: Democratic citizens and other subjects.* Ithaca, NY: Cornell University Press.

Das, Veena. 1996. Sexual violence, discursive formations, and the state. *Economic and Political Weekly* 31(35/27):2411–2423.

Dave, Anjali, and Gopika Solanki. 2000. *Special cell for women and children: A research study on domestic violence.* Washington, DC: International Center for Research on Women.

Desai, Rishikesh Bahadur. 2016, June 4. Political interference is the biggest issue, say police personnel. *The Hindu.*

Dhillon, Kirpal. 2011. The police and the criminal justice system in India. In *The police, state, and society: Perspectives from India and France,* edited by Ajay K. Mehra and René Lévy, 27–59. Delhi: Pearson.

Dixon, Jo. 2008. Mandatory domestic violence arrest and prosecution policies. *Criminology & Public Policy* 7(4):663–670.

Doniger, Wendy. 1999. *Splitting the difference: Gender and myth in ancient Greece and India.* Chicago: University of Chicago Press.

Dreze, Jean, and Amartya Sen. 2002. *India: Development and participation.* New York: Oxford University Press.

Dubbudu, Rakesh. 2015, May 4. 90% of the police force in the country works more than 8 hours a day. Factly. https://factly.in/indian-police-working-hours-90-percent-police-force-country-works-more-than-8-hours-day/.

Duvvury, Nata, Madhabika Nayak, and Keera Allendorf. 2002. *Links between masculinity and violence.* Washington, DC: International Center for Research on Women.

Elizabeth, V. 2000. *Patterns and trends of domestic violence in India: An examination of court records.* Washington, DC: International Center for Research on Women.

Engel, David, and Jaruwan Engel. 2010. *Tort, custom, and karma: Globalization and legal consciousness in Thailand.* Stanford, CA: Stanford University Press.

Evans, Peter. 1995. *Embedded autonomy: States and industrial transformation.* Princeton, NJ: Princeton University Press.

Evans, Peter. 2012. *Embedded autonomy: States and industrial transformation.* Princeton University Press.

Evans, Peter, Dietrich Rueschemeyer, and Theda Skocpol. 1985. *Bringing the state back in.* Cambridge: Cambridge University Press.

Ewick, Patricia, and Susan Silbey. 1998. *The common place of law: Stories from everyday life.* Chicago: University of Chicago Press.

Express News Service. 2016, February 18. How lawyer Vikram Singh Chauhan who led both assaults at Patiala Court sought support on Facebook to "teach traitors a lesson." *Indian Express.*

Felstiner, William, Richard Abel, and Austin Sarat. 1980. Emergence and transformation of disputes: Naming, blaming, claiming. *Law & Society Review* 15:631–654.

Ferguson, James, and Akhil Gupta. 2002. Spatializing states: Toward an ethnography of neoliberal governmentality. *American Ethnologist* 29(4):981–1002.

Foucault, Michel. 1977. *Discipline and punish: The birth of the prison*. New York: Vintage.

Fraser, Nancy. 1997. *Justice interruptus: Critical reflections on the postsocialist condition*. Cambridge: Cambridge University Press.

Freedman, Estelle. 2013. *Redefining rape: Sexual violence in the era of suffrage and segregation*. Cambridge, MA: Harvard University Press.

Fruzzetti, Lina, and Ákos Östör. 1976. Seed and earth: a cultural analysis of kinship in a Bengali town. *Contributions to Indian sociology* 10(1):97–132.

Gallagher, Mary. 2006. Mobilizing the law in China: "Informed disenchantment" and the development of legal consciousness. *Law & Society Review* 40(4):783–816.

Gandhi, Jatin. 2018, February 11. Nearly 400 vacancies for judges in high courts; 75 await govt nod. *Hindustan Times*.

Gandhi, Nandita, and Nandita Shah. 1991. *The issues at stake: Theory and practice in the contemporary women's movement in India*. New Delhi: Kali for Women.

Garcia-Moreno, Claudia, Henrica Jansen, Mary Ellsberg, Lori Heise, and Charlotte Watts. 2005. *Multi-country study on women's health and domestic violence against women*. Geneva: World Health Organization.

Garland, David. 2012. *The culture of control: Crime and social order in contemporary society*. Chicago: University of Chicago Press.

Gauri, Shalom. 2020, January 14. Fuel for the fire: Inside the community kitchen of Shaheen Bagh. *Goya Journal*. https://www.goyajournal.in/blog/fuel-for-the-fire-stories-from-the-community-kitchen-of-shaheen-bagh.

Gelsthorpe, Loraine. 2004. Back to basics in Crime Control: Weaving in women. *Critical Review of International Social and Political Philosophy* 7(2):76–103.

Ghosh, Biswajit, and Tanima Choudhuri. 2011. Legal protection against domestic violence in India. *Journal of Family Violence* 26:319–330.

Ghosh, Durba. 2008. *Sex and the family in colonial India: The making of empire*. Cambridge: Cambridge University Press.

Goffman, Erving. 1959. *The presentation of self in everyday life*. Garden City, NY: Doubleday Anchor.

Goldstein, Daniel. 2012. *Outlawed: Between security and rights in a Bolivian city*. Durham, NC: Duke University Press.

Gordon, Jon. 2020. The Legitimation of Extrajudicial Violence in an Urban Community. *Social Forces* 98(3):1174–1195.

Government of India. 2015. *Census 2011 data on marital status & fertility & head of household*. New Delhi: Press Information Bureau, Ministry of Home Affairs.

Government of West Bengal. 2009. District Human Development Report: South 24 Parganas. Development & Planning Department. Kolkata: United Nations Development Programme.

Griffiths, Paul, Michael Gossop, Beverly Powis, and John Strang. 1993. Reaching hidden populations of drug users by privileged access interviewers: Methodological and practical issues. *Addiction* 88(12):1617–1626.

Gulaab Gang. Dir. Soumik Sen. Alumbra Entertainment, 2014. Film.

Gulabi Gang. Dir. Nishita Jain. Torstein Gude, 2012. Film.

Gupta, Manjari, and Ratnabali Chattopadhyay. 2005. Law and violence against women. In *The changing status of women in West Bengal, 1970–2000: The challenge ahead*, edited by Jasodhara Bagchi, 111–129. New Delhi: Sage.

Halley, Janet, Prabha Kotiswaran, Hila Shamir, and Chantal Thomas. 2006. From the international to the local. *Harvard Journal of Law & Gender* 29(2006):335–423.

Haney, Lynne. 2010. *Offending women: Power, punishment, and the regulation of desire*. Berkeley: University of California Press.

Hannah-Moffat, Kelly. 2010. Sacrosanct or flawed: Risk, accountability, gender-responsive penal politics. *Current Issues in Criminal Justice* 22(2):193–215.

Hansen, Thomas Blom. 2001. *Wages of violence: Naming and identity in postcolonial Bombay.* Princeton, NJ: Princeton University Press.

Hansen, Thomas Blom. 2017, November 1. On law, violence, and jouissance in India. Society for Cultural Anthropology. https://culanth.org/fieldsights/on-law-violence-and-jouissance-in-india.

Hansen, Thomas Blom, and Finn Stepputat. 2005. *Sovereign bodies: Citizens, migrants, and states in the postcolonial world.* Princeton, NJ: Princeton University Press.

Harriss, John. 2013. Audacious reforms? India's new rights agenda. *Pacific Affairs* 86(3):561–568.

Harriss-White, Barbara. 2003. *India working: Essays on society and economy.* Cambridge: Cambridge University Press.

Hindess, Barry. 2010. Neoliberal citizenship. *Citizenship Studies* 6(2):127–143.

Hirsh, Elizabeth, and Christopher J. Lyons. 2010. Perceiving discrimination on the job: Legal consciousness, workplace context, and the construction of race discrimination. *Law & Society Review* 44(2):269–298.

Hollander, Jocelyn. 2001. Vulnerability and dangerousness: The construction of gender through conversation about violence. *Gender & Society* 15(1):83–109.

Holston, James. 2008. *Insurgent citizenship: Disjunctions of democracy and modernity in Brazil.* Princeton, NJ: Princeton University Press.

Holzer, Elizabeth. 2013. What happens to law in a refugee camp? *Law & Society Review* 47(4):837–872.

Houtzager, Peter, Ruth Berins Collier, John Harriss, and Adrian G Lavalle. 2002. Rights, representation and the poor: Comparisons across Latin America and India. Working paper 02-31. Development Studies Institute, London School of Economics and Political Science, London.

Htun, Mala, and Laurel Weldon. 2012. The civic origins of progressive policy change: Combating violence against women in global perspective, 1975–2005. *American Political Science Review* 106(3):548–569.

Human Rights Watch. 2009. *Broken system: Dysfunction, abuse, and impunity in the Indian police.* New York: Human Rights Watch.

Incite! 2007. *The revolution will not be funded.* New York: South End Press.

Inden, Ronald, and Ralph Nicholas. 2005. *Kinship in Bengali culture.* Orient Blackswan.

International Institute for Population Sciences. 2017. *National Family Health Survey 2015–2016: India.* Mumbai: Government of India, Ministry of Health and Family Welfare.

Inter-Parliamentary Union. 2019. Women in National Parliaments. http://archive.ipu.org/wmn-e/classif.htm

Jackson, Cecile. 1996. Rescuing gender from the poverty trap. *World Development* 24(3):489–504.

Jackson, Robert. 2007. *Sovereignty: The evolution of an idea.* Cambridge: Polity Press.

Jacob, Suraj, and Sreeparna Chattopadhyay. 2016. Marriage dissolution in India. *Economic & Political Weekly* 51(33):25–27.

Jaising, Indira. 2005. *Men's laws, women's lives.* New Delhi: Women Unlimited.

Jaising, Indira. 2007, October 26. Family against woman. *Indian Express.*

Jauregui, Beatrice. 2014. Beatings, beacons, big men: Police disempowerment and delegitimation in India. *Law & Social Inquiry* 38(3):643–669.

Jenkins, Rob. 2013. Land, rights and reform in India. *Pacific Affairs* 86(3):591–612.

Jerolmack, Colin, and Shamus Khan. 2014. Talk is cheap *Sociological Methods & Research* 43(2):178–209.

John, Mary. 2005. Feminism, poverty, and the emergent social order. In *Social movements in India: Poverty, power, and politics,* edited by Raka Ray and Mary Fainsod Katzenstein, 107–134. New York: Rowman & Littlefield.

John, Mary. 2019, May 3. Sexual violence 2012–2018 and #MeToo: A touchstone for the present. *The India Forum.*

Khan, Shamus, and Colin Jerolmack. 2013. Saying meritocracy and doing privilege. *The Sociological Quarterly* 54(1):9–19.

Kamat, Sangeeta. 2003. The NGO phenomenon and political culture in the third world. *Development* 46(1):88–93.

Kannabiran, Kalpana, ed. 2005. *The violence of normal times.* New Delhi: Women Unlimited.

Kannabiran, Kalpana, and Ritu Menon. 2007. *From Mathura to Manorama: Resisting violence against women in India.* New Delhi: Women Unlimited.

Kapila, Kriti. 2008. The measure of a tribe: The cultural politics of constitutional reclassification in north India. *Journal of the Royal Anthropological Institute* 14(1):117–134.

Kapur, Devesh. 2013, January 7. The law laid down. *Outlook India.*

Kapur, Devesh, and Milan Vaishnav. 2014. Strengthening rule of law. In *Getting India back on track: An action agenda for reform,* edited by Bibek Debroy, Ashley J. Tellis, and Reece Trevor, 247–264. Washington, DC: Carnegie Endowment for International Peace.

Kapur, Naina, and Jasjit Purewal. 1990. State violence, law, and gender justice. *Third World Legal Studies* 9:133–152.

Kapur, Ratna. 2002. Tragedy of victimization rhetoric: Resurrecting the "native" subject in international/post-colonial feminist legal politics. *Harvard Human Rights Law Journal* 15(1):1–38.

Kapur, Ratna. 2005. *Erotic justice: Law and the new politics of postcolonialism.* Hyderabad, India: Orient Blackswan.

Kapur, Ratna. 2012. Hecklers to power? The waning of liberal rights and challenges to feminism in India. In *South Asian feminisms,* edited by Ania Loomba and Ritty A. Lukose, 333–354. Durham, NC: Duke University Press.

Kapur, Ratna, and Brenda Cossman. 1996. *Subversive sites: Feminist engagements with law in India.* New Delhi: Sage Publications.

Katzenstein, Mary. 1991. Getting Women's Issues onto the Public Agenda. *Samya Shakti* 6:1–16.

Kaviraj, Sudipta. 2005. On the enchantment of the state: Indian thought on the role of the state in the narrative of modernity. *European Journal of Sociology* 46(2):263–296.

Kelly, Liam. 2014, December 10. You're most at risk of being killed when you try to leave. *The Guardian.*

Kesavan, Mukul. 2019, November 24. An all-India NRC would turn citizens into supplicants. *The Telegraph.*

Khera, Reetika. 2013. *Democratic politics and legal rights: Employment guarantee and food security in India.* New Delhi: Institute for Economic Growth.

Khilnani, Sunil. 1999. *The Idea of India.* New York: Farrar, Straus and Giroux.

Kirchherr, Julian, and Katrina Charles. 2018. Enhancing the sample diversity of snowball samples: Recommendations from a research project on anti-dam movements in Southeast Asia. *PLoS One* 13(8):e0201710.

Kirk, David, and Mauri Matsuda. 2011. Legal cynicism, collective efficacy, and the ecology of arrest. *Criminology* 49(2):443–472.

Kishwar, Madhu. 2003. Laws against domestic violence: Underused or abused? *Manushi* 28:37–43.

Klug, Heinz. 2011. South Africa's experience in constitution-building. In *Reconstituting the constitution,* edited by Caroline Morris, Jonathan Boston, and Petra Butler, 51–82. Heidelberg, Germany: Springer.

Kohli, Atul. 1990. From elite activism to democratic consolidation: The rise of reform communism in West Bengal. In *Dominance and state power in modern India,* edited by Francine R. Frankel and M. S. A. Rao. New Delhi: Oxford University Press.

Kohli, Atul. 2012. *Poverty amid plenty in the new India.* New York: Cambridge University Press.

Koshyari, Shri Bhagat Singh. 2011. *Hundred and fortieth report on petition praying for amendments in Section 498A of Indian Penal Code, 1860.* New Delhi: Rajya Sabha Secretariat.

Kristof, Nikolas, and Sheryl WuDunn. 2009. *Half the sky: Turning oppression into opportunity for women worldwide.* New York: Knopf.

Kruks-Wisner, Gabrielle. 2011. Seeking the local state: Gender, caste, and the pursuit of public services in post-tsunami India. *World Development* 39(7):1143–1154.

Kudva, Neema. 2005. Strong States, Strong NGOs. In *Social Movements in India,* edited by Raka Ray and Mary Katzenstein, 233–266. Lanham, MA: Rowman & Littlefield.

Kumar, Kundan, and John M. Kerr. 2012. Democratic assertions: The making of India's recognition of Forest Rights Act. *Development and Change* 43(3):751–771.

Lange, Matthew. 2009. *Lineages of despotism and development: British colonialism and state power.* Chicago: University of Chicago Press.

Lawyers Collective Women's Rights Initiative. 2013. *Staying alive: Sixth monitoring and evaluation report on PWDVA, 2005.* New Delhi: Lawyers Collective Women's Rights Initiative.

Lazarus-Black, Mindie. 2007. *Everyday harm: Domestic violence, court rites, and cultures of reconciliation.* Chicago: University of Illinois Press.

Leve, Lauren, and Lamia Karim. 2001. Privatizing the state: Ethnography of development, transnational capital, NGOs. *Political and Legal Anthropology* 24(1):53–58.

Levine, Kay, and Virginia Mellema. 2001. Strategizing the street: How law matters in the lives of women in the street-level drug economy. *Law & Social Inquiry* 26(1):169–207.

Levitt, Peggy, and Sally Merry. 2009. Vernacularization on the ground: Local uses of global women's rights in Peru, China, India and the United States. *Global Networks* 9(4):441–461.

Lodhia, Sharmila. 2009. Legal Frankensteins and monstrous women: Judicial narratives of the family in crisis. *Meridians* 9(2):102–129.

MacIntyre, Alasdair. 1981. *After virtue.* South Bend, IN: Notre Dame University Press.

MacLeod, Alan. 2020, January 13. In what may be the largest strike in world history, millions in India protest PM Modi's policies. *Mint Press News.*

Madan, Triloki Nath. 1989. *Family and kinship: A study of the pandits of rural Kashmir.* New York: Oxford University Press.

Maguigan, Holly. 1991. Battered women and self-defense: Myths and misconceptions in current reform proposals. *University of Pennsylvania Law Review* 140(2):379–486.

Mahapatra, Dhananjay. 2014, July 3. No arrests under anti-dowry law without magistrate's nod: SC. *Times of India.*

Majumdar, Rochona. 2009. *Marriage and modernity: Family values in colonial Bengal.* Durham, NC: Duke University Press.

Mallick, Ross. 2007. *Development policy of a communist government: West Bengal since 1977.* Cambridge and New York: Cambridge University Press.

Mander, Harsh. 2009. *Fear and forgiveness: The aftermath of massacre.* New Delhi: Penguin Books India.

Mani, Lata. 1998. *Contentious traditions: Debate on sati in colonial India.* Berkeley: University of California Press.

Mathur, Nayanika. 2020, February 20. Kambalchor Sarkar: Why UP's crackdown on protestors is unparalleled. *The Wire.*

Mbembe, Achille. 2001. *On the postcolony.* Berkeley: University of California Press.

McCann, Michael, and Tracey March. 1996. Law and everyday forms of resistance: A sociopolitical assessment. *Studies in Law, Politics, and Society* 15:207–236.

McCorkel, Jill. 2013. *Breaking women: Gender, race, and the new politics of imprisonment.* New York: New York University Press.

McKim, Allison. 2008. Getting gut-level: Punishment, gender, therapeutic governance. *Gender & Society* 22(3):303–323.

Mehra, Madhu. 1998. Exploring the boundaries of law, gender and social reform. *Feminist Legal Studies* 6(1):59–83.

Mehta, Pratap Bhanu. 2005. India's judiciary: The promise of uncertainty. In *Public institutions in India: Performance and design*, edited by Devesh Kapur and Pratap Bhanu Mehta, 158–193. New Delhi: Oxford University Press.

Mendez, Juan, Guillermo O'Donnell, and Paul Pinheiro. 1999. *The (un)rule of law and the underprivileged in Latin America.* Notre Dame: University of Notre Dame Press.

Menon, Nivedita. 2004. *Recovering subversion.* Urbana: University of Illinois Press.

Menon, Nivedita. 2009. Sexuality, caste, governmentality. *Feminist Review* 91(1):94–112.

Menon, Ritu, and Kamla Bhasin. 2011. Abducted women, the state, and questions of honour. In *Perspectives on modern South Asia: A reader in culture, history, and representation*, edited by Kamala Visweswaran, 119–133. Chichester, UK: Wiley-Blackwell.

Merry, Sally. 2001. Spatial governmentality and the new urban social order. *American Anthropologist* 103(1):16–29.

Merry, Sally. 2003. Rights talk and the experience of law: Implementing women's human rights to protection from violence. *Human Rights Quarterly* 25(2):343–381.

Meyer, John, John Boli, George Thomas, and Francisco Ramirez. 1997. World society and the nation-state. *American Journal of Sociology* 103(1):144–181.

Michelutti, Lucia. 2010. Wrestling with (body) politics: Understanding "goonda" political styles in north India. In *Power and influence in India: Bosses, lords and captains*, edited by Pamela Price and Arild Engelson Ruud, 44–69. London and New Delhi: Routledge.

Minow, Martha. 1992. Surviving victim talk. *UCLA Law Review* 40:1411–1444.

Mitra, Subrata. 2010. Citizenship in India: Some preliminary results of a national survey. *Economic and Political Weekly* 45(9):46–53.

Morrill, Calvin, Karolyn Tyson, Lauren B. Edelman, and Richard Arum. 2010. Legal mobilization in schools: The paradox of rights and race among youth. *Law & Society Review* 44(3–4):651–694.

Nandgaonkar, Satish. 2004. The day of the furies. *Telegraph India*.

Naples, Nancy. 1996. A feminist revisiting of the insider/outsider debate. *Qualitative Sociology* 19(1):83–106.

Naples, Nancy A., and Manisha Desai. 2002. *Women's activism and globalization: Linking local struggles and global politics*. New York and London: Routledge.

National Crime Records Bureau. 2008. *Crime in India full report 2007*. New Delhi: Government of India, Ministry of Home Affairs.

National Crime Records Bureau. 2018. *Crime in India 2017 full report*. New Delhi: Government of India, Ministry of Home Affairs.

National Judicial Data Grid. 2018. *Summary report of India as of November 14, 2018*. New Delhi: Department of Justice.

Neetha, N. 2014, November 22. Crisis in female employment. *Economic and Political Weekly*.

Neff, Daniel F., Kunal Sen, and Veronika Kling. 2012. The puzzling decline in rural women's labor force participation in India: A reexamination. GIGA working paper 196. German Institute of Global and Area Studies, Hamburg, Germany.

Nielsen, Laura Beth. 2000. Situating legal consciousness: Experiences and attitudes of ordinary citizens about law and street harassment. *Law and Society Review* 34(4):1055–1090.

Nilsen, Alf Gunvald. 2013. Adivasi mobilization in contemporary India: Democratizing the local state? *Critical Sociology* 39(4):615–633.

Nilsen, Kenneth Bo, and Alf Gunvald Nilsen. 2014. Law struggles and hegemonic processes in neoliberal India: Gramscian reflections on land acquisition legislation. *Globalizations* 12(2):203–216.

Obstfeld, David, Stephen P. Borgatti, and Jason Davis. 2014. Brokerage as a process: Decoupling third party action from social network structure. In *Contemporary perspectives on organizational social networks*, edited by Daniel J. Brass, Giuseppe Labianca, Ajay Mehra, Daniel S. Halgin, and Stephen P. Borgatti, 135–160. Bingley, UK: Emerald Group Publishing.

O'Donnell, Guillermo. 1993. On the state, democratization and some conceptual problems: A Latin American view with glances at some postcommunist countries. *World Development* 21(8):1355–1369.

O'Donnell, Guillermo, and Phillippe Schmitter. 2013. *Transitions from authoritarian rule: Tentative conclusions from uncertain democracies*. Baltimore: Johns Hopkins University Press.

Oldenburg, Philip. 1992. Sex ratio, son preference, and violence in India. *Economic and political weekly* 27(49/50):2657–2662.

O'Malley, Pat. 2004. *Risk, uncertainty, governance*. London: Glass House Press.

Omvedt, Gail. 1993. Reinventing Revolution: New Social Movements and the Socialist Tradition in India. New York: M. E. Sharpe.

Panda, Pradeep, and Bina Agarwal. 2005. Marital violence, human development, women's property in India. World Development 33(5):823–850.

Paret, Marcel. 2015. Violence and democracy in South Africa's community protests. Review of African Political Economy 42(143):107–123.

Paschel, Tianna. 2016. Becoming black political subjects: Movements and ethno-racial rights in Colombia and Brazil. Princeton, NJ: Princeton University Press.

Pathak, Zakia, and Rajeswari Sunder Rajan. 1989. Shahbano. Signs 14(3):558–582.

Pelley, Lauren. 2016, December 8. Leaving relationship is "most dangerous time" for domestic violence victims, experts say. CBC News. https://www.cbc.ca/news/canada/toronto/domestic-violence-victims-1.3885381.

Pound, Roscoe. 1910. Law in books and law in action. American Law Review 44:12.

Powell, Walter, and Paul DiMaggio. 1991. The new institutionalism in organizational analysis. Chicago: University of Chicago Press.

Puri, Jyoti. 2016. Sexual states: Governance and the struggle over the antisodomy law in India. Duke University Press.

Press Trust of India. 2018a, September 24. India has 19 judges per 10 lakh people. The Hindu.

Press Trust of India. 2018b, February 11. Over 120 recommendations for high court posts pending with government, SC collegium. The Economic Times.

Purkayastha, Bandana, Mangala Subramaniam, Manisha Desai, and Sunita Bose. 2003. The study of gender in India. Gender & Society 17(4):503–524.

Raghavan, R. K. 2003. The Indian police: Problems and prospects. Publius 33(4):119–133.

Raheja, Gloria Goodwin, and Ann Grodzins Gold. 1994. Listen to the heron's words: Reimagining gender and kinship in north India. Berkeley: University of California Press.

Ramesh, Randeep. 2004, November 9. Women's revenge against rapists. The Guardian.

Rankin, Katharine. 2001. Governing development: Neoliberalism, microcredit, rational economic woman. Economy and Society 30(1):18–37.

Rao, Anupama. 2009. The caste question: Dalits and the politics of modern India. Berkeley: University of California Press.

Rao, Sandhya, S. Indhu, Ashima Chopra, and S. N. Nagamani. 2000. Domestic violence: A study of organizational data. Washington, DC: International Center for Research on Women.

Rao, Vijayendra, and Michael Walton. 2004. Culture and public action. Stanford, CA: Stanford Social Sciences.

Ray, Raka. 1999. Fields of protest: Women's movements in India. Minneapolis: University of Minnesota Press.

Ray, Raka, and Mary Katzenstein. 2005. Social movements in India: Poverty, power, and politics. Lanham, MD: Rowman & Littlefield.

Ray, Raka, and Seemin Qayum. 2009. Cultures of servitude: Modernity, domesticity, and class in India. Stanford, CA: Stanford University Press.

Razack, Sherene. 1995. Domestic violence as gender persecution. Canadian Journal of Women and Law 8:45–88.

Razack, Sherene. 2004. Imperilled Muslim women, dangerous Muslim men and civilised Europeans: Legal and social responses to forced marriages. Feminist Legal Studies 12(2):129–174.

Reddy, Sanjay. 2005. A rising tide of demands: India's public institutions and the democratic revolution. In Public institutions in India: Performance and design, edited by Devesh Kapur and Pratap Bhanu Mehta. New Delhi: Oxford University Press.

Reynolds, Celene. 2019. The mobilization of Title IX across U.S. colleges and universities, 1994–2014. Social Problems 66(2):245–273.

Rhode, Deborah. 2004. Access to justice. London: Oxford University Press.

Risse, Thomas, Stephen Ropp, and Kathryn Sikkink. 2013. The persistent power of human rights: From commitment to compliance. Cambridge and New York: Cambridge University Press.

Rose, Nikolas. 1999. *Powers of freedom: Reframing political thought*. Cambridge: Cambridge University Press.

Rose, Nikolas. 2000. Government and control. *British Journal of Criminology* 40(2):321–339.

Roychowdhury, Poulami. 2013. The Delhi gang rape: The making of international causes. *Feminist Studies* 39(1):282–292.

Roychowdhury, Poulami. 2016a. Desire, rights, entitlements: Organizational strategies in the war on violence. *Signs: Journal of Women in Culture and Society* 41(4):793–820.

Roychowdhury, Poulami. 2016b. Over the law: Rape and the seduction of popular politics. *Gender & Society* 30(1):80–94.

Roychowdhury, Poulami. 2019. Illicit justice: Aspirational-strategic subjects and the political economy of domestic violence law in India. *Law & Social Inquiry* 44(2):444–467.

Ruparelia, Sanjay. 2013. India's new rights agenda: Genesis, promises, risks. *Pacific Affairs* 86(3):569–590.

Rustagi, Preet. 2013. Changing patterns of labour force participation and employment of women in India. *Indian Journal of Labour Economics* 56(2):215–241.

Ruud, Arild Engelsen. 2001. Talking dirty about politics: A view from a Bengali village. In *The everyday state and society in modern India*, edited by C. Fuller and Véronique Benei, 115–136. London: Hurst.

Sandhu, Rohan and Shamika Ravi. 2014, July 15. Missing women leaders. *The Indian Express*.

Sangari, Kumkum, and Sudesh Vaid. 1999. *Recasting women: Essays in Indian colonial history*. New Brunswick, NJ: Rutgers University Press.

Sanyal, Paromita. 2009. From credit to collective action: The role of microfinance in promoting women's social capital and normative influence. *American Sociological Review* 74(4):529–550.

Sanyal, Paromita. 2014. *Credit to capabilities: A sociological study of microcredit groups in India*. New York: Cambridge University Press.

Saravade, Nandkumar. 2015. Reinventing the Criminal Justice System (Part 2 of 2). *The Leap Blog*, https://blog.theleapjournal.org/2015/03/reinventing-criminal-justice-system_20.html.

Sarkar, Tanika. 2001. *Hindu wife, Hindu nation*. New Delhi: Permanent Black.

Schmitt, Carl. 1985. *Political theology: Four chapters on the concept of sovereignty*. Chicago: University of Chicago Press.

Schneider, Elizabeth. 2000. *Battered women and feminist lawmaking*. New Haven, CT: Yale University Press.

Seal, Lizzie. 2010. *Women, murder and femininity: Gender representations of women who kill*. New York: Palgrave McMillan.

Sen, Amartya. 1999. *Development as freedom*. London: Oxford University Press.

Sen, Rukmini. 2010. Women's subjectivities of suffering and legal rhetoric on domestic violence fissures in the two discourses. *Indian Journal of Gender Studies* 17(3):375–401.

Sharma, Aradhana. 2008. *Logics of Empowerment*. Minneapolis: University of Minnesota Press.

Sharma, Kalpana. 2019. *The silence and the storm: Narratives of sexual violence in India*. New Delhi: Aleph Book Company.

Shepard, Melanie, and Ellen Pence. 1999. *Coordinating community responses to domestic violence: Lessons from Duluth and beyond*. Thousand Oaks, CA: Sage.

Simon, Jonathan, and Malcolm M. Feeley. 2003. The form and limits of the new penology. In *Punishment and social control*, edited by Thomas G. Blomberg and Stanley Cohen, 75–116. New York: Walter de Gruyter.

Singh, Kirti. 2017, September 25. Why we need a fair law on marital property. *Times of India*.

Skaria, Ajay. 1997. Shades of wildness: Tribe, caste, and gender in western India. *Journal of Asian Studies* 56(3):726–745.

Smart, Carol. 2002. *Feminism and the power of law*. London and New York: Routledge.

Solanki, Gopika. 2011. *Adjudication in religious family law: Cultural accommodation, legal pluralism, gender equality in India*. Cambridge: Cambridge University Press.

Somers, Margaret. 2008. *Genealogies of citizenship: Markets, statelessness, and the right to have rights*. Cambridge: Cambridge University Press.

Spivak, Gayatri. 1988. Can the subaltern speak? In *Marxism and the interpretation of culture*, edited by Cary Nelson and Lawrence Grossberg, 271–316. London: MacMillan.

Spivak, Gayatri. 2004. Righting wrongs. *South Atlantic Quarterly* 103(2):523–581.

Srivastava, Shruti, and Sunny Verma. 2015, December 25. Seventh Pay Commission: Delay salary hikes, five states tell centre. *Indian Express*.

Steinberg, Jonny. 2008. *Thin blue—The unwritten rules of policing South Africa*. Jeppestown, South Africa: Jonathan Ball Publishers.

Stovel, Katherine, and Lynette Shaw. 2012. Brokerage. *Annual Review of Sociology* 38:139–158.

Subramanian, Ajantha. 2009. *Shorelines: Space and rights in south India*. Stanford, CA: Stanford University Press.

Subramanian, Kadayam Suryanarayanan. 2007. *Political violence and the police in India*. New Delhi: Sage Publications.

Subramanian, Narendra. 2014. *Nation and family: Personal law, cultural pluralism, gendered citizenship in India*. Stanford, CA: Stanford University Press.

Suk, Jeannie. 2006. Criminal law comes home. *Yale Law Journal* 116(2):2–70.

Sundar, Nandini. 2011. The rule of law and citizenship in central India: Post-colonial dilemmas. *Citizenship Studies* 15(3–4):419–432.

Sunder Rajan, Rajeswari. 2003. *The scandal of the state: Women, law, and citizenship in postcolonial India*. Durham, NC: Duke University Press.

Suneetha, A., and Vasudha Nagaraj. 2010. Dealing with domestic violence towards complicating the rights discourse. *Indian Journal of Gender Studies* 17(3):451–478.

Super, Gail. 2016. Volatile sovereignty: Governing crime through the community in Khayelitsha. *Law & Society Review* 50(2):450–483.

Supreme Court of India. 2018. *Monthly pending cases*. New Delhi: Government of India.

Tarrow, Sidney G. 2011. *Power in movement: Social movements and contentious politics*. New York: Cambridge University Press.

Tharu, Susie, and Tejaswini Niranjana. 1994. Problems for a contemporary theory of gender. *Social Scientist* 22(3/4):93–117.

Times News Network. 2012, August 27. Cops fume over low salary, heavy workload. *Times of India*.

Timmermans, Stefan and Iddo Tavory. 2012. Theory construction in qualitative research. *Sociological Theory* 30(3):167–186.

Tripathi, Shishir. 2016, August 15. CJI Thakur's remarks on PM Modi's speech: Crisis in Judiciary is not solely due to the executive. *First Post*.

Tuckman, Jo. 2019, November 5. Cowed and outgunned: Why Mexico's police don't stand a chance against drug cartels. *The Guardian*. https://www.theguardian.com/world/2019/nov/05/mexico-police-dont-stand-chance-against-drug-cartels?CMP=Share_iOSApp_Other

Uberoi, Patricia. 1994. *Family, kinship and marriage in India*. New Delhi: Oxford University Press.

Uma, Saumya, and Vrinda Grover. 2010. *Addressing domestic violence through the law*. New Delhi: Multiple Action Research Group.

Unger, Roberto. 1982. The critical legal studies movement. *Harvard Law Review* 96(3):561–675.

UN Women. 2019. Facts and Figures: Ending Violence against Women. https://www.unwomen.org/en/what-we-do/ending-violence-against-women/facts-and-figures

Vaishnav, Milan. 2017. *When crime pays: Money and muscle in Indian politics*. New Haven, CT: Yale University Press.

Van Meter, Karl. 1990. Methodological and design issues: Techniques for assessing the representatives of snowball samples. *NIDA Research Monograph* 98(51.40):31–43.

Vargas, Robert. 2016. *Wounded city: Violent turf wars in a Chicago barrio*. New York: Oxford University Press.

Varshney, Ahutosh. 2003. *Ethnic conflict and civic life: Hindus and Muslims in India*. New Haven, CT: Yale University Press.

Vatuk, Sylvia. 1972. *Kinship and urbanization: White collar migrants in north India.* Berkeley: University of California Press.

Vatuk, Sylvia. 1998. *The Indian woman in later life: some social and cultural considerations.*

Vatuk, Sylvia. 2001. Where will she go? What will she do? Paternalism toward women in the administration of Muslim personal law. In *Religion and personal law in a secular India: A call to judgment,* edited by Gerald James Larson, 226–250. Bloomington: Indiana University Press.

Verick, Sher. 2014. *Women's labour force participation in India: Why is it so low?* New Delhi: International Labor Organization.

Verma, Arvind. 2005. The police in India: Design, performance, adaptability. In *Public institutions in India: Performance and design,* edited by Devesh Kapur and Pratap Bhanu Mehta, 194–251. New Delhi: Oxford University Press.

Vishnupad, Phd. 2017, November 1. On the three political configurations in India. Society for Cultural Anthropology. https://culanth.org/fieldsights/on-the-three-political-configurations-in-india.

von Holdt, Karl. 2013. South Africa: The transition to violent democracy. *Review of African Political Economy* 30(138):589–604.

Wade, Robert. 1990. *Governing the market.* Princeton, NJ: Princeton University Press.

Waheed, Abdul. 2009. Dowry among Indian Muslims: Ideals and practices. *Indian Journal of Gender Studies* 16(1):47–75.

Weiss, Robert. 1995. *Learning from strangers: The art and method of qualitative interview studies.* New York: Simon and Schuster.

Willis, Graham. 2015. *The killing consensus: Police, organized crime, and the regulation of life and death in urban Brazil.* Berkeley: University of California Press.

World Health Organization. 2013. *Global and regional estimates of violence against women: Prevalence and health effects of intimate partner violence and non- partner sexual violence.* Geneva: World Health Organization.

Yadav, Yogendra. 2000. Understanding the second democratic upsurge: Trends of Bahujan participation in electoral politics in the 1990s. In *Transforming India: Social and political dynamics of democracy,* edited by Francine R. Frankel, Zoya Hasan, Rajeev Bhargava, and Balveer Arora, 120–145. New Delhi: Oxford University Press.

Young, Iris Marion. 2003. The logic of masculinist protection: Reflections on the current security state. *Signs: Journal of Women in Culture and Society* 29(1):1–25.

Fruzzetti, Lina, and Ákos Östör. 1976. Seed and earth: a cultural analysis of kinship in a Bengali town. *Contributions to Indian sociology* 10(1):97–132.

INDEX

renting. *See* housing
residential rights. *See* rights: residential
   See also Protection of Women from Domestic
      Violence Act
rights:
   access to, 6, 17, 75, 95, 113, 126, 152 (*see also*
      brokers)
   aspirations for, 132–34
   citizenship and, 75
   collective vs. individual, 6–7, 14–15, 74–75,
      132, 176
   entitlements and, 8, 10, 128, 170, 193
   extralegal gains and, 6–8, 112, 134, 141–44,
      149–50, 169
   extralegal tactics and, 12–13, 143
   as formal legal remedies, 6, 10, 174
   networks and
      clientelistic exchange, 12
      criminal, 6, 68, 76–77, 183
      family, 55
      feminist, 16, 182
      social, 7–8, 63, 75, 80–81, 113, 135, 155–56,
       169, 188
   post-colonial critique of, 174
   property, 13, 23–24, 44, 174
   self-transformation and, 128–30
   vernacularization of, 34–35, 68
   women's, 4–12, 14–34, 172–77
      Dowry Prohibition Act and, 192, 203n2
      knowledge of, 27
      legal reforms and, 4–6, 149
      organized support for, 32–34
      postcolonial critique of, 173–75
      violence, as against, 4, 10, 17, 28, 33, 73, 131,
       166, 173
   See also brokers; housing; Indian Criminal
      Justice System; marriage: matrimonial
      law; state capacity; women's movements;
      women's organizations; women's rights
Rose, Nikolas. *See* governance: defined
rule of law, 11, 171, 175–76
   See also brokers; capabilities; corruption;
      domestic violence law; Indian criminal
      justice system; law enforcement; political
      society; rights; sovereignty; state capacity
running a case, 15, 109–26, 155–56, 163, 167
   aptitudes for, 111, 155, 167, 171
   benefits of, 68–69, 150, 152, 155–59
   costs of, 4, 112–16, 117–21, 121–25,
      146, 159–64
   dangers of, 15, 47, 76, 123, 155, 159–64 (*see*
      also capabilities: costs of)
   gaming mentality towards and, 8, 126
   illicit outcomes of, 142–46, 149–50, 156
   incorporation and, 20, 102–3, 121–26, 155, 166
   mahila samiti and, 7, 63, 99, 109, 136
   versus running a family, 7, 63, 99, 109, 136
   social class and, 126, 129, 149–50, 170

   See also aspirational–strategic subjectivity;
      brokers; courts; gender inequality; Indian
      criminal justice system; law enforcement;
      NGOs; running a family; women's rights
running a family, 26, 28, 39–52, 69
   aptitudes for, 42, 46, 116
   commitments to, 68
   dangers of legal action in, 46–50
   logic of reconciliation in, 40, 41–46, 83
   versus running a case, 69, 168–69
   social basis of, 40, 49–52
   See also aspirational–strategic subjectivity;
      compromise; courts; gender inequality;
      Indian criminal justice system; law
      enforcement; marriage; *nari nirjatana*;
      running a case; Sita

sahya-sakti. *See* running a family: aptitudes for
sansar calano. *See* running a family
sati, 9, 174
Sen, Amartya, 14–15, 170
   See also capabilities
settlements, 141–45, 169
   child custody, 142
   empowerment and, 155–59
   extralegal, 112, 143
   financial, 6, 56–57, 146, 166
   out-of-court, 27, 149–50
   See also brokers; compromise; courts; gender
      inequality; Indian Criminal Justice
      System; justice
sexual deviance. *See* gender deviance
Shadheen (NGO), 17–18, 33, 57, 185
   casework, 59, 66, 78, 87–88, 93, 124
   community membership and, 76
   gender workshops of, 69–72, 79–80
   intra-organizational disputes, 143
   self-help groups (microfinance teams), 63, 103,
      116, 119
   women's rights initiative, 39, 48, 66
   See also AIN; Andolan; brokers; empowerment;
      therapy; women's organizations;
      women's rights
Shaheen Bagh, 176
shalishi, 56–57, 67
See also Andolan; arbitration; mediation
Shiv Sena, 34
   See also Bharatiya Janata Party (BJP)
Sita, 41, 46
social movements. *See* women's movements
   See also civil disobedience; political society;
      protest
son preference, 23, 177
   See also gender inequality
      South-24 Parganas. *See* Alipore; courts: District
       Magistrate's; methodology; Shadheen
South-24 Parganas District Magistrate's Court. *See*
      courts: District Magistrate's